History
Is
Hers

Women Educators in Twentieth Century Ontario

Rebecca Priegert Coulter

Helen Harper

DETSELIG
ENTERPRISES LTD

Detselig Enterprises Ltd.
Calgary, Alberta

History Is Hers:
Women Educators in Twentieth Century Ontario

©2005 Rebecca Coulter and Helen Harper

Canadian Cataloguing in Publication Data

Coulter, Rebecca
  History is hers : women educators in twentieth century
Ontario / Rebecca Coulter and Helen Harper.

Includes bibliographical references.
ISBN 1-55059-276-9

  1. Women teachers--Ontario--History--20th century. 2. Women
educators--Ontario--History--20th century. 3. Women in education
--Ontario--History--20th century. I. Harper, Helen Jean, 1957- II. Title.
  LB2837.C68 2005   371.1'0082'09713   C2005-902885-8

210 - 1220 Kensington Road NW
Calgary, Alberta
T2N 3P5

Phone: (403) 283-0900
Fax: (403) 283-6947
Email: temeron@telusplanet.net
Website: www.temerondetselig.com

We acknowledge the financial support of the Government of Canada
through the Book Publishing Industry Development Program (BPIDP)
for our publishing activities.

We also acknowledge the support of the Alberta
Foundation for the Arts for our publishing
program.

Cover Photo: Miss Clode and Donna, Grade 2, Faywood Public
School, North York, 1952. Photograph from personal collection of
Marion Clode Spencer. Photographer, Edwin Feeny.

ISBN 1-55059-276-9   SAN 113-0234   Printed in Canada

Dedication

For our teachers

Contents

Section II: Leadership Beyond the Classroom

Section III: Perils and Pleasures

Acknowledgments

Without the co-operation and support of the women teachers who gladly volunteered to participate in our project, this book would not have been possible. We thank all of those teachers for opening up their lives to us and for sharing their experiences of teaching in a variety of settings and circumstances around the province of Ontario. They not only granted us interviews, but willingly shared materials that documented their careers.

We also are grateful both to the family members who contacted us to share their memories of their mothers and grandmothers and to the former students who wrote to tell us about their special teachers. The ways in which so many members of the public embraced our research told us that the contributions of women teachers to the future success of their students and to wider social goals are recognized and appreciated.

We thank the Social Sciences and Humanities Research Council of Canada for the financial support offered through Standard Research Grant, No. 410-2000-0357. Without this assistance we would not have had the resources to undertake our study, nor to hire several able research assistants, Leslie Thielen-Wilson, Alice Taylor, Daphne Heywood, Ruth Mitchell and Kendra Coulter. Their work on the project was invaluable and through their efforts they provided important access to archival materials and scholarly literature, as well as substantive support for the over-all organization and management of a large project.

We would also like to thank Dr. Alison Prentice who served as a research collaborator on the team and whose wise advice was helpful. Similarly, Dr. Kathleen Weiler, who was a visiting summer scholar at Western's Faculty of Education in 2001, graciously met with the team and offered suggestions and important comment on our work.

Western's Faculty of Education remains a place where research is valued and we are happy to have been beneficiaries of a work climate which enhanced our research capabilities. Dean Allen Pearson and the Research and Development Committee awarded us seed money, as did the University of Western Ontario, to conduct the pilot study that led to the larger project. The Faculty also offered office space and other services that made our work possible. We thank our colleagues for their interest in our research and for offering us many opportunities to present papers to them for comment.

The Woman Teacher in Twentieth-Century Ontario Project Team

Principal Investigator: Rebecca Priegert Coulter

Co-investigators: Sheila Cavanagh, Helen Harper, Suzanne Majhanovich, Goli Rezai-Rashti, Aniko Varpalotai, Janice Wallace

April 2005

Foreword

Anna Hillen

I wanted to go to school from the time I could say the word. But my neighborhood elementary school back at the start of the nineteen forties had no kindergarten so that I had to wait – wait – wait – absolutely forever. Then after a morning of chaos and confusion, a couple of children (both boys) crying non-stop, and being separated by gender and forever marshalled into straight lines, straight rows, straight, straight, I decided school for five days every week was a totally nasty idea. Like Huck Finn, Scout Finch and Holden Caulfield I wanted nothing more to do with school.

Nonetheless, I had to attend and during the eternity when I did so, I began to figure out the good stuff: how to tell a story; hey, how to choose a really good story; even how to teach kids to write a really good story; how to perk up a classroom so that it no longer resembled

Anna Hillen and her colleague, Richard Dewey, about 1969. *Photo courtesy Anna Hillen.*

the inside of a beige bedroom slipper; how to converse with teenagers so that the conversations reflected back everyone's humanity yet individuality. Then I particularly wanted to teach those who seemed to want nothing more to do with school: the rebels, the freedom fighters, the cognitively challenged.

The chalkdust clouds rose and settled; the locker doors slammed; the PA announcements mumbled on, unheeded; the years, the decades passed. My back ached, my arches fell and some varicose veins popped. My elderliness and my years in the front ranks of "ed biz" totalled some magic number and I was free to rediscover myself and to taste the seven days a week freedom for which I'd long longed. Then, after a decade of retirement, suddenly I was being interviewed for a history of women teachers. You mean I hadn't just been doing a job to the best of my ability? I had also become an "hysterical" figure? I'd been a part of something much larger than my classroom, my lifetime? Who would have thought?

So, here we are, ladies. From different decades, different corners of Ontario, having herded thousands of "ankle-biters" or thousands of "hormonal six-footers" along the paths laid out by the authority figures. Tattle-talers, all of us, now.

Ever the rebel, Anna Hillen with colleague, Ron Stone and his wife, upon retirement in 1992 after 33 consecutive years of teaching secondary school English. *Photo courtesy Anna Hillen.*

Contributors

Sheila L. Cavanagh is an Assistant Professor in Social Sciences at York University who does gender and sexuality studies. Using feminist, queer and psychoanalytic theories she studies female social subjectivity, the regulation of desire and the socio-cultural politics of education. She is completing a book tentatively titled: Sexing the Teacher: School Sex Scandals and Queer Pedagogies of Female Desire.

Rebecca Priegert Coulter is an Associate Professor in the Faculty of Education at The University of Western Ontario where she teaches courses in the history of education, educational policy studies, research methods in education and critical pedagogy. Her research areas are the history of Canadian education, politics and education, and gender studies. Recent publications focus on young men and gender equity, the history of women teachers and a biography of Donalda Dickie. Coulter is also co-editor of *Historical Studies in Education/Revue d'histoire de l'éducation.*

Helen Harper, formerly at The University of Western Ontario and now at the University of Nevada, Las Vegas, works in the area of English and Cultural Studies in Education. Her research focuses on social difference and representation in the socio-political contexts of education. Her books include *Wild Words/Dangerous Desires: High School Girls & Feminist Avant-Garde Writing* (Peter Lang, 2000); with Meredith Cherland, *Advocacy Research in Literacy Education* (Lawrence Erlbaum, in press); and *Resident Aliens: Women Teachers in the Canadian North* (University of Toronto: forthcoming).

Suzanne Majhanovich teaches in the Faculty of Education, The University of Western Ontario, where she offers courses in theories of education as well as on issues in language acquisition and second language teaching and learning. Her current research interests include studying the careers of retired women teachers, especially francophone teachers, in the province of Ontario and she has published articles related to this project. She has also published in the area of educational restructuring, decentralization, and privatization in education. Currently she is co-editor of a special issue of the *International Review of Education* featuring articles on education and social justice.

Goli M. Rezai-Rashti is an Associate Professor in the Faculty of Education at The University of Western Ontario, where her teaching focuses on equity and social justice issues, theories of education, and globalization. Her research is in the areas of anti-racism, feminism, educational restructuring, and gender issues in Muslim societies. She is the author of numerous articles in books and journals. Her most recent work, "Unessential women: A discussion of race, class and gender and their implications in education," appeared in Nancy Mandell (ed.).(2005), *Feminist issues: Race, class & sexuality,* Fourth edition. Toronto: Pearson Education.

Aniko Varpalotai is an Associate Professor at the Faculty of Education, The University of Western Ontario, with a PhD from the University of Toronto (OISE). She teaches in the areas of education policies, research methods, gender issues in education, and health education. Her research interests include equity issues, and rural education. She lives on a farm in rural Ontario.

Janice Wallace completed her PhD at OISE/University of Toronto and is an Assistant Professor in the Department of Educational Policy Studies at the University of Alberta. Her research interests focus on the effects of gender and diversity issues on school policies and practices, school restructuring and globalization, and equity in bureaucratic settings. She is currently working on a SSHRC funded project that explores practices for inclusion of disabled persons in the workplace.

1

Introduction:
History is Hers and Ours

Rebecca Priegert Coulter and Helen Harper

Summer school, 1903. The feminization of Ontario teaching force is apparent. *Photo courtesy of The University of Western Ontario Archives, B740.*

While the "lady teacher" of the twentieth century continues to reside in the memories of individuals, in the story telling of families and communities, and less directly, in photographs, artifacts and records, it is an astonishing fact that the history of women teachers in Ontario, the largest and most populated province in the country, remains strangely neglected. Admittedly, Prentice, Danylewycz, Abbott, Gelman and others have written about women teachers and their work in late nineteenth and early twentieth century Ontario and a small number of studies such as those by Reynolds, Arbus and Gaskell have looked at a later period.[1] French, Staton and Light and Labatt have documented the history of female elementary teachers, particularly as it relates to their organized voice, the Federation of Women Teachers' Associations of Ontario.[2] But apart from these few works and a small number of other studies, most of which were completed in the late 1980s and 1990s, the history of Ontario women teachers over the last century, and especially since 1920, has yet to be written. It is to this task our research turned, and it did so from an understanding that history is "a story of power relations and struggle, a story that is contradictory, heterogeneous, fragmented."[3]

History is Hers: Women Educators in Twentieth-Century Ontario is based on data collected in a large scale, multi-year, oral history project conducted by a cross-disciplinary group of seven researchers and a number of research assistants from the Faculty of Education at The University of Western Ontario. Central to this project was the recording of the oral histories of nearly two hundred retired women teachers who had worked in the various regions of the province in the period from the 1930s through to the 1990s. Oral history has proven to be a particularly useful method for learning about the lives of women teachers who have worked unremarked in the province's classrooms for decades. Indeed, it was only through interviewing that we have been able to gather data on the daily and "ordinary" realities of teaching in Ontario's classrooms. It has been a fascinating experience.

For a brief period of time, we entered into the lives and memories of individual women who had taught in some instances at a time before we were born, in places we have never been. Sitting in kitchens and living rooms, on decks and patios; walking through gardens, barns and stables; sometimes over lunch, often over coffee/tea, with tape recorders going, we heard and participated in the efforts of retired and sometimes very elderly women to name, describe and bring meaning to their life's work. Many spoke of the romance of teaching – of dreams found; others offered less sanguine stories of teaching – of dreams lost. Some were passionately devoted to teaching for their entire careers; a few taught for only a short time or sporadically as circumstances demanded. Bitter or not, the earliest experiences were often the most vividly remembered and most powerfully told. It was apparent that those we interviewed had experienced or witnessed in the routine and "ordinariness" of teaching, in even the smallest of schools, the human condition in all its varieties. Even the most cynical among us would be affected by the stories of happiness and heartache, and the tales of the comical and the tragic in school and community life. The conventional and non-conventional renderings of a life's work at times left us elated and bubbling, and at other times, disturbed, frustrated, and silent.

The majority, though certainly not all of those in our study, were white women of European descent, Canadian born, English-speaking, 50-90 years of age, and from both working class and middle class family backgrounds. As is evident in the chapters that follow, we also obtained the oral histories of a small but significant number of minority, First Nations, and francophone women. The vast majority of women taught at some point in their careers in rural schools, in locations scattered throughout the province. Many also spent part of their careers in larger metropolitan schools. Some of those we interviewed were very elderly, though still leading active and independent lives. Most, but not all, had married. Several began their careers as teachers, but eventually became department heads, principals, consultants, or union leaders, and a few became senior administrators for school systems or went to work for the Ministry of Education. Some had left teaching for other careers or for motherhood. A number had happily retired early. Although not all were exemplary teachers in their own minds, most sounded like they had been wonderful teachers, and had retained connections with students, parents and the communities in which they had worked.

All of the participants struggled in varying degrees to render their experiences intelligible to researchers who were often a generation or two younger. Moreover, the teachers spoke to university professors, women who differed if not by class, race, ethnicity, and/or sexual orientation, then by the fact that we had left school teaching for life in academe. Thus each participant in our study was making meaning of a life's work that the researchers had chosen to abandon. In addition, although some of researchers had extensive personal and professional histories situated in Ontario, in particular southern Ontario, a number of us had somewhat more limited personal and professional knowledge of the province. It can be said, then, that the women in our study were often charged with explaining the kaleidoscope of their teaching lives to those not from their world.

We, too, struggled. Working with retired teachers and their stories of professional life, and with each other across different disciplinary and theoretical orientations, has been a challenge. Understanding and depicting the lives and legacy of women teachers in the twentieth century and reflecting upon our own struggles in the twenty-first century has been a remarkable, though not always easy, experience. In part, our intellectual struggles led us to consider and reconsider our knowledge and beliefs about the nature and value of history, women's history, and oral history. In hindsight, this should have come as no surprise.

The study of Canadian history has undergone considerable expansion and generated significant controversy in and beyond the field over the last thirty years. Contemporary social theorists, often politically engaged, have created new questions and perspectives and these have opened up and extended more traditional avenues of historical inquiry. Traditionally Canadian history focused on the story of nation building and on the public sphere of wars, diplomacy, politics and trade dominated by privileged men of European, most often Anglo-Saxon, ancestry. However, this approach and its vision of an objective, unified, and overarching history of Canada has given way to multiple, and particular local histories and perspectives not normally represented in historical chronicles: the history of women, Aboriginal peoples, new immigrants, workers, the poor, among others, and with greater attention paid to the private sphere. Most recently, historians, under the influence of postmodern theory, have challenged unified and stable categories of social identity that underpin both the traditional "consensus" model and the more recent "particularities" approach to history writing. Although still controversial, multiple perspectives, stories, and more fragmented and shifting identities can now legitimately figure in historical accounts. Women's history has been part of the expanding range and increasing complexity of accounts now possible at the beginning of the twenty-first century.[4]

Since the 1970s, there has been a rapid growth both of women's history and educational history. As Heap and Prentice point out, there has been a growing interaction between the two fields, as feminist historians increasingly challenge the dominant story of educational history in Canada.[5] Initially women's history functioned simply, albeit importantly, as a corrective to the androcentric bias in conventional accounts. Women's educational experience was or could be added to the educational past in order to subvert the assumption that men's experience represented the norm for humanity. Research initially focused on feminist concerns with educational access, in particular on women's admission to higher education and ultimately to the professions, economic independence, and status. However this trajectory implied a certain universality to women's experience and it has been quite rightly critiqued. Women's history thus began to turn to an engagement with differences among women based on race, class, ethnicity, and sexuality. Greater attention was given to social differences that diversified the categories of "women" and "women's history." In addition there has been a stronger focus on gender studies that examine relations between men and women. In this regard, feminist educational historians have been analyzing gender relations in educational institutions over time, examining the connections between educational practices and gendered (and other) social structures, raising questions about who defines what we perceive to be knowledge, who has control over the production and dissemination of knowledge, and what the institutionalization of schooling and learning has meant to women broadly defined.

A new emphasis in much recent research has been on language and discourse rather than experience. This line of thought suggests that it is not the historical event or experience itself that is important; nor do the multiple perspectives or interpretations of the event or the experience tell the whole story. Rather, attention shifts to the ways in which dominant and counter discourses produce what is taken to constitute historical events and their interpretations. This means recognizing historical accounts are not simple reflections of the "way it was" but are themselves open to analysis. While the past may exist, an understanding of it is not unchangeable. In other words, the lessons we learn from history may have less to do with what happened and more to do with how we interpret what happened, then and now. For some feminist historians this shift in historiography has meant examining the discursive production of masculinity and femininity now and in the past in order to understand how social structures, and social relations, as well as forms of agency and resistance are produced and reproduced in ways that have worked (or not) in the interests of women.[6]

Our project was designed to recover the histories of women teachers who numerically dominated the teaching force in Ontario. Our intention was to fill a gap in the research literature and in doing so provide a more adequate, reliable and gendered account of educational circumstances in twentieth century Ontario. These aims remain important for our project. At the same time we were cognizant of the dangers of universalizing the category of women and made efforts, evident in the chapters that follow, to include the histories of minority women and those marginalized by social, economic and geographical contexts. And, much as we might wish as feminists to celebrate the work and voice of women in the historical account, recent theoretical debates make us more skeptical and critical of the data and the effects of our research process, as well as of our own interpretive/discursive frames and those of our participants. As Luisa Passerini, argues, "The guiding principle could be that all autobiographical memory is true; it is up to the interpreter to discover in which sense, where, for what purpose."[7] Thus we were forced to question ideas about authentic voice, romanticized experiences and "true" accounts, even those offered by teachers who were present at the time of the events described.

These kinds of questions and directions challenge and change the very nature of what constitutes historical inquiry.[8] There were differences on the research team with regard to these new developments and debates about how to understand and interpret our evidence flourished. This should not be surprising since members of the team came to the enterprise from different disciplinary backgrounds and had different interests related to the broad topic of our study, the history of women teachers. As our research proceeded, the oral history method itself also produced tensions and difficulties, at times directly related to the shifts in historical understanding outlined above, at other times more practical and logistical in nature.

We turn now to describe our study in more detail and to speak of the education we have acquired through and about the research process of oral history.[9] As explained previously, our study was a large scale, multi-year, oral history project conducted by a cross-disciplinary group of seven researchers and several research assistants. The project was designed to allow for seven separate, though highly interconnected and over-lapping sub-projects, that built on the expertise of team members. The seven sub-projects focused on:

1. the social and moral regulation of female teachers as exercised through the discourse of professionalism, the application of "community standards" and the imposition of the formal authority of regulations and inspections;

2. teacher-community relationships in rural settings over time with a particular emphasis on the links between women teachers and rural women's organizations;

3. the experiences of female French language teachers, many of whom were francophones and often visible minority women recruited from former French colonies during periods of teacher shortages;

4. the lives of minority women teachers and the barriers, contradictions, tensions and dilemmas they faced during their teaching careers, particularly in circumstances where they actively used emancipatory and anti-racist pedagogies in the classroom;

5. the experiences of Aboriginal and non-Aboriginal women teachers who taught in northern and north-central communities in Ontario and their efforts to construct professional identities for themselves;

6. the ways in which the normative discourses of leadership have changed over time and how they intersected with women's understandings and experiences of school administration;

7. the efforts of women teachers, whether organizing through their unions or women's groups, to promote social reform, equity and social justice for themselves and for others.

Within each of the sub-projects, the researchers sought to explore how women understood and constructed their professional identities as educators; how female teachers' subjectivities and the material conditions of their work were shaped by the community, the state and professional associations; how women understood and negotiated their positions as teachers/workers; how teachers' personal and professional lives were integrated; and if and how teachers were politicized by their work and social location and what impact that had on their activities inside and outside the classroom.

A growing body of literature dealing with the history of female teachers raises other important and troubling questions which we pursued. How are women teachers and school systems implicated in the reproduction of gender and other inequalities? How could women teachers take pride in their work and yet practice in a system that was hierarchical and reinforced systemic patterns of discrimination? How did women teachers "make meaning" in their lives when the conditions in which they labored challenged the claim that their work was valued?

To address these questions we used evidence from several sources. We examined primary sources such as the archival records in central repositories and in personal, local, institutional and regional collections; teachers' published and unpublished autobiographies, memoirs, diaries and letters; novels by teachers about teaching in Ontario; and relevant educational policy documents produced by government departments, school boards, teacher federations and other educational agencies. However, the largest and most important source was the nearly two hundred oral history transcripts, prepared from interviews with retired women teachers who lived and worked in the various regions of the province during the twentieth century. Women teachers, like so many other historical actors who have been rendered silent in the records, have left few personal papers or other written documents about their work or their lives. The traces they have left most often illustrate their lives of service to students and to communities and take form in local histories, meticulously and lovingly prepared. Oral history, which largely owes its existence to the desire of social historians to recover the voices of ordinary people, has proven to be the only method by which we could recover important elements and ordinary moments of teachers' lives and their feelings about the work they did.[10]

Volunteer participants were solicited in a number of ways including through retired teachers' organizations, through free advertising space provided by many weekly and daily newspapers, and by a word-of-mouth, snowball technique. As we identified informants, we conducted an initial screening, either through a telephone or e-mail conversation. Once selected, informants were asked to complete a written questionnaire detailing descriptive information about their lives such as where they were born, what teacher education they received, how they got their first job, and in what schools and which grades they have taught. One member of the research team then interviewed each informant, using a semi-structured format, and tape recorded her story, which was later transcribed. Each participant was assigned a pseudonym and an identification (ACPID) number and these pseudonyms and ACPIDs are used for identification purposes throughout this book.

Almost from the start, we began to recognize a pattern emerging. The women volunteering for interviews were those who were the most self-confident, those who had been recognized in their careers, whether by being offered special professional opportunities or being elected to positions in the teachers' federations or the like, and those who were the leaders and the "movers and shakers" even in retirement. For the most part, these women represented Ontario's majority culture; they were white, Anglo-Saxon in origin and Protestant. They were also largely former elementary school teachers, an artifact of the historical occupational segregation in teaching. To increase the diversity of the informant pool, we had to become more pro-active. Because team members themselves were involved in a range of community groups and social justice activities, we were able to ask, through those groups, for assistance in identifying more marginalized, less well-known teachers, who might be interested in participating. Once we were able to locate a few informants, and establish our credibility with them, the snowball effect took over, enabling us to expand our catchment.

Because one of our goals was to examine teaching in Ontario, and not just southwestern Ontario, we were sensitive to geographic and regional representation among our informants. This has been less a problem than we imagined since teachers have turned out to be an amazingly peripatetic lot. Large numbers of our informants had worked in rural and urban areas, and in the north as well as in the south or east. Many had also worked elsewhere in Canada and several had taught in other countries. The mobility of teachers has, in fact, made it necessary for us to re-think location as an identifying category for teachers. When a teacher went to North Bay Teachers' College, taught in a northern lumber camp, Sault Ste, Marie, Orillia, Kingston and Chatham, what region is she from? And how does region within a province matter given that our understanding of terms such as "the north" is a fluid one. Indeed, "the north" in teachers' minds turns out to be everything from the Barrie area to the Yukon Territory.

The biggest challenge in identifying informants was finding women who had left the classroom after a short period of time either because they disliked the work or because they experienced problems with colleagues, administrators, trustees or the community. Women who loved teaching, who found a great deal of personal satisfaction in the work, who were supported and honored, were happy to discuss their careers. Woman who were harassed, who did not fit it, experienced classroom disasters, or were driven from communities were reluctant to identify themselves as potential informants, and even more reluctant to talk about events about which they still felt shame, guilt, anger or resentment. We were not able to recruit retired teachers who hated teaching but stayed with it because they needed the job and were unwilling or unable to try other possibilities.

The assumption that seven researchers from different disciplinary backgrounds and with very different life experiences would all conduct interviews in relatively the same way through a semi-structured format guided by a set of common questions, proved to be remarkably naïve. For two members of the team who had experiences similar to those of the teacher informants, the interviews become intimate, shared conversations about events through which they both had lived. Other team members conducted more formal or business-like interviews, asking the question, getting the answer, probing where necessary, and then moving on. Understandably, too, each team member tended to emphasize those questions about which she was most interested. Of course, this was partly because we were matching team members to informants who were likely to have information most relevant to that member's sub-project. But individual interest skewed the weight assigned to different sets of questions. This is not to suggest that somehow this renders any or all of the interviews unusable. It simply acknowledges the way in which interviews, like all historical documents, are constructed.

Sangster also reminds us that interviews are historical documents "created by the agency of both the interviewer and interviewee."[11] Nonetheless, significant power inequities can exist between the two parties and no doubt there was some disparity in many of our interviews. However, in our project this relationship was also shaped by the fact that professional women (i.e., university professors/teacher educators) were interviewing other professional women (i.e., teachers), at least some of whom have, themselves, taught at teachers' colleges or in faculties of education. Thus the power relationship in the interview dyad worked itself out in different ways in different interviews. At least one interviewee made it clear that she wished only to tell her stories and had no interest in an interview with "serious academic purpose." On the other hand, those teachers who had held senior administrative positions or leadership positions in teacher federations had a strong sense of their own historical position and recounted their lives in a well-rehearsed fashion. While a few teachers wondered if they "had anything to add to the project," for the most part teachers were anxious to volunteer for interviews and had a fairly clear sense of what it was they wanted to share.

Initially the vast majority of teachers offered an uncritical narrative, speaking in a way Di Leonardo has termed "rhetorical nostalgia" about the pleasure of teaching and the joys of working with the young.[12] Concomitantly, there was a common denial of gender discrimination, despite the fact that most interviews were replete with examples of the disadvantages that fell to women because they were women. How to disrupt romantic recall without denying the pleasures of teaching was a challenging aspect of the interview process. Respect for the age and experience of informants initially encouraged us to be too careful, to avoid reference to matters which we thought would trouble our interviewees. However, it soon became clear that this was inappropriate and that we stereotyped retired women teachers, making assumptions that explicit questions about sexual harassment or homosexuality, for example, would upset them. We quickly came to accept Portelli's argument that we respect our informants best when we are honest, straightforward and open with them, while at the same time remaining responsive to their sensitivities.[13] Hence we shifted our vague questioning about "getting into trouble with school boards and communities" to more explicit questions about sexuality and lifestyle, about abortion and pregnancy outside of marriage, and so on. Rather than ask only about classroom management, we asked more specific questions about forms of discipline and corporal punishment.

As a team we also debated how to respond to biased comments from participants. How, for example, should we respond to a racist observation from an informant about Aboriginal or black students? Some members of the team felt that the appropriate response was no response; as interviewers our task was simply to collect the views of informants. Other researchers felt that as human beings we are obligated to challenge racist observations wherever they occur or we are complicit with them. This does not mean accusing the informant of being racist but rather of asking a follow-up question to probe the comment in ways that would force the informant to become more self-reflexive. The different positions on this matter reflected an ongoing debate about the methodology of oral history and was not resolved within our team.

Each tape-recorded interview was sent for transcription. When returned, the transcript was reviewed by the interviewer for egregious errors, and then sent to the participant who was asked to read the transcript and either do nothing or correct mistakes of fact, add further information she had remembered since the interview or delete anything she did not now wish to have included, and return the transcript to us. We learned very quickly that former teachers were shocked to see the transcripts and could not believe that their spoken English did not meet the rigorous standards of their written work. Many spent long hours correcting the transcripts and the project's research assistants spent long hours making the changes on the electronic copies. One teacher fully re-wrote her whole transcript, in effect re-doing the whole interview and giving different, more complete answers. Our assumption that teachers would understand that we would only be using selections from transcripts as we prepared articles was clearly wrong. That we would protect their anonymity also escaped their notice or, at least, could not overcome their concern for correct English usage. In order to ensure our participants would not spend long hours correcting their transcripts, we prepared another, more detailed covering letter that was more explicit about how the transcript material would be used. We also assured informants that we would fix the worst grammatical errors before quoting from the transcripts and eliminate the "umms" and "ahhs." This, of course, pushes up against the consideration that quotes should be reproduced exactly as the words were spoken but it is a compromise we felt we had to make.

We also had to confront the implications of changes teachers wished to make in the content of their transcripts. Often they wanted to soften a judgment they had rendered originally or delete a critical comment or otherwise substantively edit the transcript, often to the point of changing meaning. While such changes are the prerogative of the participant, we also felt that valuable information was getting lost when words, sentences or sometimes even sections of the transcript were deleted. However, ethical considerations dictated that the wishes of the participant, expressed in the form of a revised transcript, had to be honored. While we had the original and the revised transcript and could read the former with the latter, it was the revised transcript that we were required to use as the source of our evidence, however frustrating that was at times.

In managing and interpreting the data, we had to face questions about personal and collective memory, agency and resistance, political consciousness and hegemonic discourse, namely the dilemmas that all oral historians face as they try to understand their participants as gendered, classed and racialized subjects situated in a specific socio-historical context. As researchers we were also cognizant of the fact that we exercised the power of interpretation and we acknowledge that it must be exercised responsibly, with academic humility and in a self-conscious and self-critical manner. How each of us worked out these challenges is reflected in our individual contributions to this collection.

We are aware that many of our participants and others who have encouraged retired teachers to participate in our research expect us to produce work that is commemorative, rather than critical. While we did celebrate the lives and contributions of women teachers in Ontario where appropriate, our research also was organized to explore the multiple views of women teachers who spoke from their own social locations and identities and consequently they sometimes revealed that relations among women and among teachers could be ones of conflict and pain. What teaching meant to women individually and collectively in a system based on male dominance of a hierarchical structure and how teachers both shaped and were shaped by their work and the political context of public education are the kinds of concerns we confront in the chapters that follow.

In the first section, "Different Women, Different Teachers, Different Ontarios," five chapters address the diversity of women teachers in Ontario. While they shared the common experience of work in the classrooms of the province, that work was also shaped by geographic location (chapters 2 and 3), by language (chapter 4), race (chapter 5) and sexuality (chapter 6). In her chapter "Rural Teacher/Farm Wife: 'Women's Work is Never Done'," Aniko Varpalotai explores the lives of rural women who combined a career in teaching with work on the farm and in the household, and well as in the voluntary sector of the wider community. These teachers juggled not just women's usual double burden, nor even a triple one, but four major responsibilities as their education, organizational skills and other attributes made them a key resource in their rural settings. Helen Harper turns her attention to an examination of women teaching in the north in a chapter entitled "Personal and Professional Freedom in the Hinterlands: Women Teachers in Northern Ontario." She illustrates how women negotiated the tension between isolation and autonomy, highlighting the importance of freedom in the lives of professionals. Both Varpalotai and Harper note that women teachers, having experienced professional autonomy in their careers, found it particularly hard when the educational re-structuring of the 1990s imposed significantly greater controls on teaching work.

In "For the Sake of Language and Heritage: Ontario Francophone Women Teachers Reflect on Their Careers," Suzanne Majhanovich discusses the particular and special nature of the work of francophone women teachers and emphasizes their commitment to cultural survival. For these teachers, their identity as francophones was of paramount importance and, while they experienced discrimination and exploitation in their careers, they overlooked sexism to focus on the maintenance of the French language and culture through schooling. In her chapter, "Women of Color and Teaching: Exploring Contradictory Experiences of Immigrant Women Teachers," Goli Rezai-Rashti explores the lives of five women of color who came to Canada to teach. She is concerned to demonstrate how structural constraints are mediated by individual responses and how identity is "fluid, relational and multi-positional." Consequently Rezai-Rashti emphasizes the complexities of the gendered and racialized experiences of the immigrant teachers she interviewed. Sheila Cavanagh turns attention to the intersection of sexuality and teaching in her contribution, "Female Teacher Gender and Sexuality in Twentieth Century Ontario Canada." She traces the trajectory of the ideal woman teacher from the chaste, single woman of the early twentieth-century to the hetero-normative married teacher of the second half of the century and links this shift to a growing fear of homosexuality.

The second section of this book focuses on teachers' leadership outside of the classroom. In "Assuming Leadership: Women Superintendents in Twentieth Century Ontario," Janice Wallace looks at four women who took on senior administrative positions at the school board level to see how these women "did leadership." She argues that they played out two different gender scripts – the dutiful daughter or the troubling woman – and explores how and why that was. Rebecca Coulter turns to look at women who exercised leadership in the Federation of Women Teachers' Associations in Ontario at the local and provincial levels in the chapter, "Organizing in Contradiction: Women Teachers, Unionization and the Politics of Feminized Professionalism." She analyzes how women teachers both used and opposed discourses of professionalism and femininity and related (or not) to unionism and feminism.

Turning to a different set of themes, the third section looks at the perils and the pleasures of teaching. Sheila Cavanagh, in "Nervous Narratives: Female Teacher Maladies in the Twentieth Century," directs attention to those teachers who suffered from psychological disorders and had, as she states, a "rendezvous with madness." Cavanagh thus reminds us that some teachers had real mental health difficulties and she examines a few specific cases with a view towards explicating the social and historical construction of female madness in the mid-twentieth century. The book concludes with a chapter by Rebecca Coulter called "'Girls Just Want To Have Fun': Women Teachers and The Pleasures of the Profession." As an antidote to pessimistic and negative renderings of women's experiences of teaching, Coulter points to the many pleasures a job of one's own could offer and argues that to fully understand the history of teachers, we must look not only in the classroom but beyond it.

Taken together, the chapters in this book offer a variety of readings of women teachers' lives and suggest so many more questions that must be pursued. One thing is clear, however: women teachers have been central to knowledge development and promulgation, and through their work they have contributed to the making of Canada, for better or worse. Understanding historically how they experienced their lives as gendered, racialized, sexualized subjects, how they made sense of their lives as women and as teachers, what they believed about the meaning of their work and its relationship to state formation and citizenship, is an important task that must not go unfinished. After all, "Without history we are infants. All good news becomes ecstasy and all bad news disaster."[14]

Notes

[1]See, Alison Prentice and Marjorie R. Theobald, "The Historiography of Women Teachers: A Retrospect," in *Women Who Taught: Perspectives on the History of Women and Teaching,* ed. Alison Prentice and Marjorie R. Theobald, 3-33 (Toronto: University of Toronto Press,1991) for a useful, though now somewhat dated, review of the literature and Susan Gelman, "Select Bibliography" in the same book, 285-301. See, also, Alison Prentice, "Workers, Professionals, Pilgrims; Tracing Canadian Women Teachers' Histories," in *Telling Women's Lives: Narrative Inquiries in the History of Women's Education,* ed. Kathleen Weiler and Sue Middleton, 25-42 (Buckingham and Philadelphia Open University Press, 1999); Marta Danylewycz and Alison Prentice, "Teachers' Work: Changing Patterns and Perceptions in the Emerging School Systems of Nineteenth- and Early Twentieth-Century Central Canada," *Labour/Le travail 17* (1986): 59-80; Alison Prentice, "From Household to School House: The Emergence of the Teacher as Servant of the State," in *Gender and Education in Ontario,* ed. Ruby Heap and Alison Prentice, 25-48 (Toronto: Canadian Scholars' Press, 1991); John R. Abbott, "Accomplishing 'A Man's Task': Rural Women Teachers, Male Culture and the School Inspectorate in Turn-of-the-Century Ontario," in *Gender and Education in Ontario,* ed. Heap and Prentice, 51-72; Susan Gelman, "The 'Feminization' of the High School: Women Secondary Teachers in Toronto, 1871-1930," *Historical Studies in Education 2* (1990): 119-148; Cecilia Reynolds, "Hegemony and Hierarchy: Becoming a Teacher in Toronto, 1930-1980," *Historical Studies in Education 2* (1990): 95-118; Cecilia Reynolds, "In the Right Place at the Right Time: Rules of Control and Woman's Place in Ontario Schools, 1940-1980," *Canadian Journal of Education 20* (1995): 129-145; Judith Arbus, "Grateful to be Working: Women Teachers During the Great

Depression," in *Feminism and Education: A Canadian Perspective,* ed. Frieda Forman, Mary O'Brien, Jane Haddad, Dianne Hallman, and Philinda Masters, 169-190 (Toronto: Centre for Women's Studies, OISE, 1990); Sandra Gaskell, "The Problems and Professionalism of Women Elementary Public School Teachers, 1944-1954" (EdD thesis, University of Toronto, 1990).

[2]Doris French, *High Button Bootstraps: Federation of Women Teachers' Associations of Ontario, 1918-1968* (Toronto: Ryerson Press, 1968); Pat Staton and Beth Light, *Speak With Their Own Voices: A Documentary History of the Federation of Women Teachers' Associations of Ontario and the Women Elementary Public School Teachers of Ontario* (Toronto: FWTAO, 1987); Mary Labatt, *Always a Journey: A History of the Federation of Women Teachers' Associations of Ontario, 1918-1993* (Toronto: FWTAO, 1993).

[3]Janice Newton quoted in Kathleen Weiler, *Country Schoolwomen: Teaching in Rural California, 1850-1950* (Stanford: Stanford University Press, 1998), 5.

[4]See. for example, discussion of these topics in Kathryn McPherson, Cecilia Morgan and Nancy M. Forestell, "Introduction: Conceptualizing Canada's Gendered Pasts," in Gendered Pasts: *Historical Essays in Femininity and Masculinity in Canada,* eds. Kathryn McPherson, Cecilia Morgan and Nancy M. Forestell, 1-11 (Don Mills, ON: Oxford University Press, 1999).

[5]Ruby Heap and Alison Prentice, "Introduction: Gender and Education in Ontario's Past," in *Gender and Education in Ontario,* ed. Heap and Prentice, v-xix.

[6]For a very useful discussion of recent debates see Kathleen Weiler, "Reflections on Writing a History of Women Teachers," in *Telling Women's Lives*, ed. Kathleen Weiler and Sue Middleton, 43-59.

[7]Luisa Passerini, "Women's Personal Narratives: Myths, Experiences, and Emotions," in *Interpreting Women's Lives: Feminist Theory and Personal Narratives*, ed. Personal Narratives Group (Bloomington and Indianapolis: Indiana Univesity Press, 1989), 197.

[8]For a good introduction to the current debates about historical inquiry see, Richard J. Evans, *In Defence of History* (London: Granta Books, 2000).

[9]Much of the following discussion about our project appeared in an earlier version as Rebecca Priegert Coulter, "Learning Our Lessons: Oral History and the Women Teachers of Ontario," *Oral History Forum 21-22* (2001-2002): 87-99.

[10]For an excellent discussion of the importance of oral history in understanding teachers and teaching see, Philip Gardner, "Oral History in Education: Teacher's Memory and Teachers' History," *History of Education 32* (2003): 175-188.

[11]Joan Sangster, "Telling Our Stories: Feminist Debates and the Use of Oral History," in *The Oral History Reader,* ed. Robert Perks and Alistair Thomson (London and New York: Routledge, 1998), 92.

[12]M. Di Leonardo, *Varieties of Ethnic Experience* (Ithaca, NY: Cornell University Press, 1984), 233.

[13]Alessandro Portelli, *The Battle of Valle Giulia: Oral History and the Art of Dialogue* (Madison: University of Wisconsin Press, 1997).

[14]Simon Jenkins quoted in Richard Aldrich, "The Three Duties of the Historian of Education," *History of Education 32* (2003): 137.

Section One

Different Women,
Different Teachers,
Different Ontarios

2
Rural Teacher / Farm Wife: "Women's Work is Never Done"

Aniko Varpalotai

Annual Fair of Westminster Township Schools. *Photo courtesy of The University of Western Ontario Archives, London Free Press Collection, Sept. 9, 1938.*

Introduction

The rural and agricultural landscape in Ontario has undergone significant changes during the twentieth-century. The definition of "rural" varies from person to person, and place to place, and can mean anything from the proximity of the nearest urban centre, the community economic base, size of the local population, and other factors defining the geography and social fabric of the community. Rural communities are found throughout Ontario, from the most isolated in the far north, around mining sites, lumber camps, and Aboriginal settlements, to the more densely populated agricultural areas of southern Ontario. For the purposes of this chapter, "rural" will pertain primarily to those areas that are dependent on farming and related enterprises for economic survival.[1] Most of the interviews cited in this chapter are with rural women teachers/farm wives living and working in southwestern Ontario rural communities.

Canadian Farm Women

A number of historical studies have been written on the lives of farm women in Canada.[2] These studies make mention of rural women's longstanding advocacy and support for rural education. Langford notes that "the educational opportunities provided in rural areas were as important as health care to farm women."[3] Halpern states that farm women:

> supported the modern view that "farmers' daughters" should receive the best education possible.... Teaching was the most common career for farm daughters, proving attractive because in addition to there being a teacher shortage ... training was not overly costly to fund. Moreover, within the farming communities, a woman schoolteacher, while poorly paid and subjected to trying working conditions and little privacy, was always considered "a good catch."[4]

Despite farm women's support for higher education for their children, farm daughters were sometimes required to stay home from school in order to help with chores and younger siblings. And the consolidation of rural schools during the second half of the century created a further problem for farm wives: as the yellow school buses began to take farm children further away from their homes to school, "this deprived farm women of the much-needed children's help around the house, yard, barn, and farm. In 1951 only 29.6 per cent of this population had nine years of education, compared with 55 per cent in urban areas" – still, farm women tended to have more formal education than farm men.[5]

Despite numerous references to the education, aspirations, and paid and unpaid work of farm women, what has been missing until now is the voice, through oral histories, of the rural woman who was both farm wife and teacher in the province of Ontario. This chapter, then, will focus on selected interviews and the themes, stories and issues as recounted by retired rural women teachers and farmwomen in Ontario during the twentieth century.

Rural Education in Ontario

The early twentieth century schools of Ontario were organized around the agrarian roots of much of the society of the time – the school year was interrupted for the summer farm season, and one-room schoolhouses were to be found throughout rural Ontario during the first half of the century. According to the Annual Reports of the Provincial Departments of Education (1909-1910, 1910-1911) the majority of rural teachers across the country were women, with Ontario recording the largest percentage at 80.9% followed by Alberta at 63.3% and Saskatchewan with 57.4%.[6] A Federation of Women Teachers' Associations of Ontario study shows the turning point for women teachers in rural schools. In 1957-58: 3 516 teachers were teaching in one-room schools (which represented 59.6% of all schools in Ontario at that time), just a few years later, in 1960-61, the one-teacher/one-room schools had declined to 2 976 and 52.3% respectively. In 1945 there were 5 081 one-room schools in the province, and only 224 schools with 4 rooms/teachers.[7] Of the close to two hundred retired Ontario women teachers interviewed for this study, the majority had at least some rural teaching experience – particularly those who began their careers in Ontario during the first half of the twentieth century.

With advances in technology and transportation, and as the province became increasingly urbanized, the family farm began its decline, and schools were consolidated and centralized in the closest towns and cities. Most of the one-room rural schools closed and/or were amalgamated during the 1960s and 1970s, but even today, the issue of rural school closures continues to be a concern in single school communities where students are already spending up to two hours riding school buses each day to and from their homes and/or farms.[8] Then, as now, urban based education policy makers promoted this as the pedagogically progressive and economically efficient thing to do, while the local citizens lamented their loss of control and the impact of school closures on their community.[9] Road improvements led to increased school bus transportation, further amalgamation of both the schools and local school boards, and the creation of larger, centralized (often in the nearest urban centre) and even more distant schools.

The rural teachers who were interviewed during this study lived through the political and social upheavals surrounding these decisions, and experienced the autonomy, and the loneliness, of the one-room, multi-grade schoolhouse, as well as the collegiality, and improved resources, of the larger central schools. Those who were from rural and farming backgrounds themselves faced the combined challenges of working as both schoolteacher and farm wife, particularly when their school was no longer located in their immediate community. Rural women played a pivotal, though sometimes invisible role in farming, community building, and of course, teaching in the rural schools.[10] This chapter focusses on those women who served in all of these capacities as rural teacher and farm wife – their trials and tribulations, their joys and sorrows, their stories.

The Rural Woman Teacher

Reference to the Canadian rural woman teacher of the twentieth century can be found scattered through various education and rural histories, but they are also frequently romanticized in celebrated works of fiction. Perhaps the best known Canadian examples are the much loved stories of Lucy Maud Montgomery[11] and her heroine, *Anne of Green Gables* who developed from feisty schoolgirl to respected teacher in a one-room school on Prince Edward Island. To some extent, the experiences of the rural woman teacher were internationally enjoyed by young readers – even *Heidi,* of the Swiss Alps, in the lesser known sequel,[12] returns to her beloved village in the mountains, her Grandfather and his herd of goats, to teach in a challenging one-room school, when barely out of school herself. These youthful teachers were required to win the respect of students close to them in age, some of the older, and bigger, country boys were a particular challenge, as well as sceptical community members, who served as trustees, landlords and parents. Of the rural women teachers surveyed by the Federation of Women Teachers' Associations of Ontario (FWTAO) in 1961, only 1.2 per cent of them "had the equivalent of a university degree or better, and the vast majority (71.8 per cent) had what one would consider minimum qualifications for elementary school teachers."[13]

The Women's Institutes, found in almost all rural communities throughout Canada, and other countries worldwide, played a significant role in promoting education, supporting local women teachers, and educating farm women. Through their Tweedsmuir Histories, housed at local libraries, they documented the comings and goings of the local teachers, as well as other important community events, saved newspaper clippings, and other noteworthy items in their scrapbooks, as well as narratives. As noted in the Centennial History of the Women's Institutes in Ontario[14]:

> A third area where the Institutes worked in their communities was schools. This was an area that was close to the hearts of mothers particularly, as they extended the concerns of caring for their families outside their homes and into the schoolyards. "The Women's Institutes have done considerable by visiting the schools and offering suggestions to the trustees to improve the conditions surrounding the rural schools. The sanitation of the school has been much improved and scholars and teachers have cooperated in beautifying the school grounds as a result of suggestions by the Women's Institute."

Still another perspective on this time and place is through the eyes of rural children.[15] Collections of children's letters, stories and photographs documented both farm life and schooling, as experienced by rural children and shed further light on the working conditions of their teachers. As Cochrane notes, "Country schools were not at all like the schools in towns. For one thing, everyone who attended was a neighbor, including the teacher."[16] Both the students and the teachers shared recollections of the daily chores, school fairs, school pranks, 4-H clubs, and the strap! The schools had a role to play in both ensuring that children became literate and numerate, but also to convince them to stay on the farm, despite the hard work that entailed. The exodus from farms and rural communities became a concern as early as the 1920s.

> Farm propagandists did everything they could to keep the young ones down on the farm. There were lessons in school and competitive

school fairs to teach farming techniques and to help lend an air of excitement. There were stories and poems and talks and sermons promoting the mythical image that still exists of the freedom, dignity, and virtue of life on the family farm.[17]

Rural women teachers were more or less successful in these sometimes contradictory goals, depending on their own roots in a farming community or conversely, their awareness of what the beckoning city had to offer.

The women whose stories are reproduced here, were either from farming backgrounds themselves, married into farming families, or found themselves teaching in farming communities. They will be the first to suggest that their stories are neither dramatic nor particularly unusual for the times – yet, throughout each interview, local dramas, and important glimpses into the history of both schooling and society during the various decades of the 20th century emerge as insights worth preserving.[18] Their views of changing educational policies and curriculum, the double and triple work day experienced by women working within the home, on the farm and teaching, community relationships, and additional contributions to the wider community all emerge through their life stories and histories as rural teachers and farm wives.

"I didn't know a horse from a cow!"

Many of the close to 200 teachers interviewed for this study spent at least a portion of their teaching careers in rural schools, and there were some who had not had previous experience in the countryside, or in farming communities. The insights and observations of newcomers to rural life are especially valuable as they saw rural schools as novel institutions. Thus they recounted in great detail the unique features of the typical rural school. Those who had themselves attended one-room schools, took the various expectations and hardships for granted; this is how they had been taught, and they took their eight grade classrooms in stride. Teachers whose only exposure to rural life was through brief practice teaching experiences during their teacher education programs, had this to say about the one-room rural school in the late 1940s:

We all went together, [six of us student teachers], and these would be one-room country schools. The teacher in the morning lit the fire and she sat up on a raised platform and the grade 8s sat on one side by the windows. The little kids went home early and then the older students got personal attention. In between they helped with teaching the little ones. And I was fascinated. These kids were so good, all their work was on the board, and I couldn't believe there was no nonsense. They were wonderful kids. I was captivated by the whole thing, that was in the country.... I don't know what I would have done. I couldn't have tackled eight grades. Of course most of the teachers had been raised in the country. (Mavis, ACPID 130)

Another teacher, Lauren (ACPID 050) recounts her first teaching assignment in a rural (two-room) school in the early 1950s:

[Grades] one to eight, that's all we knew. It was a rural school. On top of that I was assigned, we were put up in a farm house and I had never been on a farm in my life [laughter], and the one thing I must say they fed us very well, wonderful food, but in the mornings we got up and had to chip the ice off the basin and the only place it was warm to get dressed was under the covers. We got to the school and we had to light the fire before we could get going. We never got going in the morning til about 10 o'clock because it wasn't warm enough to take off any clothes til then, so it was quite an experience, and fortunately because the kids seemed to be so lucky in reading, you could just pick up and just work individually with the kids, but I don't think we ever taught any structured lessons.... Literally flying by the seat of our pants ... You were just sort of guiding them through a type of individualized program, which wasn't bad experience, simply because at a later date and when we got into the open concept schools, technically that's what we should have been doing.

Ashley (ACPID 198) completed teachers college in 1934-35, and began teaching in a remote, northern Ontario one-room school at the age of 19. Her aunt found her this job through the Chairman of the School Board, from whom she bought her vegetables and eggs. Ashley's only exposure to rural schools had been through a few brief practice-teaching assignments ...

so it was a real eye-opener when I had my own school. I got, oh, there was a desk there for the teacher, with a bell on it, a hand bell that I would have to, when I'd lift it up I would yell [laughter]. Once there was a snake under there, then they'd put frogs and different bugs and all this sort of thing. I used to screech, oh boy! But ... I would have

to handle those things because I didn't dare show them how fright-
ened I was . . . I made a garden, and I taught agriculture [laughter] I,
who had never been on a farm for any length of time. I didn't know
anything about gardening or anything like that. I taught agriculture. I
didn't know a horse from a cow, you know, the names of them, but I
learned. Oh boy, I worked.

Not only did rural women teachers have to deal with their own
fears and uncertainties, but also with community members who were
equally, if not more frustrated with their own situation. Ashley recalls
a confrontation with one mother:

did she bawl me out, and finally she became so abusive I ordered her
out of the classroom . . . oh, I was just shaking . . . But she was mentally disturbed, I'm sure . . . because she didn't want to come to
Canada, and she was a city-bred girl, and married this man and they
decided to try farming in this God-forsaken section . . . There were
some good farms there, people had been looking and got them, but
it wasn't a place, I often thought that the British certainly didn't think
very much of their soldiers to give them land like that, as a reward for
having fought in the [World] War [I]. . . it was pathetic, those children . . . I let it be known that I was going to visit every family in the
school. . . . so every week I visited one family . . . oh, some of the
meals were pathetic . . . but I was willing to share what they had – I
had bear meat, I had beaver meat, I had possum meat. . . .

Despite the hardships, and after having spent the latter part of her
teaching career in city schools, Ashley reflects:

I thought it would be heaven to teach in a city school with one class,
but I found it wasn't. . . . I much preferred my rural school teaching
. . . Because the pupils were different. They were much more pliable,
and you were a young God to them, Goddess to them, and if you
noticed anything and made a comment, oh but that was wonderful. . . ."

With memories of lighting the woodstove, inspecting outhouses,
dealing with head lice, and cooking hot lunches for her pupils, the
rural school remains among the fondest memories of her teaching
career.

Farm Women and Rural Teaching: Seamless Realities and Professional Issues

The usual caveats applied for a farm girl who wanted a career for herself: ". . . maybe it was the way I was raised, or something, a girl had to be either a nurse or a teacher, that's all that was open to them" (Ruby, ACPID 174). Ruby was encouraged to pursue a career rather than stay at home or work on the farm. She attended normal school in 1943-44, and was tempted to join the war effort. While she attended normal school in Toronto, where she had already lived and worked for a year, ("Oh yes, I value those years in the city very much") – she returned to her home community to teach, initially in a one-room schoolhouse, grades 1-8. Having grown up on a farm, herself, and engaged to be married to a farmer from her community, Ruby returned home to teach and farm. "Oh I was married the first year I

Teacher Noreen Conlin and her class in 1952 at the school on Highway 4 and the Roman Line, Lucan, Ontario. *Photo courtesy James Van Bussel, a student in that class.*

taught, you see, so, to a farmer. . . . Yeah, and I've lived on a farm ever since I was married, so there you are." [chuckle]

Ruby taught through the era of the transition from the one-room schoolhouse where she was in charge, to the multi-room schools with principals, and superintendents from the larger school boards exerting more influence over her worklife. As younger teachers began to arrive with university degrees, the older teachers, like Ruby, were pressured to take summer courses to upgrade their qualifications. This is when Ruby decided that she was going to take early retirement from teaching:

> Well there was one superintendent . . . that's why I quit, actually, why I got out of teaching, and he said, you know, when are you going to upgrade your qualifications? Well he was meaning why aren't you taking more summer courses, and I didn't have a BA and had no intentions of getting one, and then I thought well now this, you know, I should get out when I get enough years in there that I can get some kind of pension, so that's why I got out, because I could feel the pressure, and I thought well it's just gonna continue and get greater, you know.. . . . I think it was a system-wide pressure, and actually in a small school like that I was the only one who didn't, who wasn't taking summer courses, and there were only eight, nine of us . . .. lived on a farm, I enjoyed my summers and I mean while I had taken courses like, short courses, there's no way I was going to ever end up with a university degree. . . .

> Int.:.Were you also active on the farm?

> Ruby: Oh, yes . . . I worked with the livestock, and had a garden and I didn't, you know, run some machinery, not like when I was a child, we used to, you know, drive the horses and all these types of things. Milk cows and so on . . . I didn't have to do it, I just, what I did on the farm because I did, I wanted to do it, type of thing.

Ruby also incorporated the farm into her teaching:

> Well, I always took them out to the farm, for the trip, you know, every year. They always came here, they always came to my farm . . . and like where I live it's a Century Farm and there was some historical significance to that too, and the location of the farm with regard to the county, was a good way to teach the local geography because it was right, it's right on the edge of Perth, and there's Wellington over here, so, and we have a different township across the road and actually we had four townships to consider . . .

Ruby also made sure that her rural students were exposed to the city, and took them on trips to Toronto, where they were able to tour the museum, the Royal York Hotel ("they were really good to us, a bunch of kids travelling through this, and on the elevator, showed them rooms, the dining rooms, the kitchens even!") and other landmarks.

Other rural teachers had the sense that their career options were restricted due to their rural background. Nancy (ACPID 008) followed the family tradition (her mother and two older sisters were also teachers), and for the most part, she was happy with her "choice." She became a secondary school teacher, working for most of her career in the community in which she had been raised.

> There were some days I was wishing I was doing anything but teaching, but in general terms, yes, I enjoyed teaching and I enjoyed working with kids and my colleagues. . . . I think now [pause] that I'm retired and have more time to think [slight laugh] about it, if I were growing up right now I might do things differently. Yeah. I'm very interested in genetics. . . . I might have chosen that path now. . . ."

Nancy also attended normal school in Toronto, and has vivid memories of her practice teaching experiences there:

> But oh, talk about fear and trepidation. They had just had, now this, and you've gotta remember this was '58/'59. They had just had a stabbing on the front steps of the school . . . and of course, that was in the red light district, Jarvis [St.], at that time. . . . Like this happened just before I went there for my practice-teaching assignment – little girl from the country. Oh, boy!"

Nancy moved back to her home farm with her husband who was also from the area. She had anticipated a short-term career.

> Well, you know, it was funny. This is another female thing. When I started teaching, I thought, 'Oh, I'll teach for five years' which [pause] I did, [laugh] 'And then I'll quit teaching and become a lady of leisure.' [slight laugh] Notice, the plan never came! Although, I, [pause] at that time, when you became pregnant and it became obvious, you had to resign. I mean you were a bad model for the students. So, I did teach for five years, and then I had a baby, so I quit that year. But I found . . . I don't know. I just found that I was missing something. I know that's awful to say when you're talking about your own daughter, but anyway [laugh] and so I stayed off for one year and then went back. . .

so it was going to be a short term career and it turned into a long term career. And you know, I don't think it was from the point of view of finances that I went back. No, it wasn't. It was, I don't know, just felt, I guess, that I missed something and, you know, I wanted to get back in at it again.

The political climate surrounding education reached into the countryside, as well. Nancy notes her frustrations with Conservative Premier Mike Harris's educational policies, towards the end of her career:

And I get so, every time, too, this Harris,. . . . when he's going on about the state of the educational system in Toronto, and every time I would meet an ex-student and what are they doing, well, they're chemical engineers or Deputy Minister of Agriculture, you know, in Ontario, you know. And I just, oh, God. Well, I wrote to him once, but I know it doesn't do any good, so I've given up. Yeah. . . .. And I just love to, you know, write to him and list all these students that we produced in our school and what they're doing, you know, to show him that education wasn't so bad in this province.

Politics was a source of frustration from the time the rural boards were merged in the 1960s. When the Board was centralized in the nearest town, Nancy said it became "more remote." Prior to that,

all of the Board members were local people, and you know, it seemed as though you could. . . . they would come into the school and . . . you knew them, you could talk to them, more approachable. Then once it moved. . . . And this, the way it is now, [referring to the large scale Board amalgamations that took place in 1998] I just cannot, I cannot believe it.

Living and working in the same rural community has often been likened to a "fishbowl." Teachers were (and continue to be) public figures, well-known throughout their small community. Their lives were subject to public scrutiny, and gossip, and more than one teacher talked about having to be on their best behavior, especially in social circumstances. Inevitably, in a small community, everyone was somehow connected to the school, either directly or indirectly.

Nancy was aware of this concern but was not troubled by it herself:

Well, you know, I've heard some people say that living in a rural area, that is the real disadvantage, is if you live in the area where you teach, particularly in a rural area. But you know, I've had teachers tell me this that came [here] to teach, that they found that they were like in a fish-bowl, you know. But I never particularly felt like that. . . . Although, you know, I think sometimes it comes down to the fact that if you don't do anything stupid (laugh) I mean, you're not going to be the focus of public opinion. Like, I can remember once I went up to the Post Office and this was on school business, and it was during my spare, and meeting this man, and he said, you know, I mean, he made a big deal "Oh it must be nice to, you know, be a teacher, get off whenever you feel like it . . ." And I just said, very nicely, "Well," I said, "Go and take the training and join the profession!"

A common perception, echoed by many of the teachers, including Nancy, was

that rural students were more teachable . . .(furthermore), like in the '60s and '70s, a significant proportion of our school population would be first generation people. . . . And I mean, they had a work ethic.

Several teachers commented on the hard working immigrant families within their communities. Various farm settlements, particularly in southern Ontario, attracted immigrant families from Europe, primarily from the Netherlands, Germany, and Eastern Europe. Though there were a few communication issues noted, and many of the families were very poor, with many children, for the most part it was the work ethic, and the discipline of the children that stood out in the teachers' memories.

Nor was the rural community immune from "scandal!" Nancy, and each of her two sisters, recalled one fellow teacher who was both an alcoholic and a lesbian, but who was nonetheless a brilliant teacher. "We used to try to cover for her . . . she'd come to school late, and we'd cover for her," but ultimately, she left the school – and it was never clear whether she was dismissed or resigned voluntarily.

Nancy's eldest sister, Georgina (ACPID 005) became the first secondary school vice-principal in her County and served in this capacity until she retired (1976-85). She attributes her success in this predominantly male culture to her farming background. She describes her experience as the only female at a weekend retreat for school administrators:

I couldn't complain, I expect likely their language was a lot better because I was there. I never found, uh, how shall I put it . . . I never found working in a, in what was really a men's milieu, didn't bother me that much. For two reasons I think: one because I was brought up on the farm as a boy, the three of us, you know, we had no brothers, so we worked. There was nothing we couldn't do most days in general farming. . . . and plus, I don't know, I guess maybe it's my nature because I mean, I don't think I'm aggressive but I mean if somebody's attacking me I'm not going to back down. So I mean I always stood up for myself.

Despite this assertive demeanor, it took many years of applying before Georgina was finally chosen to attend the principal's course. Various excuses were given: a quota with the recent dissolution of the local boards and the move to County boards; denials about gender or age being factors (by now she was in her forties). She invited Superintendents to her class to observe her teaching ("So, you see, you just have to push.") Finally, she confronted one of the original trustees from the local board:

There were only six Board members at [that] Board, and we really had a good relationship. . . . The Board usually entertained the whole staff, dinner, you know, and a social evening in the Fall, and we always entertained the Board. So, I mean, you knew your Board members. And I remember, I taught. . . . [board member], I had taught his son and I figured he was a straight guy to tell the truth. And I remember after the second year [of applying] I remember going out to see him, and asking him, "Now, why do you think, why do you think they wouldn't send me on that course? Is it because I'm a woman?" "Well," he said, "probably . . . You know, . . . You have to be outstanding if you're a woman if you want to get on it." He told me that. . . ."

Even after she was finally successful in being selected to attend the course, it was several more years, and several more applications before Georgina finally was appointed to an administrative position.

Georgina preferred to teach rural and working class students; she recounts her experience at a large consolidated high school which bordered the city and rural area that included

kids from [the city] who did think they were God's gift to creation, eh, because they were well to do, you had the rural kids, and you had the kids from the east, the industrial section. . . . there was friction, definitely. . . and when I went over to [the other school] I was never aware of that. . . it was rural rural and we got rid of the snobs.

Her preference for teaching in a rural community was two-fold:

The kids, first of all, were not so sophisticated. . . . And the numbers are small, you know, smaller numbers, and I don't care what they say . . . bigness is not better. I can remember when they consolidated the schools here, you know, and they talked about all the wonderful advantages, you know. They would get shops, they would get better libraries, they would get labs, and so on. . . . They didn't look at the disadvantages. For example, if I were a parent now with a young child, I would never let them ride the buses. . . .

Despite having lived and taught in various parts of the province during her career, Georgina felt most comfortable in the country:

[I] was much happier . . . if you're a country girl at heart, you know, I mean, like I'm used to, when I finish mowing the lawn here, I go out on my back patio and shed all my clothes and shake the grass out of them. See you haven't got your neighbor looking over the door at you. . . .

Though she did not return to live on a farm, as her sister Nancy had, Georgina spent the remaining years of her career living and teaching in a rural community.

Ruth (ACPID 003) also completed her teacher training during the war years, and spent the early years of her teaching career in one-room schoolhouses in farming communities in southwestern Ontario. Since the nearest high school was more than twenty miles away, most of her students ended their education after completing grade eight. She also experienced working with a local school board, directed by members of her own community, a township board, and then the county system – she retired before the most recent amalgamation took place in the late 1990s. "It went from a local school board in the first four years, which was just people in the community, to a township school board. When the schools went central at first they were controlled by the township, and that was a really good system. But then they needed to improve on it, you know. They never want to leave anything alone. Then it went to a county system . . . Each time they went to a new system, I felt you had less contact. I think when the Township was in charge, you knew the trustees better than when it was the County. And the Township was always very good on supplies you know, getting anything you wanted."

She recalls practice-teaching in a one-room, eight grade school-house for two weeks

> Yes, I did, and it was a killer! (Slight laugh) But it was such an artificial situation. . . . you had to spend so much time getting that lesson ready and printing it out in exact printing form or you'd be criticized, and I guess we learned how to make up a lesson plan, but after you get out into a rural school with eight grades, you don't have time for lesson plans.

Ruth did not feel well-prepared for her first teaching position, she describes it as:

> Terrible. (laugh) Nightmare. It was in the Township, and oh I suppose there were thirty children, and not a lot of . . . . I like teaching really bright children, and there were not a lot there. (Slight laugh) And books to mark, you know, and it would be so discouraging – they couldn't get their math right and they couldn't spell, and of course I didn't know what I was doing either which didn't help. . . . I was all by myself. And no resources, no library, I don't know whether there was even a set of Books of Knowledge or any kind of encyclopedia. I can't remember that there were. No visual aids. . . . I did have a music instructor who came around once a week or once every two weeks. . . .

Ruth taught in one room schools from 1944-48 and then interrupted her teaching career until 1967 while she raised her four children. In 1967 she began teaching in a larger central school, but still in a rural, farming community. "They closed the country schools and brought in children from the surrounding district. . . . I'd say about two thirds of our students . . . maybe even four fifths, were country kids, and they were nice kids to work with, you know. They were usually on farms and had good work habits and so on, whereas today I'm sure it isn't like that."

The newer central school boasted "a huge library. It's a library that's divided between the County and the school. Now, it was the first one they'd ever done that way, and they didn't think it would work, they said "It just won't work," but they got it and it has worked well."

Ruth recollects that among her teaching colleagues "most of the ladies were farm wives," however, she did not participate in farmwork herself:

Well, I would get the meals, but not work out in the barn or anything like that. . . . I don't think any of them did. They were teachers and it was about all they could handle – look after the children. . . . After my girls left I had to get a cleaning lady – that was my salvation!

While many of the other women had to make various child care arrangements with other women in the community, Ruth's husband was farming at home and was there to greet the children when they came home from school, and her daughters cooked the meals. To ensure that other household chores were done by the time she came home, the family worked together while she taught school.

Donna, (ACPID 007) also began her teaching career in the early 1940s in a one room rural school.

I was very unhappy my first year teaching – very lonely, and I felt while I was in a community next to my home community, I felt alone and without young people to relate to. . . . I felt unprepared. . . . if I hadn't gone to a rural school, I don't know how I'd've ever managed to make a timetable and make it all fit together. But I went to a two-room rural school, and I remembered what the teachers had done there. But we learned very little about timetabling . . . I guess we were all supposed to teach one grade in a city some place. . . . The first year I just had six grades, and it was a small school, and I didn't have a grade 3 and I didn't have a grade 7, but I had all the other grades. I'm afraid the grade 1 and 2 reading got neglected often when I was teach-ing something else. Of course, in a rural school, some of the smart ones in Grade 8 or Grade 6 get their work done, you can have them go over and listen to the reading, but then the teacher's not seeing where a child's having a problem. . . .

Unlike Ruth and her colleagues, Donna was very active on the family farm, and felt that this hindered her professional education:

I've always felt that the Department of Education courses I took should've been equated with university courses, and I could've had my BA. However, I was a busy farm wife, I was raising two girls, and by the time I could take Department of Education courses, because you could take them at a school somewhere nearby during the winter or in the spring. And the university courses. . . . well, they worked into a farm wife's busy time on the farm, and so I never, I did take six uni-versity credits, and I had ten or eleven Department of Education credits, so I would've almost had my BA, but they would only count five of the Department [credits]. . . .

Donna always lived and worked in her home community, and remained active in local church work and "ladies' clubs." Juggling the roles of farm wife, mother and teacher entailed some sacrifices:

> Well, your kids give up some things. I gave up taking university cours-
> es, because my kids were at an age by that time that it was either I
> would be away from home in the summer and take university cours-
> es, hire somebody to do meals for threshers and silo-fillers and that
> sort of thing plus your house-cleaning for the year. And so I opted
> that my kids would be able to go to 4-H and do those things, and I
> wouldn't be off to night classes, and so I ended up with a Class C cer-
> tificate or something and I was always well-paid. And I have a good
> pension, and it would've been better if I'd had my BA, but I didn't so.
> . . . It was my own choice.

Like most farms at the time, Donna's family had a mixed farming operation:

> We ran a partly cash-crop, partly beef cattle. We'd have cash crop
> beans every year to sell. Some corn to sell, but most of it, a lot of it
> went into the silo for the beef cattle. And so, you'd have the different
> meals for different men that came to look after the crops . . . and it
> was always a busy time around the farm in the summer time. That
> time you canned and you pickled and you did all those sorts of things,
> and. . . I don't know. You just juggled it until it worked out.

Though she seldom worked with the animals,

> I did work in the harvest. I loved driving the tractor and I loved get-
> ting the tan that you could get driving the tractor all day, but other
> than that, I hadn't been brought up on a farm, so I didn't really know
> anything about caring for animals or that sort of thing, so I never did
> work in the barn, but I did help with harvesting the crops.

Donna returned to work for economic reasons, and was a rarity in her community:

> I was the first woman in our community that went out to work away
> from home. At the time farming wasn't great, and we didn't have a
> large farm, a hundred and fifty acres, but there was no reason for us
> to buy more land and become bigger because we didn't have any sons
> to go on with the farming. And so, we talked it over and I just knew
> that if I didn't go back to teaching my girls wouldn't get a university
> education, and that was all there was about it, and I didn't get one and
> I wanted them to have one, and so did my husband. . . .

But there was also guilt, and community disapproval:

Well, it wasn't necessarily frowned upon, but there were sort of jibes about it, you know. . . . if there was a school bus trip or something I had to hire a high school girl that was out of school in June and there was one particular girl that used to go with my girls on the school bus trips. And I remember one time, and it made me feel kind of badly. . . . the kids were having a Valentine party at school. So I said to [my] student- teacher, "Would you feel okay if I were to leave at one thirty and be gone until three thirty?" She said, "Yeah." . . . . And I didn't realize how much it meant to my girls to have Mom at the Valentine party because I'd never been there before. . . . I don't think I ever was on a school bus trip with them. . . Anyway, there's certain things you have to give up and maybe the kids felt it more than I did. And it used to be thrown up at them too. . . .. "Oh, well, no wonder you get along well in school, because your mother's a teacher." Teacher probably has less time to help her kids than anyone else!

Lessons to be Learned?

The experiences recounted by these, and many other teachers who participated in this research are from another century, a different place, a different notion of what it was to go to school, to become a teacher, and to live and work in a rural community in Ontario. Rural communities continue to evolve. Farmers and farm communities are feeling the effects of globalization, and struggling to maintain their farms. Off-farm jobs are the norm for both men and women on the farm – no longer a "choice." Women, on the other hand, have many more career options. While teaching, nursing, and clerical jobs continue to be female dominated, these are no longer the only, or even main choices, for young women today. As noted earlier, even the centralized, rural schools populated with five hundred or more students from the surrounding countryside, are fighting against yet another round of school closures. Nancy, who vowed during the interview to have given up on political activism, is once again featured in a local newspaper, lobbying on behalf of the school where she taught during the latter part of her career. It too, is undergoing an "accommodation study" – the precursor of a school closing. Meanwhile, the retention and recruitment of teachers to rural schools is an ongoing concern for rural school administrators. Most rural teachers live elsewhere, commuting from the nearest city, no longer an integral part of the rural community and its generational history. Some of these teachers claim that it is the "fishbowl" environment, lack of privacy and anonymity which they crave in their private lives which motivates them to live elsewhere. Others are eager to transfer to an urban school when the opportunity arises. Are there lessons here for contemporary educators? Working conditions are now vastly different – and certainly, life for most is much easier physically, at least, than it was for the solitary rural woman teacher of early and mid 20th century Ontario. Still, many of these women preferred the conditions of their work then, over the expectations, politics, and changing society of today. Most of the women featured in this chapter chose to take early retirement, due to pressures to seek further education, the unfriendly political climate, and a fatigue due to the many educational changes endured during their lengthy careers. Though their career choices were very limited, most were satisfied with their teaching careers. They opted to continue after they had children of their own (whether or not this was economically necessary), and worked for many decades in a variety of educational contexts: different kinds of schools, school boards, and curriculum policies.

In retrospect, they argue that "bigger is not better," that distant administrative centres do not serve the schools well, and that sending children out of their communities to attend school via lengthy bus rides is neither sensible nor healthy. As Ontario and other provinces continue to review small and rural schools for more closures in the name of economic efficiencies, they might heed the words of those who worked and succeeded in much smaller and much poorer schools in bygone days. Adventurous, hardy, and open to diversity, the rural woman teacher in Ontario's one-room schools was able to maintain her sense of humor, and her sense of dignity, in the face of some trying moments – and she ably educated a substantial segment of Ontario's citizenry. Juggling teaching challenges in multi-grade schools, with family life, farmwork and community activities, the twentieth century rural woman teacher was resilient and dedicated, whether she was born and raised in a rural community, or transplanted from elsewhere – her legacy should not be forgotten.

Notes

[1]For various perspectives on the changing dynamics of 'rural' Canada, see: Raymond Blake and Andrew Nurse (eds.) *The Trajectories of Rural Life: New Perspectives on Rural Canada* (Regina: Canadian Plains Research Center, 2003); Harry P. Diaz, Joann Jaffe, and Robert Stirling, (eds.) *Farm Communities at the Crossroads: Challenge and Resistance,* (Regina: Canadian Plains Research Centre, 2003).

[2]See the following for research on farm women in Canada during the twentieth century: E.A. Nora Cebotarev, "From Domesticity to the Public Sphere: Farm Women, 1945-86," in *A Diversity of Women: Ontario, 1945-1980,* ed. Joy Parr, 200-231 (Toronto: University of Toronto Press, 1995); Louise I. Carbert, *Agrarian Feminism: The Politics of Ontario Farm Women* (Toronto: University of Toronto Press, 1995; Nanci Langford, *Politics, Pitchforks and Pickle Jars: 75 Years of Organized Farm Women in Alberta* (Calgary: Detselig Enterprises, 1997); Monda Halpern, *And on that farm he had a wife: Ontario Farm Women and Feminism, 1900-1970* (Montreal & Kingston: McGill-Queen's University Press, 2001); and Naomi Black & Gail Cuthbert Brandt, *Feminist Politics on the Farm: Rural Catholic Women in Southern Quebec and Southwestern France* (Montreal & Kingston: McGill-Queen's University Press, 1999).

[3]Langford, *Politics, Pitchforks and Pickle Jars,* 68.

[4]Halpern, *And on that farm he had a wife,* 49.

[5]Cebotarev, "From Domesticity to the Public Sphere," 207.

[6]James Collins Miller, *Rural Schools in Canada: Their Organization, Administration and Supervision,* (New York City: Teachers College, Columbia University, 1913, 61).

[7]Educational Studies Committee, Federation of Women Teachers' Associations of Ontario, *A Survey of the Problems of Female Rural Elementary School Teachers in Ontario, 1960-61,* 1961, 20-21.

[8]For further discussion of the impact of rural school closures and consolidation historically and at the present time, see: Aniko Varpalotai, "From Consolidation to Amalgamation: The Experiences of Rural Women Teachers in Ontario," in *Leadership from Within, Proceedings of the Seventh National Congress on Rural Education,* (Saskatoon: SELU, 2002); and Aniko Varpalotai, "Phoenix Rising? The Anatomy and Aftermath of Threatened Rural School Closures in Ontario," in *Designing our Future... Making the Right Decisions,* Proceedings of the Eighth National Congress on Rural Education, (Saskatoon: SELU, 2003).

[9]See R.D. Gidney, *From Hope to Harris: The Reshaping of Ontario's Schools,* (Toronto, University of Toronto Press, 1999), 13, 28-29, 48-49.

[10]See: Nora Cebotarev & Kathleen G. Beattie, "Women Strengthening the Farm Community: The Case of the 'Concerned Farm Women' Group in

Ontario," in *Farming and the Rural Community in Ontario: An Introduction,* ed. Tony Fuller, 255-268 (Toronto: Foundation for Rural Living, 1985).

[11]Lucy Maud Montgomery, author of the well-known "Anne" books, herself grew up on a farm on Prince Edward Island, and while still in her teens taught in a rural school on P.E.I. in the 1890s. The Women's Institute, *Lucy Maud Montgomery, "The Island's Lady of Stories,"* (Springfield, Prince Edward Island, The Women's Institute, 1963), 7; L.M. Montgomery, *Anne of Green Gables,* (Toronto, The Ryerson Press, 1908).

[12]*Heidi Grows Up,* was written by the original author Johanna Spyri's translator, Charles Tritten, after her death. It chronicles Heidi's life away at a boarding school, her longing for her home in the remote Alpine village, and her eventual career as the local teacher in the one-room school. (New York, Grosset & Dunlap, 1938).

[13]FWTAO, *Problems of Female Rural Elementary School Teachers in Ontario,* 28.

[14]Linda M. Ambrose, *For Home and Country: The Centennial History of Women's Institutes in Ontario,* (Erin, Ontario, Boston Mills Press, Federated Women's Institutes of Ontario, 1996, 59).

[15]For example: Norah L. Lewis, Editor, *"I want to join your club,"* Letters from *rural children 1900-1920,* Waterloo, Wilfred Laurier Press, 1996.

[16]Jean Cochrane, *Down on the Farm: Childhood Memories of Farming in Canada,* (Calgary: Fifth House Publishing, 1996).

[17]Jean Cochrane, *Down on the Farm: Childhood Memories of Farming in Canada,* Calgary, Fifth House Limited, 1996, 2. See also: K. Bonner, *A Great Place to Raise Kids: Interpretations, Science and the Urban-Rural Debate* (Montreal-Kingston: McGill-Queen's University Press, 1997).

[18]For additional stories from rural women teachers, see: Aniko Varpalotai, "Happy Stories and Haunting Memories.... Women Teaching in Rural Schools in Twentieth Century Ontario," *Oral History Forum 24* (2004) 30.

3

Personal and Professional Freedom in the Hinterlands: Women Teachers in Northern Ontario [1]

Helen Harper

A teacher in search of his/her own freedom
may be the only kind of teacher
who can arouse young persons
to go in search of their own.

Maxine Greene, 1988[2]

Teacher Penny Petrone (on right) with colleague, Hazel Chalmers, eating lunch while out skiing, Chapleau, Northern Ontario. *Photo courtesy Penny Petrone.*

This chapter examines the ways in which personal and professional freedom featured in the lives of women who taught in the northern hinterlands of 20th century Ontario. Northern Ontario provides a particularly apt context for the study of professional and personal freedom in part because "the North" has always been associated with freedom. As noted by literary critics, among others, the North in the Canadian imaginary has been depicted as a place of few constraints, of many open doors – an unbounded place where freedom can find expression and the true and natural self can be established.[3] The dominant image of the North is of a vast and pure land, "where the disenchanted individual can hope to escape from the false utopia in which he seems trapped ... where a man can yet pursue a personal dream – where he can hope to be an individual."[4] It has been said that "the wide open spaces of the North [are] where men could go to escape the world"[5]; moreover, that the North "imparts an element of freedom to Canadian life, even for those who never go there, a "psychic freedom" that forms the real basis of Canadian life"[6] Whether the North is psychically or actually a place where women, more particularly, women teachers can escape the world, can be individuals, can open doors and search for, if not discover, freedom is a question not often considered.[7]

For purposes of this chapter, the northern hinterlands encompass the resource-based cities, towns, and rural communities in northern and north-central Ontario, including Thunder Bay, Sudbury, Sault Ste. Marie, Hearst, Kapaskasing, Timmins, and Kirkland Lake and their surrounding area, the small resort towns and villages in the Muskoka area, as well as the more isolated, fly-in communities in the most northerly section of the province, where greater numbers of First Nations people (e.g., Lowland Cree) reside. These communities, although very different from each other, share a social and geographical distance to the large urban centres of Toronto and Ottawa where provincial and national political power is dispensed, as well as to the long settled, and densely populated agrarian communities of southwestern and eastern Ontario.

To various degrees the northern hinterlands, particularly the far North, can be seen as politically, socially, and economically marginalized from southern Ontario, what is sometimes referred to as the "heartland" of the country. As will be made evident, the marginalization and isolation of the hinterlands offered an unusual blend of freedom and restriction, possibilities and limits in the personal and professional lives of Northern women teachers. These possibilities and limits tell us much about the nature and conditions of women's choices in their time, but also in ours.

In our times there has been increasing attention paid to the professionalism of teachers and their autonomy.[8] One prominent view considers teacher professionalism as the rational capacity and ability to conform to the norms and standards of the state and of the field. A neoliberal concept, Jo-Anne Dillabough suggests that this view of professionalism "tends to be defined in terms of the instrumentality of the teacher as reform agent and his/her role in subverting personal interests (e.g. political concerns, personal wisdom) to accord with objective standards of practice."[9] Many, including Dillabough, contend that this view of the teacher professional, although it portends to offer teachers greater status and autonomy, is a thinly disguised political device that turns teachers into technocratic agents, with only limited discretion.[10] That is, with increasing standardization, regulation and surveillance, teachers cannot attend to local educational circumstances nor to the political nature of education more generally, without threatening their status as professionals since to be a professional within this discourse requires standardizing teaching practices and policies to external norms and demands. Drawing on the work of Michel Foucault, it can be argued that the teacher's body in this view becomes "more obedient as it becomes more useful and conversely" more useful to state interests as it becomes more obedient.[11]

Related critique suggests that professionalism is often tied to masculine identity and a disembodied subject that places women teachers at odds both with femininity, autonomy and professionalism. The argument is that rationality, objectivity and autonomy have been values associated with professionalism, masculinity and the public sphere; qualities associated with the feminine – emotionality, irrationality and relational capacities – have been viewed as a part of domesticity and the private sphere. Professionalism thus is incommensurate with femininity. The teaching of small children, "Woman's 'True' Profession," was made possible only because the very traits aligned with femininity came to be seen as more suitable for this "sacred office"[12] than those associated with masculinity. Teaching was viewed as an extension of mothering and as such, was in direct opposition to conventional understandings of professionalism. Dillabough comments, "women teachers' professional identity can only be found amid the so-called 'virtues' of the private sphere, which is ultimately viewed as contemptible in the context of a 'real' profession."[13]

The incongruency between femininity and professionalism makes the ongoing and contentious efforts to "professionalize" women teachers an important theme of our oral history project. In part, this chapter focuses on one aspect of professionalism, what is arguably the most important, autonomy. More generally this chapter explores the professional and personal freedom in the lives of women teachers, specifically those who taught in the northern hinterlands of 20th century Ontario. In this effort I draw on the work of feminist theorist Nancy Hirschmann, in using the term freedom synonymously with autonomy, to refer to the ability to make and actualize choices, with the understanding that choice is socially constructed, that is, external (social, physical, discursive) conditions and internal (psychological: desire, will) circumstances interact to determine "the construction of choice itself; what choices are available and why, what counts as choice, [and] who counts as a chooser."[14] Thus the nature and conditions of choice in the lives of those women who taught in the northern hinterlands of Ontario are important in understanding their freedom. As I hope to show, the history of these teachers offers an important resource, for in narrating their 20th century working lives, the women in our study provide a means of rethinking the nature and conditions of the choice, and the challenge of ensuring the ongoing search for freedom for both teachers and students in our 21st century.

I begin with a discussion of the first professional "choice" for the women in the study: the decision to become a teacher, and in this instance, to become a teacher in the northern hinterlands of Ontario.

Choosing to Teach in the Northern Hinterlands

Although the vast majority of the women interviewed for the study enjoyed teaching immensely, the decision to become a teacher or to teach in the northern hinterlands was not much of a choice. Like many other women, teachers in the hinterlands spoke of external factors that ultimately directed and determined their occupation:

> You know in a little town in northern Ontario there were not too many career openings for women that we could think about ... So teaching was about the best thing that we could consider at the time, you know, in the 40s. (ACPID 183)

> At that time most girls that I had been to school with were either going to be nurses, teachers or secretaries. There wasn't much encouragement for an alternative career. (ACPID 089)

> Well, I guess back when I was growing up teaching, bookkeeping, nursing were the three big things for girls ... We came from a very small town, so I suppose our experiences were limited in exploring what else was available. (ACPID 043)

Evidently growing up in northern Ontario did not offer expansive career opportunities for young women, certainly no more than elsewhere, and indeed according to these women perhaps less, considering that small town life in the hinterlands did not appear to them to present many options. Moreover it appears that the choice of career was limited to the "helping" professions that replicated in the public sphere, women's work in the domestic sphere. In addition many of those interviewed spoke of financial considerations that limited their career choices further:

> I really wanted to be a nurse or work in a library. But then my parents told me that they could pay only for one more year because my other sister was already in boarding school. (ACPID 174)

> I wanted to go to university but my father died and at that point my mother didn't have the money to send me to university but you could go to teachers' college after your high school and you didn't have to pay tuition. (ACPID 062)

> And then as a young woman, I didn't see many opportunities for careers in other areas. I had two brothers and my dad always let me know that any money to be spent for university would be spent on the boys and not the girls. (ACPID 042)

> I guess it was about 1963, and I was accepted at the University of Toronto, [but] my dad said, "I'm not sending you to university. I think you'll be married in a couple of years. You just go off to teachers' college" And like a good little girl – I was only 17 and I was too young – off I went. (ACPID 030)

The normal school training of teachers was shorter and less expensive than a university education and this made teaching a viable option for the daughters of financially strapped families. Moreover, as evident in the last two quotes, for much of the 20th century women's ultimate occupation was as housewife and mother; therefore, time and money spent pursing other options was viewed as an extravagance in some families. Teaching was evidently one of a limited number of choices that economically and socially served as an acceptable alternative or precursor to women's ultimate or ideal occupation.

Although relatively inexpensive, the specialized training increasingly required for a teaching career was not easily obtained in northern Ontario. Many of the women were forced to go south for their education. The establishment of teachers colleges in North Bay, and in what would later be renamed Thunder Bay made training more accessible and a teaching career imaginable. But for many in the hinterlands, even these cities were still a long way to go, and the accessibility did not always compensate for the distress of often very young women leaving home, a pain many still remembered. One woman noted: "I took the train to normal school in September, 1934, and I cried all the way to Port Arthur, now Thunder Bay, at the idea of leaving my family behind" (ACPID 033). Difficult, but the travel nonetheless offered new experiences and the expansion of one's horizons, as one teacher described. "So off I went to summer school. Left Kirkland Lake. I'd never been out of the community before. We had never travelled ever, any of us . . . never been on a train before . . . and Toronto was very overwhelming" (ACPID 189). Undoubtedly it took some courage for women in the North to actualize a decision to become a teacher.

Although not much a choice, and even then not always an easy choice, teaching did offer an escape from manual labor, as one elderly retiree recalled:

> My mother didn't want me to be a farmer and work hard, like a horse. So she made sure I went to high school and encouraged me all along the way [to teachers college]. (ACPID 037)

Evidently teaching was understood by this woman's mother, as a more feminine and genteel occupation where one would not be working "like a horse." The strong influence of parents on their daughter's career is evident in this quote and several of those cited previously. Fathers and/or mothers decided the course of their daughters' working lives. Parents and family circumstances along with related financial concerns, logistics, and most obviously the social assumptions about women's ultimate and ideal role, and perhaps the more genteel nature of the work, organized teaching as an acceptable option for many women in our study. None of the women spoke of extensive, independent deliberations in which they considered a wide range of alternatives for their career. It was simply the best of the limited options offered women in small northern communities.

Some of those interviewed spoke not of social, economic or geographical factors that influenced their career choice, but of personal feelings and inexplicable desires, what might be termed a "calling" that could not be easily or rationally explained:

I think it [the profession] chose me. (ACPID 025)

I decided at a very young age I was going to be a teacher ... I wanted to be a teacher, just felt I wanted to do this. (ACPID 189)

One woman, when asked if she wanted to be a teacher, replied with some hesitation, "Well I think, I don't know, I really can't tell you because I enjoyed teaching so it must have been in me" (ACPID 201). Another interviewee, after describing all the difficulties of her job, exclaimed, "It had to have been a calling" (ACPID 053).

Rather than a calling, a few spoke of teaching as a "duty." One woman commented, "I thought it was my duty to go teach after going through normal school" (ACPID 227). Another interviewee, stated, "When I started, I knew it was my duty. Certainly I wanted to fulfill my duty, that's for sure" (ACPID 037).

While evidently deeply felt, a calling or a duty to teach removes decision making from the individual since one is compelled by forces beyond one's control. What one might want personally becomes insignificant. Individual "choice" cannot be easily entertained within such a discourse. There well may be religious undertones to the notion of a calling or duty. But while such a "calling" may serve to indicate the value of public service, exalting the profession and the professional, it also renders the profession an oddly irrational endeavor, and the inductee as passive and self-sacrificing. Moreover, talk of a duty or calling in a largely women's profession may well work to reinscribe the feminine as passive, self-sacrificing, irrational, and, albeit dedicated, in need of careful monitoring by others (men). In addition if the circumstances of who does and does not become a teacher is a matter of answering the call of destiny rather than one of social norms and economic conditions, then change cannot be considered. Human efforts to expand opportunity will do little if destiny will have it otherwise.

This is a troubling idea for those of us who work to expand women's choices in public and domestic life. Of course a calling or a duty to teach can be socially constructed, although the women in our study did not speak of it in such a way. But if a calling or a feeling, albeit deeply felt and experienced by individuals, is socially produced and organized, then it is possible to alter what seems otherwise unalterable, and choice and therefore freedom can be expanded.

The women in our study were not passive to the circumstances and contexts that determined for them a teaching career. From the interviews it was apparent that, as limited as the choice was to become a teacher, even if it was "a calling," many women were able to find scope enough in teaching to pursue their own interests, desires, and agendas, as noted vividly by one retiree:

> My girlfriend wanted to be a teacher, and, of course, I wanted to be something like an artist, but anyhow, we were great friends so at some point I decided I'd go with her and we both became teachers. I always wanted to be an artist, and then I became the Arts and Crafts teacher. And I loved to read so I wanted to be a librarian and finally I became a librarian at the school, so it all came true. (ACID 058)

Another commented about her desire to "see the world" and "meet new people" and that by teaching in different places she could do so: "You see when I started to teach, I wanted to see the world ... I said: 'I'm going to teach two years [in one place] and them I'm going to move [to another]'" (ACPID174). Another retired teacher with a similar desire, used her salary to finance her travels. "I've done a lot of traveling and if I was told when I was a kid that I'd ever see the world the way I have, you know I couldn't have believed it. So with teaching I had the money, you know, to go" (ACPID 037).

For many women in our study the decision to teach in the northern hinterlands was, like the decision to teach, tightly circumscribed by social and economic conditions. Many of the women I interviewed for the study were born and raised in small towns and villages in North-central Ontario, and after leaving for teacher training, generally returned to their own or nearby communities. And most, though not all, of those interviewed had retired to the same communities or at least in the same general area. In short, they were, and are locals. By contrast those who taught in the most northern sections of the province were outsiders and, as will be discussed, came for specific purposes and often did not stay long. However, for those in North-central Ontario the decision to teach in the area was simply a decision to stay with the "home" they knew, or to create a home with husbands whose employment kept them in the hinterlands:

> It was just that I got work here, and I was used to The North … I was born here. I was used to the climate and that, so it wasn't any adjustment. (ACPID 210)

> Well I came back [North] because in teachers college, R--- and I met. We got married the year after so I went to Kapuskasing with him. (ACPID 189)

> My husband worked in the mines …. I was happy to stay in Timmins. I didn't want to teach in the city. I have friends who have taught in the south, but I have never lived out of Timmins. (ACPID 201)

Ethnic and racial factors also influenced where one could get a position. At a time when there were few teaching positions available, one teacher remembers that her ethnic background helped her secure a job:

> And then I knew also that a [nearby] Slovakian settlement was going to be looking for a teacher, and because I'm of Slav descent, I'm Bulgarian, they offered me a job before they even had a school. (ACPID 201)

On a less positive note, when there a pay discrepancy between male and female teachers, women were cheaper to hire. On reserves, local First Nations teachers incurred less expense. One teacher explained:

> If they hired a white person they'd have to set up a house and every-thing but for a Native girl teacher, like me, they just paid my salary … only eighty dollars a month. (ACPID 229)

Teaching in the Hinterlands: Professional Responsibility and Freedom by Default

The teachers in our study were happy to secure a teaching position, and entered the profession with great hope and youthful confidence: "When you're young, you don't feel daunted by too much. I probably would be far less ready to jump into that situation, knowing what I know now, but I think I did a good job" (ACPID 056). Another teacher commented, "I was so young and naïve, I probably didn't know that I wasn't prepared for the job … But I think I was probably as competent as the others" (ACPID 030).

Confident or not, teaching in the hinterlands proved demanding. The responsibilities were immense, particularly in one- and two-room school houses.

> I had to teach the 8 grades and I have to say I was alone. I mean they talk about prep time and they talk about relief time [nowadays] and here you were by yourself all day in the bush with no relief, every day, and you do it.... Well, you had to want to love that job. I loved it. (ACPID 189)

Another retired teacher commented, "young teachers had to oversee a learning environment that would make today's teacher shudder. We had 8 or 9 grades all in one room. Think of what we were doing each day" (ACPID 033). It was hard work made more difficult by a lack of resources:

> I worked late every night and got to school at 7:30 or 8 in the morning to get everything on the blackboard, and we had limited resources as far as books were considered. The I.O.D.E. (the Imperial Order of the Daughters of the Empire) used to send books north … [but] a lot of them weren't very satisfactory. Some were discards from the schools down south. (ACPID 161)

> It was a sad little school … it wasn't a log school, it was timbers but we had only a blackboard and the small library, very small library, and we had one big map that you could pull down. We had very little equipment … It was a very poor community, and actually I didn't get paid until Christmas … My salary was $460 a year. (ACPID 119)

With the demise of the one-room schools, one teacher stated candidly, "Well it had to come. I mean who's going to live in the country like that and be responsible for everything, I mean it's silly" (ACPID 106).

In the North not only were teachers confronting heavy teaching responsibilities, they also faced isolation and a harsh climate. Their stories were remarkable.

> It's a very cold spot in the winter time, and I had to walk about a mile and a half to school and there was no transportation into this area, and the ore train would come by at the end of this long street and the men on the ore train knew I was the teacher, and of course, they, some of them couldn't speak English at all, [but] they stopped the train and they'd take me the other mile, and then I'd just have a little two or three blocks to walk . . . . But you know the winters there were very, very bleak . . . you'd have a lot of indoor recesses. (ACPID 011)

> I boarded in a house about a mile away from the school . . . I remember the first year, we had one of those blasts of snow . . . we were, I think, six weeks before we were ploughed out . . . and I remember praying for the snow plough (laughter). (ACPID 204)

> It was lonely . . . in the fall my father would drive me to 3 miles within the school and then I would walk on a wagon road, with rubber boots and I didn't wear pants then, wore a skirt, and my skirt would have 2 inches of mud on the hem, you know. And then in the winter I would ski, I skied 8 miles into Hearst and back again. But I enjoyed the children. (ACPID 201)

While many women teachers in the early part of the century faced such difficulties, conditions remained a challenge for at least some of those teaching in the northern hinterlands through much of the century. One retired teacher described the conditions of her first year of teaching in 1959:

> A couple of the fathers would come and have to lead me out [from the school] at night at 4 o'clock because I couldn't get through the snowdrifts. I had to walk 2 miles out to the road to catch the bus to get back to Kirkland Lake. The bus would never come in and get me . . . I got dropped off on the side of the road, we're talking 30 below zero in Kirkland Lake, walk to my school, start the stove, carry the water and keep the stove going all day, and teach. I think there were at least 20 some children in that school and they were extremely poor . . . I never had a telephone. . . . no indoor plumbing. I had an inspector come once and he sort of said, 'well, you know, it's a poor community' and off he went. (ACPID 189)

Another teacher remembered how glad she was when the inspector visited. "I was so really glad to see him. You're glad to see anybody from the outside when you're alone like that in the community" (ACPID161). Another woman who had recently retired from teaching in the far north, spoke of how the isolation and darkness was considered mentally debilitating and that teachers would become "bushed" or experience "cabin fever" and need to be pulled out of the community permanently, or for a brief holiday (ACPID 211).

Although the job was demanding, and the isolation difficult, many women in the study remembered considerable professional freedom. Of course it was the very isolation and harsh conditions that ensured a lack of surveillance by state and district educational officials and created, by default, considerable teacher autonomy. Left alone, they could make their own professional decisions.

> Teaching in a rural school is wonderful because face it, you're the boss, and I don't mean that you don't have somebody that inspects you and you do but the inspector comes a couple of times a year but you're going to teach the best you can because it's survival and teaching 8 grades is very difficult and you have a lot to cover and you have to work out a scheme that really works. (ACPID 052)

> This is one of those things that I hated about the school system – the inspectors. They didn't know dip about what we were dealing with. I wasn't allowed to let children skip a grade . . . Well the way I did it, it was seamless. Like if you're finished grade 1 work, you go into grade 2 and so on. And so he'd come along and say no, you're not allowed to let the children skip classes, skip grades. I did it anyway, and the same with the exams. Well you weren't called the principal, but yeah, you were it. That's it. Whatever happened there was your baby. (ACPID 106)

> You were given a lot of freedom as to what you would offer the students. So I did things that today may seem marginal but most appreciated by the people of the community. I had shorthand and typing . . . we obtained enough funds to purchase typewriters . . . and these children were given this extra opportunity so that when they completed their grade 10, they were able to go directly into work, but had a skill to offer to the employer. I think in this sense, they were much further than we could expect from a rural area. (ACPID 053)

> I started very independent in a three-room school. I could teach children until five o'clock, and it was no problem, I would tell them the day before: "Tomorrow we'll be working until five, tell your parents." And we'd work until five. Now, try and do that . . . there is too much bureaucracy now. (ACPID 054)

The first year I had 43 kids in Grades 1, 2, and 3 and the grade 1s had never been to school before. It sounds almost terrible, but it wasn't. The first three years there were great. I think we had more leeway…I think you felt you had more control, maybe, of the whole situation. (ACPID 043)

It is recognized that in the most northerly communities teaching positions were filled by default; that is, with few applicants, less qualified teachers would be hired. One teacher commented:

Now back in the '60s most of the jobs were posted in February. Have you heard how huge the job listings were in the Globe and Mail? If you had good qualifications you tended to get jobs in southern Ontario. If you didn't quite match that hiring pool then you'd move further north. (ACPID 211)

But the northerly and more isolated communities did offer women teachers substantially better incomes and that drew some to take positions there, as one woman explained:

I had a daughter who was accepted into college, and if I didn't do something then there'd be no money to pay for it. So I applied, got the job and went north. (ACPID 211)

The comments offered by women in the study suggest that the choice of occupation and the job location were generally organized by the social and economic circumstances of the times. With rare exceptions, it was not much choice. Certainly it appears that the decision to enter the profession and teach in the hinterlands was well contained within the bounds of what was considered practical and possible for women at the time. Even as a subjective decision, a teaching career was viewed as a commonsense desire or calling for young women. Although viewed perhaps as better than farm or factory work, the women in our study did not speak directly in terms of teaching as a "profession" rather, it was a job that simply made sense for a particular group of young women at the time. But whether the job was considered a profession or not, in the northern hinterlands it carried both immense professional responsibilities and at the same time considerable professional freedom through much of the 20th century.

As is evident from their words, many of the women in the study, spoke about the difficult teaching situations they faced, but in the same breath often remembered with great pleasure their professional freedom – the choices they had, the control they could exert over at least some aspects of their work. Being the "boss" meant they had power to affect the curriculum, scheduling, and, in general, to improve and fashion learning for their charges. The independence, the freedom, the agency was "wonderful" and this seemed to compensate in considerable ways for the difficult teaching circumstances of the North.

Leadership and Professional Development

As challenging as their situations may have already been, several of those interviewed assumed additional administrative responsibilities, often not by choice, but simply because there was no one better qualified available.

> We were two women in the school and [in addition to] the general aspect of being in a school that had no telephone and having all these children, I was classed as the principal, being a senior teacher in the school. Senior, because I taught the higher grades, not because I had the longest teaching experience. Both of us were brand new teachers. (ACPID 089)

One Aboriginal teacher became an administrator at her school simply because "the principal got ill" and "I knew the school" (ACPID 228). Another teacher, who became a leader in special education in her district, commented on the source and nature of her freedom.

> I know there's not the freedom today. And I think why I had the freedom is 'cause nobody else knew what to do...I was always one to find my own way . . . I went out and found out what the best people were doing and brought it back and generated it myself. (ACPID 025)

In direct opposition to traditional notions of femininity, women teachers in the hinterlands had to display considerable initiative, assertiveness and resourcefulness, if not outright courage, in attending to teaching and administrative tasks in situations and circumstances in which one learned the job on the job. One teacher lamented:

I had no training. I think you should have some training, you should do the vice [principalship]. I had no one, the principal had left town. I had no vice [principal] so again I'm thrown into a situation with no background . . . The only person that could help me actually, when I was the principal up there was the secretary, because she was the only one who knew what was going on. (ACPID 189)

With the demands of increasing professionalization, understood in terms of increasing credentialing, and as indicated above the need for additional administrative and other forms of training, teachers in the hinterlands we interviewed, had spent considerable time and energy upgrading their qualifications. Again this was not much of a choice, but necessitated by circumstances of the profession and of life in the North. Many women in the study completed degrees and gained additional qualifications by attending summer school or through year-long correspondence courses from southern Ontario. "I went to summer school nearly every summer . . . Every summer I spent all that hot weather down in Toronto" (ACPID 058). When courses were offered locally, instructors had to negotiate vast distances and tight schedules. One woman recalled,

I was able to give courses, which I don't think anybody else would try to do today because on Monday I taught in Timmins, on Tuesday I taught in Kirkland, on Wednesday I taught in North Bay, on Thursday I taught in Sudbury. It had to be a calling. (ACPID 053)

Upgrading one's qualifications demanded considerable commitment from those in the hinterlands; moreover, the reception of northern teachers in the "heartland" was not always encouraging. One teacher who spent six summers expanding her qualifications noted how those from the hinterlands were treated.

I was from the "North," quote "from the North," and it was almost as if you're just not quite up to what we're doing. You're just not as experienced or as worldly . . . we, coming from the North, were learning a lot about the South. We were very open to their ideas, but I don't know if they appreciated our ideas . . . we're talking isolation, we're talking about how difficult it is to come down here to learn, whereas they had to go down the street to go to [summer] school. I was traveling, leaving my family [behind] . . . it was really important to me. (ACPID 189)

Although this teacher was a powerful person in her northern class-room, there seemed little recognition of her knowledge, expertise or of her commitment to the profession. Evidently her professionalism needed confirmation by southern ideas and standards. In relation to professional freedom, that is, the choices this teacher could make, her choices, in order to be considered valid and "professional," would need to align with ideas and standards from southern Ontario. There is a long history of suspicion concerning the professionalism of non-urban teachers, despite the fact these teachers were the majority. Cavanagh notes with regard to FWTAO, "These early years [1930s] of federation history marked the beginning of the disciplinary processes set up to curb the wayward tendencies of the unprofessional teacher believed to populate rural school communities."[14]

It is evident that the isolation and marginalization of the hinter-lands limited contact with educational resources, both human and material, and thus kept bureaucracy at bay. In turn this allowed for greater professional freedom within the limits of what was possible in the circumstances of the North. Undoubtedly greater support could have made teaching considerably easier for women teachers in the hin-terlands. Without such support, the women relied heavily on their own personal/professional resources to improve their teaching and their status, if only in the community in order to secure professional free-dom and respectability.

The Community: Promoting and Restricting Personal and Professional Freedom

As with other women teachers in the twentieth century, those teaching in the northern hinterlands had to maintain strict decorum in their personal and professional life. Standards were made clear in teachers' college but also in the community as well. Often this was expressed in terms of a woman's attire and living situation.

> It was made very clear in assemblies [at teachers' college] that we were not allowed to be in certain places in the city . . . pubs, probably. We had to wear . . . dresses and nylons, very much a dress code . . . the overall feeling was that you had to be very prim and proper.(ACPID 043)

Skirts of any fashion were fine. I could never understand why mini-skirts were OK and trousers weren't. Obviously as a primary teacher, trousers were wonderful ... I mean if you're doing finger painting that's not very practical. And on yard duty, a mini-skirt in Muskoka, it's ridiculous. (ACPID 042)

Your personal life was scrutinized ... For one of our women teachers, the boarding place wasn't suitable, so she rented an abandoned farmhouse and lived there. And the [school] board said she couldn't live there without a chaperone because she had a boyfriend. So she had to hire a young girl, who wasn't going to school, to be there as a chaperone. (ACPID 059)

In the hinterlands as elsewhere, the community had much to say about the new teacher and the Christmas concert was an important test, at least according to one teacher.

One of the teacher's duties in those years was to have a Christmas concert and every child must be a part of the entertainment, must have a part to play. If the concert pleased the parents, the teacher would be asked to return to teach the following year. (ACPID 230)

Provided the teachers observed decorum, and evidently could produce a successful Christmas concert, they could garner considerable respect and support in the community. According to those in the study, this was particularly true in the early part of the twentieth century when there was tremendous respect for teachers.

In Sudbury, it was amazing how the parents appreciated the least little thing you did for them ... But back then, in my first school I could have been the queen, you know. I was really the important person in the village. I'd be invited out to all the homes. The teacher was very important. (ACPID 058)

But in the community I was very well known. I taught the parents and the children and then almost the grandchildren, and then I was principal ... I was a very high profile person in the community. (ACPID 189)

It was a small town; we had tremendous support from parents. Very local school boards where you knew all the people. It was more a community, family feeling. Which sort of got lost in the shuffle later. (ACPID 043)

Many of those interviewed believed that the professional status and the autonomy of teachers slipped in the last decades of the twentieth century:

> I think that when I first started teaching, you weren't really questioned about what you did. You were supposed to know what you were doing and I think in this 21st century, and even before that, parents began questioning. (ACPID 062)

> I want to state it again . . . in the beginning as a teacher, I was trusted. And when I left after teaching in a classroom for 33 years, I did not feel that I was trusted. I felt that I was questioned. I felt that I was being monitored . . . I didn't feel teachers were treated as professionals. (ACPID 060)

Professional freedom on the job was made possible by the geographical and economic conditions in which the women in the hinterlands taught – the isolation, harsh climate, sparse population, that secured curricular and pedagogical choices. With the increased development of the hinterlands and greater centralization, regulation and standardization, the decision-making powers were increasingly taken away from local teachers. But, in addition, professional freedom in the hinterlands was garnered in large part by the respect, trust and ultimately the status of women teachers locally and in the greater society. However, as indicated in the previous quotes, the trust and status of teachers seems to have declined, at least in the opinion of those we interviewed.

Despite their community involvement and leadership, despite their efforts to seek further professional development and additional credentials, and comply with professional standards, greater status or increased professional freedom did not evidently occur. Consider that amazing quote: "when I left after teaching in a classroom for 33 years, I did not feel that I was trusted. . . . I didn't feel teachers were treated as professionals" (ACPID060). Such an acknowledgment is a challenge to the neoliberal notion of professionalism and its insistence on increasing the regulation and standardization of practice.

Professional and Personal Freedom for Women Teachers in the Northern Hinterlands

The northern hinterlands offered women in our study limits and opportunities, choices and restrictions in their personal and professional lives. It was not an open and empty wilderness where the pursuit of any option was possible, at least not for the women interviewed. Because of its climate and isolation, the northern hinterlands in the early and mid-part of the century seem to have provided opportunities for women to exercise more professional autonomy in curricular, pedagogical, and administrative decisions within the material limits of their own classrooms and schools than might well have been possible in more populated and accessible sites. With little interference from educational officials, many teachers remembered the pleasure of being their own "boss," although they were regulated by community standards and expectations. Career choice, location, working conditions, career development and enhancement seem to have been largely restricted by social, economic and geographical circumstances. Although it is predictable that the northern environment would feature as a powerful factor in women's personal and professional freedom, what is also apparent is that social and economic circumstances factored strongly into the choices and freedoms possible for women teachers, even in the North.

This suggests that if teachers and their students seek freedom in their personal and professional lives, as suggested by Maxine Greene at the outset of this chapter, it well may be that such a search begins with the social and discursive contexts of their lives, where freedom may not be found as much as it is forged.

Notes

[1] An earlier version of this chapter appeared in *Oral History Forum, 24*, (2004): 46-66.

[2] Maxine Greene, *The Dialectic of Freedom* (New York: Teachers College Press, 1988), 14.

[3] See for instance, Margaret Atwood, *Strange Things: The Malevolent North in Canadian Literature* (Oxford: Clarendon Press, 1995); Sherrill Grace, *Canada and the Idea of North* (Montreal: McGill-Queen's University Press, 2001) and Sherrill

Grace, "Gendering Northern Narrative" in *Echoing Silence: Essays on Arctic Narrative,* ed. J. Moss, 163-180 (Ottawa: University of Ottawa Press, 1997).

[4]Allison Mitcham, *The Northern Imagination: A Study of Northern Canadian Literature* (Moonbeam, Ontario: Penumbra Press, 1983), 17.

[5]R.A. Phillip, *Canada's North* (Toronto: Macmillan Press, 1967), 196.

[6]Daniel Francis, *National Dreams: Myth, Memory and Canadian History* (Vancouver: Arsenal Pulp Press,1997), 153.

[7]I'm drawing on a discussion by Margaret Atwood in her book *Strange Things:*, pp. 87-88 in which she tells what happens in the written North, a place inhabited primarily by men, when women enter the northern landscape as authors or protagonists.

[8]Oddly enough there is little consensus about what constitutes a profession although neoliberal concepts are gaining prominence. See Jo-Anne Dillabough, "Degrees of Freedom and Deliberations of Self: The Gendering of Identity in Teaching," in *Revolutionary Pedagogies: Cultural Politics, Instituting Education and the Discourse of Theory,* ed. Peter Trifonas, 315, (New York: Routledge Falmer Press, 2000) and Jo-Anne Dillabough, "Gender Politics and Conceptions of the Modern Teacher: Women, Identity and Professionalism," *British Journal of Sociology of Education, 20* (1999): 375.

[9]Dillabough, "Gender Politics and Conceptions of the Modern Teacher," 375.

[10]Dillabough, "Gender Politics and Conceptions of the Modern Teacher," 376.

[11]Michel Foucault, *Discipline and Punish: The Birth of the Prison* (New York: Vintage Books, 1979), 138.

[12]Nancy Hoffman, *Woman's "True" Profession: Voices from the History of Teaching* (New York: McGraw-Hill Books, 1981), 3-4.

[13]Dillabough, "Gender Politics and Conceptions of the Modern Teacher," 381.

[14]Sheila Cavanagh, "The Gender of Professionalism and Occupational Closure: The Management of Tenure-Related Disputes by the Federation of Women Teachers' Associations of Ontario 1918-1949," *Gender and Education, 15* (2003), 48.

4

For the Sake of Language and Heritage: Ontario Francophone Women Teachers Reflect on Their Careers

Suzanne Majhanovich

Grace Gerrard and three friends at Normal School, 1939-40. *Photo courtesy of The University of Western Ontario Archives, B740.*

Background and Introduction

This chapter focuses on a particular population of teachers over-looked in most studies of women teachers in Ontario, namely, fran-cophone women who taught French as a first or second language.[1] It explores the careers of three francophone women in particular, two who entered the teaching profession during the 1940s, and one in the early 1950s. All three are native speakers of French; one, whom I call Arlette, was born in Quebec, and the other two, whom I have named Anne-Marie and Colette, in francophone regions of Ontario. As we shall see from their stories, teaching French in anglophone Ontario provided a main challenge and focus of their careers. But as women who entered teaching in the mid-twentieth century, they also had to contend with systemic obstacles based on their gender.

Some Historical Context of French Teaching in Ontario

Before turning to the stories of Arlette, Anne-Marie and Colette, it is helpful to place into context the teaching of French in elementary schools in Ontario. Although the percentage of the Ontario popula-tion that designates itself as French speaking has been decreasing dur-ing the last century,[2] Ontario, as the most populous province of Canada, still has the largest francophone population outside Quebec. By the end of the twentieth century only about 5% of Ontario stu-dents were francophones. The Ontario francophone population tends to cluster along the border with Quebec, across the central northern area of the province, and in a few pockets in the South West around Windsor, Midland, Welland and St. Catharines. Since 1910, there has been an association, L'association canadienne-française d'éducation de l'Ontario (ACFEO)[3] dedicated to the preservation of francophone culture, protection of the rights and privileges of Franco-Ontarians, and the promotion of French language interests in Ontario. As a minority group in Ontario, Franco-Ontarians sensed that they were being overwhelmed by the Anglo Saxon majority. The Ontario gov-ernment was encouraging assimilation with the result that even in their French language schools, there were insufficient resources to teach young Franco-Ontarians to read in French, and families of French Canadian origin were rapidly losing their francophone identity.[4] Consequently, a major concern has been to secure the right of francophone Ontarians to receive their education in French. The English majority had not been particularly sympathetic to these aspirations, and both Protestant and Catholic English-speaking groups demanded English-only education. However, matters would deteriorate soon after the founding of the ACFEO in 1910. In 1912, the Conservative government of Ontario passed Regulation 17, which limited the use of French as the language of instruction to the first 2 years in elementary schools.[5] An amendment in 1913 permitted French as a subject of study for one hour per day only. Clearly, this regulation was aimed at assimilating francophones into the English-speaking population.

The harsh ruling was furiously opposed by Ontario francophones and the ACFEO, and was reflected in the celebrated Desloges case of 1915.[6] The sisters, Béatrice and Diane Desloges had been hired to teach in a bilingual school in the French-speaking area of Ottawa. They made it known that they were prepared to defy Regulation 17 and would teach in French. It appears that the school board was inclined to look the other way, but the provincial government sent in a small committee of three Anglophones to overrule the local school board, and to oust the sisters Desloges from their classrooms, replacing them with other teachers who would teach the young francophones in English. The sisters were threatened with prison if they resisted, but not ready to give up, they decided to hold classes in French in a nearby parish hall. All their students followed them. The local president of the French Canadian Education Association declared to the local French language newspaper:

> Nous, Canadiens-français de l'Ontario, nous sommes en guerre. Nous combattons aujourd'hui pour la défense de notre langue et pour la protection de nos enfants que l'on veut nous arracher pour les livrer à l'anglicisation.[7]

The sisters continued to teach their students in French in make-shift quarters until the Christmas break. In January, 1916, the parents escorted the two teachers and their pupils back to the original school, forcing their way past three police constables sent by the "committee" to "protect" the school. The parents re-established the sisters in their original classrooms. Reinforcements of 25 police officers were unable to dislodge the teachers. The mothers, armed with hat pins rebuffed the police and declared themselves guardians of their children's right to an education in French. They maintained guard over the school for several months. The Desloges sisters received threats of arrest from the police, the government revoked their teaching certificates and cut off their salary but they did not give up. The school became the symbol of Franco-Ontarian opposition to Regulation 17. In the Fall of 1916, the Judicial Committee of the British Privy Council in England declared that the imposed three-man committee of Anglophones was illegal. The Desloges sisters and the Ottawa francophone community had won.[8]

However, Béatrice and Diane Desloges were not the only teachers in Ontario to resist Regulation 17. The French Language Teachers' Federation, the AEFO (l'Association de l'enseignement français de l'Ontario) in *Femmes de Vision*,[9] recognized Ontario francophone women of the twentieth century who have contributed to the preservation of the French identity in Ontario. Jeanne Lajoie is cited as "the heroine of Pembroke" for having defied Regulation 17 and set up an alternate school in a private home for the 55 francophone students who would have been deprived even of the one hour per day of French as a result of the blatantly discriminatory action by the local separate school board. The board comprised mainly of Irish Catholics had fired Jeanne Lajoie and installed in her place an English speaking Irish nun whom they claimed could teach the one hour of French along with the English curriculum. Despite a petition to the board requesting that Mlle Lajoie be reinstated or a truly francophone teacher be hired in the place of the Irish nun, the board refused, forcing the community to set up their alternate school where Mlle Lajoie taught in French for three years.

Another "Femme de Vision" cited in the collection is one Ida Drouin (Preseault) who began teaching primary grades at the age of 16 after completing Grade 10 and teacher preparation in a model school in the area. She taught in French for nine years in Eastern Ontario during the period of the imposition of Regulation 17.

It is interesting to note that some of the strongest opponents to bilingual [French language] schools in Ontario were English-speaking (Irish) Catholic clergy. Stéphane Lang notes that as early as 1912 Monsignor Michael Fallon stated his opposition to the aspirations of Franco-Ontarians who demanded French language education for their children. Msr Fallon declared bilingualism to be the main enemy of elementary education in Ontario.[10]

Undoubtedly, Regulation 17 served to strengthen the convictions of Franco-Ontarians that they would have to remain united and continue to exert pressure on the government if they were to survive as a Canadian French-speaking group outside Quebec. The ACFEO recognized that education was the key to survival and hence articulated a series of recommendations related to education that would strengthen their cause. Besides working for fifteen years to overcome the most stringent requirements of Regulation 17, the AFCEO labored tirelessly to ensure that a reasonable and equitable program of bilingual education for Franco-Ontarian children was available (one that permitted more than one hour per day of French in the lower primary grades only). They recognized that a supply of teachers educated to deliver programs in French was crucial, and so they sought the establishment of a French language teachers' college in the province to prepare teachers for bilingual schools. Anglophone Ontarians are probably not generally aware that until the late 1920s, francophone teachers in Ontario normally received teacher preparation in the so-called bilingual model schools near their homes where they would effectively apprentice themselves to practising bilingual teachers before starting to teach on their own – as did Ida Drouin, mentioned above. The ACFEO did not consider model schools an appropriate teacher preparation, but the alternative meant attending an English-language normal school where teachers would be prepared to teach only in English. Francophone teachers graduating from English normal schools often had less than adequate proficiency in their native language, and were ill equipped to deliver school curriculum in French. Hence, the ACFEO made as one of its goals the establishment of an "école normale" associated with the University of Ottawa where francophone teachers could receive preparation in French to teach in the elementary bilingual schools. By 1923 the University of Ottawa took steps to open a "School of Pedagogy" run by the Oblate Fathers.[11] The School of Pedagogy became the Ecole Normale in 1927[12] after the relaxation of Regulation 17, and was associated with the University of Ottawa, although its orientation remained Catholic. However, Regulation 17 only disappeared from the record in 1944 [13]

It was not until the late 1960s that a French language college of education, comparable to the Ontario College of Education (OCE) in Toronto was established at the University of Ottawa to prepare French secondary teachers. Indeed, the Department of Education did not even grant certification in teachable subjects[14] in French, other than "Advanced" or "Special" French until late in that decade.

It is in the context of the language struggles that two of the women featured in this study received their elementary education, and the third, originally from Quebec, came to teach in the province at a time when the major issues of Francophone teacher education in Ontario were still unresolved. Although they began teaching in Ontario after Regulation 17 was officially removed from the Education record, it is clear from their stories that they experienced the continuing effects of this discriminatory and assimilationist bill.

The Teachers and Their Role in Maintaining and Promoting French Language Education

Arlette's Story

Arlette (ACPID 251) was born and raised in Quebec and, in fact, received initial teacher preparation at a normal school in Quebec where she began teaching in 1945. By 1948 she took a position in a bilingual (French) school in Kapuskasing in northern Ontario because the salary ($1 200 per year) was double her salary in Quebec. Her early years of teaching took place in one-room schools where she was acting principal as she was responsible for all the grades. Since she did not speak English well, but according to the rules of bilingual schools in Ontario had to teach the majority of the subjects from grades 5 to 8 in English, this presented quite a challenge for her. In those days (the 1940s and 1950s) there was an entrance examination for high school and it was entirely in English, even for students from the bilingual schools. Arlette had to prepare her students for a totally English high school. Two years after her first Ontario position, she moved from north eastern Ontario to a four-room bilingual school in the extreme west of Ontario in a small town near the Minnesota border. There she taught grades 1 and 2 in French to children of francophone parents.

She essentially had to develop an immersion second language program for them as the children did not really speak good French, but their parents were concerned that their children retain the French heritage language. Arlette speaks fondly of this experience with helpful, cooperative parents and three other francophone teachers all living in a "teacherage" which had formerly been a religious mother house.

After a six-year hiatus from teaching during which she married and had her children, Arlette came to central Ontario in the mid 1950s to set up French second language programs for anglophone children. She had to acquire Ontario English teaching certification, an Ontario Secondary Honours Graduation Diploma (Grade 13) and then eventually a BA degree. She remarked that when she was required to pick up the Ontario Grade 13 diploma in English, she had to write English literature and composition, chemistry and history. Studying Ontario history provided some surprises because, as she commented, the history she had learned in French in Quebec was from quite a different perspective. Arlette rose in her profession to become a master teacher, and then a consultant for a large school board just north of Toronto.

She recalls her career affectionately; she loved teaching and helping young teachers become competent French second language teachers. Still, she also acknowledges the prejudice she encountered because she was a francophone, as well as the unnecessary obstacles she faced when she tried to advance in her profession – problems she attributes partly to her gender and partly to the bureaucracy of Ontario certification which has separate qualifications for teachers in the French and English school systems.

Anne-Marie's Story

Anne-Marie (ACPID 252) was born and raised in a francophone family in south western Ontario. Because of Ontario's bilingual schools regulations, she was educated in both French and English in elementary school, and English in secondary school. She received her teacher education in French at the University of Ottawa Normal School, graduating with an elementary teaching certificate for bilingual (French) schools in 1944. She began teaching the following year at the age of 18 in a four-room bilingual school in south western Ontario. Her starting salary was only $800. Her school was a Roman Catholic elementary school, grades 1-8, with four teachers – herself and three nuns, one of whom served as principal. Anne-Marie changed schools frequently, usually to improve her salary, as in the 1940s and 1950s, every town or parish had its own school board with different pay scales for teachers.

She married in 1956. Although the marriage bars in Ontario were relaxed in the 50s, married women were still expected to resign when they became pregnant and Anne-Marie complied. However, her services were valued, and the local school encouraged her to come back to teaching, although she could only be hired on short-term contracts because she had two young children. That meant that she received less pay and no benefits, even though she was teaching full time. In the late 1950s she switched to the public school board and taught fully English classes and special education until she was encouraged by a superintendent to develop a pilot program in French as a second language for anglophones. By 1958, she had to qualify for her English teaching certificate – elementary. To do that, she had to pass examinations at a teachers college about 200 kilometres from her home. She subsequently took special courses in French second language teaching and also completed her BA degree by extension in 1976. In 1978, she left the public school board and became the French language coordinator in a nearby semi-rural Roman Catholic Separate School Board. She was instrumental in improving the basic French second language program offered from grade 1, for developing the French immersion program in that board, and for working with the French language schools in the area. She worked as a sessional instructor at the local Faculty of Education, continuing to teach there for a few years after her retirement from the school board in 1991.

Anne-Marie regarded teaching as her vocation and found it a privilege to be able to contribute to students and young teachers over the years. Perhaps because she is such a positive person, and because she grew up in the bilingual (French) system, she did not feel she faced prejudice because she was a francophone so concerned with promoting her language and the francophone culture. However, she was sensitive to restrictions placed upon her because she was a woman and a married woman teacher with children. She recalled the remark of the inspector who came to evaluate her in her first year of teaching before she married, and who called her "his little unclaimed pearl," a remark that might be considered sexist – Anne-Marie, certainly felt it to be such. She believed that women teachers, especially married women teachers in the 1950s and 1960s were not encouraged to improve themselves by taking additional qualification courses in teaching, or to aspire to become principals. In one school, the principal, a nun, wanted her to teach a special education class but forbade her from taking a course to learn how to work with children with special needs. The nun told her that she was already qualified enough. Anne-Marie felt that superintendents and inspectors – usually men – would encourage young men teachers with little experience to gain qualifications as a principal. It never occurred to them that women might wish to become principals as well. Anne-Marie never did get her principal's papers. In those days, one could only take the course on the recommendation of an inspector. Although no inspector ever encouraged her to work in school administration, they thought nothing of assigning her to mentor younger teachers in difficulty, encouraged teachers to come to observe her teach, and expected her to present workshops on French second language teaching after hours. When she left teaching to become a coordinator of French, it was on the urging and invitation of one of the rare woman superintendents of the time. Nevertheless, she does pay tribute to one or two male principals and Ministry of Education officials who appreciated the work she was doing for French second language teaching.

Colette's Story

Colette (ACPID 240) is an Ontario francophone born in Timmins in northern Ontario. She was educated in bilingual schools up to the end of Grade 10, and appears to have had the majority of her schooling in French to that point. For the final years of high school, she switched to a public English high school and found it very difficult to do all the courses in English, especially mathematics and sciences. She felt that the teachers in that school and the anglophone students were racist because they always labeled the francophones as "stupid, dumb French kids." She said that no help was offered to francophone students who had difficulty with English and for that reason, the majority of francophone students from the north never finished high school but simply dropped out. Colette, speaking of her experiences in the English high school said:

> So I think out of my grade 8 class, I probably am the only one that continued and got a degree. Because once they went to the high school, you lost them. . . . We spoke English and the writing was OK. It's when you got in the terminology, in the maths and sciences. It took you a while, so if you didn't do a lot of extra work . . .

> So I think a lot of the students just gave up. If you asked questions in the class, many, many times you were humiliated because we didn't know the terms. It was not a positive experience. I hated it.

In 1954, after grade 12, Colette accepted a primary Grade 1 and 2 teaching position in a bilingual school and taught everything in French. Apparently teachers for bilingual schools were in short supply, and so it was easy to get hired without formal teaching preparation. This situation reflects the concerns of the ACFEO expressed back in the 1920s when they lobbied to have a bilingual normal school set up to prepare francophone teachers for French-language schools. Evidently even in the 1950s when Ottawa had such a facility, qualified francophone teachers were still difficult to recruit. However, the following year, Colette did attend the Ottawa Normal School and graduated in 1956 with her elementary teaching certificate for bilingual (French) schools. After her graduation she taught for a number of years in elementary bilingual schools, then became an itinerant French second language teacher for grades 7 and 8, and then moved into the secondary school teaching both French first and second language courses. In the meantime, she also gained her BA degree through extension courses. At the end of the 1960s, she went to Germany to teach French on one of the army bases and loved the experience. When she returned to Canada, she taught junior high school and then became a consultant with a major urban board in south central Ontario. She continued in that position until her retirement in the 1990s.

Perhaps because she was younger than Arlette and Anne-Marie, Colette seemed more aware of the limitations placed on her career because she was a woman. She also mentioned more instances of overt anti-French sentiments. As was the case with the other two teachers, her elementary French teaching qualifications were not accepted once she switched to the English school system, and, in addition, began to teach in the secondary panel. She had to take a number of courses over two summers to receive her secondary teacher qualification for English schools, and also had to take special make-up courses in French as a second language teaching. Colette explained that she really preferred teaching the older students in junior high school and high school, but as there were no French language high schools in the areas where she was teaching, she had to become qualified for the English system in order to teach the age level she preferred.

Of the three women interviewed, Colette seemed perhaps less positive about teaching although she did certainly gain satisfaction from the successes of her career. She explained that when she was a girl there were really only three choices for women – nurse, teacher, or secretary, and at the time, teaching seemed the best choice. If her family's financial circumstances had been different, and if she had had a choice, she would have become a doctor.

Discussion

Language Issues

As for issues particular to francophone teachers, we see three women who qualified as elementary teachers for French or bilingual schools. It is clear that the assimilationist intent of the 1912 Regulation 17 was still alive for these women despite the fact that it had been removed from the official record in 1944. Colette mentions her difficulties in completing secondary schooling in the early 1950s because she had to attend an English-only high school for grades 11 and 12, and further noted that the majority of Ontario francophones simply dropped out without completing high school at all. She also gave as one of the reasons for switching to an anglophone board the relatively small number of francophone schools. Probably the geographical location of the majority of francophone schools mainly in the north, along Ontario's eastern border and in the south west of the province, along with the lower salary also contributed to her decision to teach in the Anglophone system.

Anne-Marie and Arlette mentioned the need to prepare their francophone pupils for the high school entrance examination all in

English. Anne-Marie spoke about holding special Saturday classes to prepare her students. Arlette, as a native Quebecer did not speak English very well, but knew that her students would be going to an English high school. Arlette reports:

> There wasn't such a thing as a French school. They were called bilingual schools.

> Not like we have now . . . .They needed to do all these subjects in English, because then they were going to an English high school, and that's why these children had to be prepared to go to the English schools.

> . . . That was a real challenge for me . . . because I didn't really speak English enough. Then we had to help each other. And I was taking a course at the high school in English, I knew the science. I knew all of this in French, but for them to do it in English was really [hard].

> . . . . But you know, these children went to write these exams, and they succeeded so well, and they just passed like. . . . probably better than if they would have had an English-speaking person.

All three speak of the lack of materials for their pupils and how they had to develop materials themselves. Of course, that gave them excellent experience for their subsequent positions teaching anglophones French as a second language. All three switched from the bilingual schools to work in teaching French as a second language with anglophone students. In the 1960s after the Canadian Royal Commission on Bilingualism and Biculturalism was created (1963) resulting in the *Official Languages Act of 1969,*[15] some areas in Ontario began to offer French Second Language courses in elementary schools. Board administrators sought out French-speaking teachers to set up the programs and Arlette, Anne-Marie, and Colette were three who took up the challenge. However, as their teaching qualifications were for French language (so-called bilingual) schools, their certificates were not recognized in the English school system even though their tasks only involved the teaching of French. That meant that all three had to re-qualify for the English language teaching certificate. Anne-Marie had to go to another centre in Ontario to write the examinations; Colette took two summer courses and at the same time received qualifications to teach in the secondary schools. For Arlette, it was the most difficult since her original qualifications were from Quebec. She had to get her Ontario secondary school diploma, and then after teaching for two years, the Ontario Ministry of Education decided to grant her equivalency. Now she thinks that she was badly advised and should have proceeded directly into university studies. As Arlette said,

> What I went through for these qualifications, I could write a book because nobody at the Ministry knew what to do to give me qualifications in Ontario. Instead of advising me to start my degree right away . . . I was over twenty-six at that time, – I had to go back and write my Grade 13 exam.

It is interesting that because of the entry into the Ontario teaching force of a number of francophone women teachers from Quebec or abroad – women who had teaching certification but not Ontario certification, the Ministry created a special diploma called "The Certificate for Teachers of French as a Second Language to English-Speaking Pupils." This diploma could be taken in one summer, but was actually very restrictive, since the teachers who held it could only teach French in an elementary school (no other subjects), and in addition, were restricted to the school board that had originally hired them to teach French. If they moved to another region, their certificate was declared null and void. Arlette took that course to gain the certificate although she felt that she actually could have taught the instructors how to teach it. Later, she took the three-part French second language additional qualification courses offered through the Ontario Ministry of Education and found them much better.

Arlette, Anne-Marie and Colette were obviously excellent teachers, and were recognized as such by their school boards that entrusted them with the task of setting up French second language programs for anglophones, who encouraged them to provide in-service presentations for other teachers, and who appointed them as language consultants. They were passionately devoted to teaching French language and culture. Still, they all refer to the difficulty of teaching French to anglophone students often because of anti-French feelings of the principals and some of the teachers. Colette mentioned that as a teacher in Southern Ontario in a dual-track school – half English, half French language, she found that the English principal and some of the Anglophone teachers were openly hostile and would tell the francophone teachers to "speak white"[16] whenever they would speak French among themselves. She also mentioned one particular teacher who used to put on an exaggerated French accent whenever he would speak to her until she confronted him and told him to stop.

Other teachers interviewed confirmed the prejudices against francophones. Berthe (ACPID 054) reported: "I was told when I came to Ontario that since we had lost the war on the Plains of Abraham that maybe we should quit insisting." Above, I referred to the belief among Franco-Ontarians that Irish Catholics were undermining their aspirations to receive instruction in French as far back as 1912. Berthe, speaking of a problem she ran into in the late 1960s remarked that a low point in her career came when she discovered the Irish versus French situation. She believed that the Irish superintendent went after her because she was a francophone.

French teachers often face serious discipline problems in French second language classes because of hostility toward the subject from students and their parents. Arlette does relate a success story she experienced with a young girl who was particularly difficult in one of her French second language classes, refusing to participate or do any work at all, and disrupting others until Arlette had a chat with her asking her more or less to "Try it, you might like it." Years later when Arlette was a language consultant organizing the immersion program, she again met the woman, now a parent, who was determined to enroll her children in the immersion program so they could learn French. This was a gratifying experience for Arlette. Unfortunately, however, far too many FSL teachers in Ontario still have to combat the anti-French feelings that continue to exist especially in small town Ontario since the English-only days of Regulation 17. Several of my graduate students have researched the area during their Master of Education studies, and have found some parents in rural Ontario to be quite racist in their treatment of the French teacher, and totally dismissive of French language programs in schools.[17]

Another challenge, particular to French teachers, and referred to by all three informants was the paucity and quality of materials for teaching their French classes whether in a first or second language program. All spoke of having to develop and write their own materials. Colette eventually became one of the writers of a commercial French second language text series for anglophones. Resources are more available now, but at the time when these women taught, they had to use all their ingenuity to produce interesting and worthwhile curriculum for their French classes.

Gender-related Issues

The women profiled here faced particular challenges because they represented minority teachers involved in the education of a minority group or in delivering a minority language as a subject in Ontario. As women, they also faced the challenges of their sister teachers. Arlette and Anne-Marie both resigned their positions as teachers once they married. Anne-Marie soon reentered the teaching force but without the security of a regular contract. Arlette's reentry involved switching to the English language system and resulted in her trials described above to gain appropriate certification.

All three women were called upon to provide leadership in French second language program development. None was ever invited to become a principal. Anne-Marie noted how men with little teaching experience would be approached by the inspector and encouraged to advance. Regarding the issue of women administrators in education, Colette noted the same thing and stressed how important it was to have contacts and the support of colleagues in order to be accepted into the Principal's course. She was well aware of ways in which the system discriminated against women. She explained:

> When I was at DM school, there were men because it was 7, 8, 9, but the women were never encouraged to go into administration. Because I . . . can't remember how many years I had been in [that board] and one of the math teachers, B, he got promoted. Then they got promoted. I don't know how they did it. They just talked to you and that was it. He was hand picked. Nobody went around and talked to the women and there were lots of women there that were just as capable as this person.

As to how one could enter the Principal's course, she said:

> Well, it was hard to get into those courses because there was a quota to take the Principal's course. The Board sponsored so many people. . . . I forget how many people the Board could sponsor, so obviously you couldn't submit your name. Well you could, but you wouldn't get in. So that was the biggest problem because I think there were centres where they offered the courses and you had to go to these centres. I know some people got their qualification [by] going to the francophone centres because they hadn't reached their quota, and if

> you were French speaking, sometimes you could get in . . . A friend
> of mine did that because she wanted the qualifications and she could
> never get in the English centres so she went to a francophone centre.
> So that was the barrier there. I think they did [admit] a few token
> women.

Colette also mentioned that the centres were rather isolated and if you
could not go to the designated centre, you could not take the qualification. This obviously discriminated against women with children who
could not easily leave their children in the summer to go to a distant
centre to take the Principal's course.

> My sister went and she had four kids and she had to go to Sudbury. I
> think Sudbury offered both [francophone and anglophone principals'
> courses]. She took her course there. She was lucky her husband was
> home to take care of the kids because otherwise you wouldn't be able
> to go.

However, eventually things did change because in her board a program was started called "Women in Leadership" to encourage women
teachers to go into administration. Eventually through lobbying from
the Federation of Women Teachers' Associations of Ontario
(FWTAO), the boards and faculties of education began to offer the
Principal's course locally, and so more women could become qualified
as principals. Colette did complete the Principal's course although she
never became a school principal but remained as a coordinator until
retirement. With regard to the importance of the Women's Leadership
Network, she noted:

> I think the men used to have the old boys' club and . . . I remember
> that VL had given a workshop and . . . she was encouraging women
> to continue – maybe she was a principal at the time – . . . . and she
> was saying how the men support each other and they help each other.
> So if you are a new kid on the block . . . and the principal sits down
> with you and he goes over and talks about the staff and gives you
> pointers how to handle [things],well you've got a lot of ammunition
> to help you, but if you don't have that support, you're probably going
> to fail because nobody is helping you. And this is [how] she was
> encouraging women to help each other that way.

Arlette mentions how although she had been hired to set up the elementary French second language program, when it came time to
appoint master teachers to oversee the program, two male high school

teachers were chosen over her. They knew little about the elementary program and would direct other elementary French teachers to her for after school workshops which she gave gladly. They had the authority and the prestige, but she did the work. Anne-Marie recalls similar experiences in her board before she left to become the coordinator in another board.

During the interviews the women were asked about their involvement in one of the Ontario teachers' federations. None had been particularly active in the federation nor did they mention any support they received from them in, for example, their problems with gaining appropriate certification for an anglophone board. Perhaps in the case of Arlette and Anne-Marie, it is because they switched from francophone to anglophone boards and between public and Roman Catholic Separate School boards. Moreover, they taught in the 1940s and 1950s when boards were very small, often representing just the local town, so perhaps there was no active federation member in their school to whom they could turn. Colette did mention the "Women in Leadership" program but seemed to connect it more to the efforts of a woman principal in her board. According to her, it was the women in the leadership program who successfully lobbied the board to allow more women to be chosen for the principal's course, and to have it held locally rather than in remote areas around the province so that it would be accessible to women with family responsibilities. She did not connect this work to a particular federation, and certainly not to the FWTAO. Of course, at that time she was a member of the secondary teachers' federation, the Ontario Secondary School Teachers' Federation (OSSTF) that included both men and women secondary teachers. She saw the issue of women in administration as a gender issue, one that women had to address themselves in their own boards and not through a teachers' federation.

Final Observations: Pondering Priorities

In interviewing the three women, I was aware of a dilemma that always arises when one engages in research involving personal narratives. I wished to give them voice to express what they found significant and valuable about their lives as francophone women teachers. But as an anglophone, albeit a bilingual one with experience in teaching French, I could identify with Petra Munro's discomfort when she says: "In fact, the notion of 'giving voice' has been particularly unsettling because it actually underscores my perceptions of those I was researching as disempowered and conflicted with my understanding of them as meaning makers."[18] How much of what the three women told me represented their construction of their experiences designed to justify their careers in teaching and the life choices they had made? How much reflected their attempts to provide me with information they thought I wanted, information that would confirm my assumptions about the lives of women teachers in the times when they taught? As Kathleen Weiler has noted:

> A theoretical reading of the narratives of women teachers raises questions about the complexity of the construction of meaning and identity through discourse. But a feminist approach addresses not only the contradictions of competing discourses, but also the context in which narratives are produced and the relationships of power through which various accounts are given. This approach raises a number of questions for researchers: what kinds of knowledge do narrative texts provide? How can we read them? How are we as researchers implicated in the creation of social knowledge? A recognition of the situated quality of narratives demands not only that historians be conscious both of their own assumptions as they gather 'evidence,' but also that they consider the context in which such evidence (as texts or narratives) is produced.[19]

I have tried to pay heed to the context of the stories Arlette, Anne-Marie and Colette told. However, I may have skewed their intentions by the parts of their narrative I highlighted, and the quotations I selected to support my reading of their lives as teachers. Despite their marginalization as francophone women teachers (a marginalization that Anne-Marie, at least, did not seem to recognize) their stories are positive ones. The women profiled in this study enjoyed successful careers and were highly respected by their peers. As mentioned before, their respective school boards recognized their quality: they were all chosen to develop French second language programs; they provided professional development for other teachers in their boards, and they all became board consultants or language co-ordinators. Arlette and Colette rose in the Ontario Modern Language Teachers' Association (OMLTA), Colette to Secretary-Treasurer. Anne-Marie and Colette taught courses at faculties of education in the province and all three taught courses for the Ministry of Education. Colette, as mentioned above was hired to write French second language texts. I sought them out as participants in this study because they had been recommended to me by other teachers. It is a tribute to their strong spirit that in reflecting on their careers which they recall with great fondness, they highlight their successes with problem students, their ability to survive and even thrive while teaching in less than ideal conditions with few resources. They celebrate the contributions they were able to make to the teaching of French in Ontario and the efforts they expended in trying to improve the French second language teaching cohort.

However, their happy and proud accounts are interspersed with episodes of injustice they all experienced – the precariousness of their jobs, often because of certification regulations, assumptions of inspectors and supervisory principals (usually male) that women teachers, even when well qualified, were not suitable for administrative positions; the active discouragement from gaining additional qualifications; the marriage bars that dictated resignation for a woman teacher when she married, harassment from superiors, and problems encountered when teaching in a minority language.

In speaking to the three teachers who began their careers half a century ago, I was keen to find evidence of obstacles they encountered as women first, and as minority teachers second. They confirmed my expectations and gave me examples of discrimination, exploitation and inequities they had faced. However, I must admit that their priorities were different than mine. From their point of view in reflecting on their careers, such "problems" were minor, and, in any case, they overcame them. I believe that they wanted their stories told to celebrate their successes. To them, the most important thing about their lives as teachers lay in the way they championed their francophone heritage and were able to promote the French language and culture in Ontario schools. All other problems they faced seemed insignificant in comparison. Given that they had experienced first hand the effects of the repressive Regulation 17, even long after it was no longer law, it is not surprising that these francophone women would focus on that area. Each in her own way contributed to making French language and culture in Ontario a positive element for their many students over the years. They were proud to report how they stood up to those who tried to disparage French and francophone people. Whether or not they were consciously aware of the goals articulated by the ACFEO early in the twentieth century regarding promotion and preservation of the French language and identity in Ontario, they certainly devoted themselves to such aspirations and considered their contributions to those goals a main justification for their success as teachers. It should be noted that other francophone women teachers whom I interviewed for the larger project, but who are not profiled for this chapter, confirmed that language and culture furnished a powerful "raison d'être" in their teaching careers.

Marielle (ACPID 220), a francophone woman who only began teaching in the 60s but who rose through the ranks to become a principal, superintendent and then Deputy Minister of Education in charge of francophone schools and "francisation" of the French language curriculum, perhaps expressed the notion of mission for francophone teachers best. She said:

> I have always told people that to be a teacher is not a profession, it's a vocation, especially in the French language schools, because it is much more than to be simply a teacher, particularly in minority regions. Perhaps a bit less in regions like Ottawa, but as francophone teachers in French language schools, you have to get involved a great deal more in the life of the community, rather than simply saying "I am a teacher and that's all." These things involve cultural activities at the level of the French centres, of the parish, of the Catholic school, etc. Sometimes I think that teachers of French have to be real cultural facilitators as well who would encourage the children to maintain their language, [tell them] that they should be proud of it, etc. Then I always repeated this to the teachers "if you choose to go to teach in a French language school, you have to accept the additional responsibilities that you would not have in the English language schools." [translation, mine]

Arlette, Anne-Marie and Colette accepted these responsibilities and lived a career in service to them.

Notes

[1]The author acknowledges with gratitude funding support from the Dean of the Faculty of Education, and an award from the Vice President's UWO Research Committee which supported initial research into this area.

[2]The percentage of Ontarians who designate themselves as francophones has been falling during the twentieth century. For example, according to the 1911 Census of Canada, Vol. 2, Table XIII, p. 371, out of a total Ontario population of 2 523 274 people, 202 442 or 8% identified themselves as French speaking; by 1941 (1941 Census of Canada, Vol 4, Table 14, p. 226) out of a total population of 3 787 655 people, 289 146 or 7.6% were French speaking; and by 1996, the figure was 5% (Info-Stats "Statistical Profile of the Francophone Community in Ontario," http://www.ofa.gov.on/ english/stats/infostaats1.html (accessed February 27, 2005).

[3]The group later changed its name to "L'association canadienne-française de l'Ontario (ACFO) once it affiliated itself with various French Canadian groups in Ontario which were not necessarily associated with education issues. Such groups included La Fédération des Sociétés Saint-Jean-Baptiste de l'Ontario; L'Union des Cultivateurs Franco-Ontariens, La Fédération des Femmes canadiennes-françaises, L'Association de la Jeunesse Franco-Ontarienne; along with the educational groups such as the AEFO. Cf *L'Ecole Ontarienne. Revue pédagogique de l'Association de l'Enseignement de l'Ontario* (mars, 1953), 54.

[4]*L'Ecole Ontarienne* (mars, 1953), 52-53.

[5]M. Barber, "Ontario schools question" in *The Canadian Encyclopedia,* Vol. 3, ed. M. Hurtig, 1578 (Edmonton: Hurtig, 1988); Ontario Royal Commission on Learning, *For the Love of Learning. Report of the Royal Commission on Learning,* Vol. 1, Chapter 2 (Toronto: Queen's Printer, 1994), 18; R. D. Gidney, *From Hope to Harris. The Reshaping of Ontario's Schools,* (Toronto: University of Toronto Press, 1999), 143; Stéphane Lang, "La communauté Franco-Ontarienne et l'enseignement secondaire, (1910-1968)" (PhD diss., Université d'Ottawa, 2003), xii, 7-12.

[6]*Infomag,* Vol. 3:3 (2000), 20; also available at http://www.infomag.ca/magazine/chroniques/grands_personages/gra_v3n3_1.asp (accessed February 27, 2005).

[7]"We, French Canadians of Ontario are at war. We fight today to defend our language and to protect our children who will be torn away from us and delivered over to anglicisation." (translation, mine), quoted in *Infomag,* vol. 3:3 (2000), 20.

[8]*Infomag,* op. cit., and M. Barber, op. cit.

[9]AEFO, *Femmes de Vision. Fiches biographiques et strategies d'intervention pédagogique,* Ottawa: AEFO (2000).

[10]Stéphane Lang, "La Communauté Franco-Ontarienne," 8.

[11]Stéphane Lang, "La Communauté Franco-Ontarienne," 22.

[12]"Les écoles normales" http://www.uottawa.ca/academie/crccf/passeport/IV/IVC1c/IVC1c.html, accessed February 27, 2005.

[13]Ontario Royal Commission on Learning, *For the Love of Learning,* Vol. 1, Chap. 2 (Toronto: Queen's Printer, 1994) 18; *Infomag* 3:3 (2000), 20.

[14]Teacher education programs in Ontario require candidates preparing to teach in the intermediate and senior divisions (grades 7 to 12) to complete pedagogical qualifications in subject areas (such as history, science-biology, art, etc.) taught in secondary schools. The subject areas are called "teachables."

[15]Office of the Commissioner of Official Languages, "Language Policy" in *The Canadian Encyclopedia,* Vol.2 (Edmonton: Hurtig, 1988), 1175.

[16]Michèle Lalonde, *Speak White, poème affiche* (Montréal: Editions de l'Hexagone. 1974).

[17]Cf Laurie E. Finn, "Beyond 'masculin ou féminin'; gender and the teaching of the core French programme" (Unpublished MEd thesis, The University of Western Ontario, 1994), Elisabeth M. Richards, "The Devaluation of Foreign Languages: An Overview of the Issues Surrounding Foreign Language Teaching in the Elementary Grades" (Unpublished Directed Research Project, The University of Western Ontario, 1994). Elisabeth Richards' EdD thesis, "Positioning the Elementary Core French Teacher: An Investigation of Workplace Marginality" (Unpublished doctoral thesis, OISE/U of Toronto, 2001) also makes reference to the area of prejudice against French teachers and the teaching of French in Ontario.

[18]Petra Munro, Subject to Fiction. Women Teachers'Life History Narratives and the Cultural Politics of Resistance, (Buckingham: Open University Press, 1998), 12.

[19]Kathleen Weiler and S. Middleton, Eds., *Telling Women's Lives: Narrative Inquiries in the History of Women's Education* (Buckingham: Open University Press, 1999), 47.

5

Women of Color and Teaching: Exploring Contradictory Experiences of Immigrant Women Teachers

Goli M. Rezai-Rashti

I am proud to be a Canadian woman. Yet I am seldom treated as a full Canadian. I still encounter comments about how I must hate the winter, and love the hot temperatures since that is what I am viewed as "used to" in my homeland. At forty-two, I have lived only twelve of those away from Canada. My skin color still forms the basis for quick judgment about my likes and dislikes, my strengths and weaknesses . . . [1]

Rania Gameil, a Sudanese Canadian who immigrated in 1995 and is part of the new diversity of teachers in Ontario. *Photo courtesy of Faculty of Education, The University of Western Ontario.*

This paper examines the oral history narrative of five women teachers of color who immigrated to Canada, started teaching in the 1960s, and retired in the 1990s. The main objective of the paper is to show how the lives of these women of color were shaped by this experience, and how they accessed the teaching profession and worked as teachers in the Canadian education system. As important as their stories are in and of themselves, my intention is to analyze some of the contradictions and complex articulations of these women's gendered and racialized experiences while teaching in schools in Canada.

In recent years, a consensus has formed that women are not unitary categories, devoid of race and social class.[2] The work of those in cultural and postcolonial studies suggests the complexities of a race, class and gender analysis, and the contradictions and instabilities of these categories. Research on race, identity and the politics of anti-racism by Hall, McCarthy, Said and Shohat[3] are helpful in situating and interpreting the lived narratives of these five retired women teachers. One of the most interesting developments in anti-racist and feminist struggles in recent years has been the move away from the concepts of identity and community as essentialized and fixed, to a consideration of them as fluid, relational and multi-positional. As Shohat argues, "communities of ethnic, racial, national, and sexual identity are not fixed, nor are all identities analyzable within an either/or (black/white, hetero/homo) binarism."[4] This way of thinking about race and gender has created a situation in which some women (Latin American, Middle Eastern, North Africans) have been denied status as women of color. Shohat concludes that "tension within and between communities obliges us to go beyond a discourse of "common oppression' sisterhood."[5] She further argues that some of those well versed in gender theories still lack a basic understanding of colonialism and its aftermath:

Despite symptoms of irritation with the mantra of race, class, gender, and sexuality, many of those eager for a next wave theory still lack a basic materialist understanding of colonial history and its aftermath. Students in my seminars are often well versed in gender and sexual theories, but they often know little about anti-colonial writings (Cesaire, Memmi, Fanon), or history of imperialism and its relevance for feminist theorization, or about feminists such as Audre Lorde,

Angela Davis, Gloria Anzaldua, Assia Dijebar, or Fatima Mernissi. Those of us bringing postcoloniality and race into women's and gay/lesbian studies tend to work in an intellectual and institutional vacuum, just as those bringing gender and sexuality to ethnic studies area face marginalization.[6]

McCarthy criticizes both mainstream and radical approaches to racial inequality and offers a more relational and contextual approach to the operation of racial inequality. Such an approach he argues, allows us "to better understand the complex operation of racial logics in education and helps us to explore more adequately the vital links that exists between racial inequality and other dynamics – such as class and gender – operation in the school setting." As well, Cohen criticizes existing theories of racism for their reductionist approach; that is, for "trying to explain a complex and multifaceted phenomenon by resorting to a single, simple cause. These explanations are therefore limited, since they tell only part of the story, leaving out those elements which do not fit into their chosen line of argument."[7]

In addition, in recent years an increasing number of oral history projects dealing with women teachers' histories and their life choices have emerged.[8] There has also been much theorization and writings about women teachers.[9] The work of Weiler is of particular interest to this study.[10] In her analysis of oral history accounts she exhibits an awareness of the complexities and contradictions inherent in analyzing these accounts and the multidimensionality of gender and its articulation with race and social class. She argues that the notion of "subjectivity" is useful in understanding oral history because it captures the social construction of the self which is constantly in a process of struggle over the unstable notion of identity, and "suggests the incomplete and sometimes contradictory quality of our lives both in the present and as we construct our past through memory.[11] She further cautions oral history researchers to recognize the situated nature of the narrative; to consider their own assumptions as they gather data, and to be conscious of the situation within which these narratives are produced.[12] In addition, several other feminist researchers[13] have raised the question of the relationship between researcher and subjects, and the responsibility of these researchers in terms of interpretation and making judgments about the meaning of produced narratives. My own experience as a woman of color teaching in Ontario schools in the 1980s facilitated my ability to interview teachers with comparable backgrounds. As a teacher with a relatively "shared location," I was well aware of the context of some of their narratives, and this fact might have helped the interviewees feel relatively comfortable when narrating their teaching experiences as immigrant women of color to me. Of course, my teaching experience and my history, like that of many other immigrant women, is far messier than this simple description suggests. As Mohanty points out, "the very process of constructing a narrative of oneself – of telling a story – imposes a certain linearity and coherence that is never entirely there. But that is a lesson, perhaps, especially for us immigrants and migrants: that is, that home, community and identity all fall somewhere between histories and experiences we inherit and the political choices we make through alliances, solidarities, and friendships."[14]

Immigrant Women Teachers

Participants in this study were five women of color (two from Trinidad, two from Jamaica and one from Pakistan). They all came to Canada as immigrants in the 1960s, and all but one came as trained and experienced teachers in their countries of origin. All were educated in colonial style institutions, and in some cases, the degree awarded to them was from an educational institution in England. The narratives of these women certainly direct us to some of the discussion in postcolonial studies about the nature of community, identity, gender, race and other matters of social difference. These women teachers experienced their lives and teaching careers in Canada, and specifically in Ontario differently than one another and from white teachers. Although all experienced racism and sexism, their level of analysis and their political position towards these issues were different. While one teacher could analyze her experience as an example of institutional and systemic racism, another would describe the experience as an attitudinal and individual problem. For example, in terms of access to the profession, it was relatively easy for two women: Laura (ACPID 088) from Jamaica and Blanca (ACPID 079) from Trinidad, as they were both math teachers. Donna (ACPID 117) who was not able to secure a permanent teaching position, decided to go to school and complete a university degree before entering the teaching profession. Claudia

(ACPID 103), who already had a university degree from Trinidad, and had worked as an economist in her own country, decided to obtain her teaching qualifications from the University of Toronto and became a business teacher at the secondary school level. Meena (ACPID 084) was a secondary school teacher in Pakistan who did supply teaching at first and then became an elementary school teacher specializing in special education.

How their qualifications were accredited by the Ontario Ministry of Education is an interesting issue to consider in the analysis. Laura, who was a math teacher and secured a teaching position obtained her teaching qualifications in Canada after completing an intensive program over two summers. Blanca also did not face difficulty in obtaining a teaching position because she had lived and worked as a teacher in England for seven years. Therefore, she did not have to complete any upgrading in Canada. She had two years of teacher training in Trinidad and in addition had completed some math courses at the college level. After immigrating to Canada, she decided to complete her university degree, and after teaching grades 7 and 8 for a number of years, taught at the secondary school level. Claudia, who came to Canada with a degree in economics, worked as a clerk until she decided to go to school, and complete her teacher's qualifications, after which she taught business at secondary schools; later, she became the department head. Meena came to Canada with a BA degree from a university in Pakistan and teaching experience in a private missionary Christian school at the secondary school level where she eventually became a head mistress. In Ontario, accredited to teach at the primary/junior level because her BA degree was recognized as only equivalent to grade 13, she started at category one (out of six) on the salary scale and was told that if she took university courses, she would be able to advance on the salary schedule.

Why in the case of Meena who had been prepared for and taught at the secondary school level in Pakistan, she was assessed as being qualified only for primary/junior (grades 1-6) level teaching? And why were other teachers of color assigned to special education classes? Perhaps it was because special education programs are often one-on-one teaching, and a teacher's accent or appearance might not be seen as significant an issue as it is in a regular classroom. The status of special education programs might also be another issue that warrants consideration. Was it that these programs were seen as of lesser value and therefore more suitable for a minority teacher? Certainly Laura's early experience had a significant impact in her future desire to teach in an academic school, or to become an administrator. After teaching for two years in rural Ontario, and finishing the required courses in the summer, she applied for jobs in Toronto where math teachers were in short supply.

> I started to apply for jobs to come into Toronto. I couldn't get a job in an academic school, this was my first choice. And if I were not willing to take a position in a special school, I probably would be still trying to get into Toronto, you know.

> Starting my career in [name of high school] had really influenced my entire career because once you got into [name of high school] it was impossible to get out. I have become the head of math and I wanted so desperately to get out, I couldn't get a headship, not even an assistant headship anywhere else. And I decided I would just in order to get out, take a position as a teacher. (ACPID 088)

Donna, after finishing her degree at one Ontario university, did supply teaching for three years, and when she could not get into a regular teaching position, accepted a position in a psychiatric institution that had a special education classroom run by the Ministry of Education (it later came under the control of the local board of education). She explains that there was a very small number of teachers in that institution, and those who came often remained:

> It was a small group, and actually at the beginning it was more like a family, because people who were there, stayed there. Like you know, like the way I stayed. A lot of people just stayed and we were like a big family, and we still are.

> I had lots of opportunities to leave [name of institution] and go out into the board which a lot of people were doing, but for some reasons I never really wanted to. I felt happy there, I felt secure there, and I don't know, it might have been better for me if I had done that and you know, taught normal children, and then not feel so bogged down by the time I was ready to retire. I retired before I was 65, because I began to feel overwhelmed, and then the class that I had when I retired had to be one of the worst classes I'd ever had. And I felt I was not able to give it my best then. (ACPID 117)

While Laura became very much aware of race, class and gender dynamics, and could analyze her experience in a more sophisticated way, others did not see it that way and seemed to be content with their job and the prospect of full employment. One of the reasons might have been related to income, since the differences between a teacher's salary in their country of origin and Canada was significant. As Donna says:

> When I started here, our pay with the Ministry was less than [board's name], but every course that we took, the ministry gave us extra money for that, so that in the long run you know, you got more.

When asked about the salary, and if the money was sufficient, she replied:

> Well it was for me. I mean having come from Trinidad and you know, this was a lot of money. Definitely!

> Just to mention that in Trinidad we didn't have all the materials, and all the benefits that teachers have here, so our classrooms weren't as pleasant. (ACPID 117)

Race, Gender and the Contradictions

In terms of race, gender and other issues of social difference, there seem to be various levels of understanding and analysis among these women. While most of these teachers had a few incidents that they would explain as a result of their difference from mainstream society, some would rationalize it as a lack of understanding of cultural differences, individual attitudes or personality. Only in Laura's case can a more theoretical analysis of social difference be detected. This is likely because, while teaching in the special school, Laura completed her MEd degree at the University of Toronto and worked for a board of education in which trustees were addressing issues of social difference in a more substantive manner.

Meena, who as a practicing Christian, was part of a minority group in Pakistan, appreciates Canadian multiculturalism and prides herself on her extensive experience in Canadian schools organizing multicultural events which celebrate cultural differences, mainly in terms of food and customs. She has always dressed in the traditional sari and she claims that although the school board that she worked for had a dress code, no one forced her to change. Several instances of contradictory experiences in her working life are illustrative for our analysis though. One is her strong belief in teaching Bible stories in the public school system, as she believes it is only through studying the Bible that students will acquire the proper values.

> So, I started introducing a little bit of stories, you know, moral stories, some Bible stories. And they [the students] would say to me Mrs [teacher's name] . . . you tell such nice stories. And they would be in the Bible. And they would say: "Oh, we have that at home too, but we don't read it." And one of the teachers, she said, "you're not supposed to have a Bible in the classroom." And I said, "Too bad, my children wanted to see what a Bible looked like, so I wanted to show them." (ACPID 084)

This story raises questions and contradictions. While Meena was promoting a multicultural understanding of customs and food, religion was not part of her understanding of multiculturalism. In fact, having been a minority Christian in Pakistan, she felt empowered in Canada. She negotiated her religious identity and her colonial experience in order to overcome a difficult relationship she had with one of her principals. As she stated to the principal:

> I thought I would have trouble with you, and my teaching career would end here. But then I learned that you were an Anglican, and I am an Anglican. . . . And I said you worship the Queen of England, because you think no other person is as good, and I was ruled by that Queen, I was a British subject. (ACPID 084)

She talks about how these statements changed the principal's behavior towards her and how they became good friends. Later on, after he found out that she had been a head mistress, he put her in charge of the school in his absence (he was attending a meeting at the board office).

She describes another incident with a teacher in the school.

> Staff, I had problems sometimes. Well, one teacher especially gave me a hard time. One day, I'm no good with directions, and you know how they would say north side? So and so, the yard duty timetable would say that, so I went to the wrong side, and she was mad. "Don't you know what is north and what is south? In this country you have to go learn north-south." . . . I cried and cried . . . I must say God has been great to me, because of my principals, they had been so good principals; "What is the matter? I said, "So and so said this that to me." "Go

and sit down in my office, I'll take your class.".…. And he said, "You had to be really gentle, she's been in a concentration camp, was German, and she has suffered, too." And I said, *"I am a Christian coming from a Muslim country, I have suffered too, and that is why I came to Canada. But that hasn't made me a bad person or a better person, I think I've learned from the experience, that no matter where I go, I will have some kind of a problem. Whether it be my color or my religion, so I will have to accept, and live each day as it comes. I can't be bitter about these things. So, it depends on your personality.* (ACPID 084)

This description of her experience shows that Meena was aware of differences, but she believed that she had to cope with the situation because "it depends on your personality." Indeed, while she was promoting multiculturalism, she practised assimilation.

In my school there was nobody from Pakistan. There were some from the Island, from Africa. I know some of the teachers did have a chip on their shoulders, and did not as easily assimilate as I did. And I think that's again how you take it. (ACPID 084)

Laura, who was more articulate in talking about structural and systemic racism, claimed that she did not face individual racism or sexism because her "colleagues were fairly sophisticated, more sophisticated than average classroom teachers … more careful and more knowledgeable and more accepting." However, she argues that she could see structural racism as one of the major issues blocking her promotion to an administrative position.

You don't know, it is hard to say. What I would say, If I'm to pinpoint racism, I would hang it more to administration. I would point at things at more at the structural racism within the board. I would say definitely when I was trying to seek promotion, I was going to an interview with four white males, and I knew, I walked in and I saw them and I knew I wasn't getting the job. Now that's where the gut feeling comes in. I think I definitely had the gut feeling more in terms of trying to gain promotion. (ACPID 088)

Laura, who later became a math consultant for the board, describes her getting into this position as a result of some progressive trustees who made it possible to promote more minorities. In addition, they had seen her creative work as a math teacher and decided to use her expertise.

I think the year before that appointment, the first report, the first multiculturalism came, report came done, and the trustees at that time they were a very progressive set of trustees, and they began to talk about how we put minorities to positions, and there were a few of us that were, right around that time I remember there was one black man who at that time became a vice-principal, as I said there were two of us in the math department. . . .

So, I decided I would take the consultant position, but the other way that this starting my career at [school's name] influenced the rest of my career was that when I decided to, when I had got my qualifications for principalship, and started to apply for that, then again I hit a wall because you don't have any experience in a secondary school, in an academic five-year program, you don't have any experience in a four-year program, and now if you look at [name of school board] schools, the majority of them, you know, they're either academic schools they are five or four year programs, and very few special schools. So basically what, I remember one year I applied for something like twelve positions. I got some interviews, but you know it was always the same thing, you got the feedback, well you don't have experience in any of these groups. So by having had to start my career in a special school, I was literally, that literally excluded me from. (ACPID 088)

Although Laura chaired the status of women committee for a number of years in her board and is sensitive to gender issues, she believes that it is white women who have benefitted more from feminism than minority women. She said that since the 1980s, there has been a change, but white women still don't support minority women. Some of them probably do, but again when feminism took hold, the women became a bit more militant and vocal and the board began to feel under pressure to promote them.

Who did they promote? White women! I mean we really didn't benefit from that change at all. White women benefitted and the data is there to show it. I mean clearly principals and vice-principals, the numbers have increased considerably. (ACPID 088)

It is, however, important to mention that although Laura was not promoted to a principalship, she became involved in the National Council of Mathematics Teachers, and was seconded to a university position as a teacher/educator, and then worked for a few years for the Ministry of Education, returning to her board in 1996. She approached the director of the board and asked him about the possibilities for promotion. I told him, "Now, I have all this experience, I have done this, I've done that, what do you have for me?" But he did not encourage her to pursue her dream. When a principal's position came up, she heard only after the submission date had passed. It had been advertised for only four days. She filed a grievance and while in process, a coordinator's position was advertised, which she was offered. She was still in this position when she retired in 1998.

The issue of promotion was also a serious one for Claudia who became a department head. She commented that while she was taking the principal's course, her principal discouraged her by saying, "what is the point of doing these things, because you are not going to get it anyway" (ACPID 103).

All of these narrative accounts contribute to our understanding that gender and race are not fixed and essentialized categories. Some of the fixed assumptions about race and gender oppression are called into question in these narratives. The fluid notion of identity and the multipositionality of the community of women of color are clearly articulated here. While Meena experienced religious oppression in Pakistan, and stated it as the cause for leaving, Canada provided a relative escape but brought a new form of racialization. On the other hand, she asserted that other immigrant teachers had a chip on their shoulders and could not assimilate as well as she did. The question is how one can embrace multiculturalism and diversity, but at the same time expect assimilation? In addition, while she celebrated cultural diversity and promoted multiculturalism in her school, subversively she brought religious education to her classroom and claimed she was teaching children moral values. As a strategy, when trying to mend relationships with her principal, she talked about shared colonial and religious identities. It appears as though Meena resorted to a colonial discourse since it was available to her in the context of being originally from Pakistan, and also being a British subject.

Another issue that warrants further analysis is the impact of differences in material rewards for teaching positions in Canada, as contrasted with those of developing societies. This is especially evident in the narrative of Donna, who emphasised that there was a difference in terms of pay, physical conditions at the school, supplies, etc. These factors can also bring a relative improvement in working condition and might explain why the two women of color who were placed in special education programs did not change jobs, but rather stayed until their retirements.

All of these narratives should be read in their historical context and in relation to both the material and discursive situation in which these women found themselves. Their racialized and sexualized experience should be investigated in relation to their previous experience in their home countries as women and teachers in order to understand how they constructed their experience in a new social environment.

These narratives suggest a complex articulation and intersection of gender, race, immigration, and religion but also show the women's individual power to resist discrimination, negotiate identity and overcome some of the educational barriers in their new environment. They all expressed teaching as a rewarding experience in Canada.

It should be noted that all of these women taught in Canada at a time when awareness of gender oppression had grown and women's organizations and teacher federations were pushing for greater changes. Although, as Laura stated there was little chance of promotion for minority women, they managed to take advantage of material rewards and working conditions that other women enjoyed.

Articulating the contradictions in the lives of women teachers implies moving away from neat binarism, and to remap "the shape-shifting modalities of oppression and empowerment, recognizing that "oppression" and "empowerment" are themselves relational terms. Individuals can occupy more than one position, being empowered on one axis (class, say) but not on another (such as sexuality). Instead of a simple oppressor/oppressed dichotomy we find a wide spectrum of power relations among and within communities."[15]

Notes

[1]Ramrattan Smith, S & R. Bickram Ramrattan, *"When We Chose Canada": A Mother and Daughter Share Stories That Shaped Their Lives in Their New Homeland* (City: Press, 1999), 48.

[2]Mohanty, C.T. "Crafting Feminist Genealogies: On the Geography and Politics of Home, Nation, and Community," in *Talking Visions: Multicultural*

Feminism in a Transnational Age, ed. E. Shoat, 489-500 (New York: The MIT Press, 1998). Mohanty, C, *Third World Women and the Politics of Feminism* (Bloomigton: Indiana University Press, 1991). Bannerji, H, *Returning the Gaze: Essays on Racism, Feminism and Politics* (Toronto: Sister Vision Press, 1993). Hill-Collins, P, *Fighting Words: Black Women and Search For Justice* (Minneapolis: University of Minnesota Press, 1998). Ng, Roxana, "Racism and Nation Building in Canada," in *Race, Identity, and Representation in Education*, ed. C. McCarthy & W. Crichlow, 50-59 (New York: Routledge, 1993). Shohat, E, *Talking Visions: Multicultural Feminism in a Transnational Age.*(Cambridge: The MIT Press, 1998).

[3]Hall, S, "New Ethnicities," in Stuart Hall: *Critical Dialogue in Cultural Studies*, ed. D. Morley & K. Chen, (London: Routledge, 1996). McCarthy, C. T, *The Uses of Culture: Education and the Limits of Ethnic Affiliation* (New York: Routledge, 1998). Said, E, *Culture and Imperialism* (New York: Alfred. A. Knopf, 1993). Shohat, E, *Talking Visions: Multicultural Feminism in a Transnational Age.*

[4]Shohat, E, Talking Visions: Multicultural Feminism in a Transnational Age, 31.

[5]Shohat, E, Talking Visions: Multicultural Feminism in a Transnational Age, 35.

[6]Shohat, E, *Talking Visions: Multicultural Feminism in a Transnational Age,* 40.

[7]McCarthy, C.T, *The Uses of Culture: Education and the Limits of Ethnic Affiliation,* 61-62. Cohen, P, "It's Racism What Dunnit":Hidden Narratives in Theories of Racism," in *"Race," Culture and Difference,* ed. J. Donald & A. Rattansi, 77 (London, UK: The Open University Press, 1992).

[8]Henry, A, *Taking Back Control: African-Canadian Women Teachers' Lives and Practices* (Albany: State University of New York Press, 1998). Weiler, K, "Remembering and Representing Life Choices: A Critical Perspective on Teachers' Oral History Narratives," in *Critical Theory and Educational Research,* ed. McClaren, P.L. & J.M. Giarelli, 127-44 (Albany: State University of New York Press, 1995). Theobald. M, "Teachers, Memory and Oral History," in *Telling Women's Lives: Narrative Inquiries in the History of Women's Education*, ed. K. Weiler and S. Middleton, (Buckingham: Open University Press, 1999). Pierson, R.R, "Experience, Difference, Dominance and Voice in the Writing of Canadian Women's History," in *Writing Women's History: International Perspectives,* ed. Offen, K Pierson, R.R. & Rendall, J, 79-106 (Bloomington: Indiana University Press, 1991).

[9]Acker, S, Gendered Education. (Toronto: OISE Press, 1994). De Lyon, H & F. Widdowson Migniuolo, *Women Teachers: Issues and Experiences* (Philadelphia: Open University Press, 1989). Thiessen, D. Bascia, N & Goodson, I., *Making a Difference About Difference: The Lives of Racial Minority Immigrant Teachers* (Toronto: Garamond Press, 1996).

[10]Weiler, K, "Remembering and Representing Life Choices: A Critical Perspective on Teachers' Oral History Narratives," in *Critical Theory and Educational Research,* ed. McClaren, P.L. & J.M. Giarelli, 127-44, 1995. Weiler, K, *Reflections on Writing a History of Women Teachers* (Cambridge: Harvard Educational Review, Winter 1997), 635-57.

[11]Weiler, K, *Reflections on Writing a History of Women Teachers,* 646.

[12]Weiler, K, *Reflections on Writing a History of Women Teachers,* 647.

[13]Casey, K,I *Answer With My Life* (New York: Routledge, 1993).

[14]Mohanty, C.T. "Crafting Feminist Genealogies: On the Geography and Politics of Home, Nation, and Community," in *Talking Visions: Multicultural Feminism in a Transnational Age,* ed. E. Shoat, 499.

[15]Shohat, E, *Talking Visions: Multicultural Feminism in a Transnational Age.* (Cambridge: Th MIT Press, 1998), 4.

6

Female Teacher Gender and Sexuality in Twentieth Century Ontario Canada

Sheila Cavanagh

Card game played by student teachers, circa 1930s to 1940s, in Normal School. *Photo courtesy of The University of Western Ontario Archives, B750.*

Before 1950, marriage bans for women were common in North America. The influence of organized religion, the belief that married women were adequately supported by husbands, and widespread agreement that women were not long-term workers – all these help explain why female teachers were imposed upon to be single and chaste. But by the 1950s, career teachers no longer had to be celibate

111

and unmarried, but instead to suit an ideal of heterosexual marriage-ability. School administrators, mental hygienists, parents, teacher federation leaders, psychologists, and concerned citizens all demanded that Ontario female teachers adopt a gender and sexual identification in keeping with the heterosexual ethos governing the post-war period.

The worry was now about female teacher masculinity and homosexuality, and about the "masculinizing" influence of the spinster teacher. The pressure to conform to normative gender and heterosexual identities was evident in postwar discussions about the institution of marriage, professional literature published by the Ontario teachers' federations, archival source documents for these organizations, psychological studies of female teacher sexual deviance published in North America and Britain, mental hygienist writings about "wholesome" family values, and in female teacher oral history testimony.

Sexologists like Havelock Ellis and Richard Von Krafft-Ebing wrote about a phenomenon they called gender inversion and their writings seeped into the North American public consciousness in the early twentieth century. The gender invert was said to display characteristics regularly attributed to the "opposite" sex. Female masculinity, like male femininity, was believed to reveal an inverted gender identity and the spinster teacher was, sometimes, thought to be such an invert. Gender inversion was, also, thought to be associated with a homosexual object choice, as sexologists influenced by Freudian psychoanalysis, argued. For this reason, a gender identity transgression, on the part of a spinster teacher, could signal to a homosexual disposition. Although teaching was seen to be women's work in the early twentieth century, the spinster-like (or masculine) demeanor of some career teachers, in the postwar period, triggered anxieties about female homosexuality in North American schools.

Economic necessity coupled with teacher shortage in the 1940s lead to the demise of the marriage bans as educational historians have argued[1] but there was also worry about the mannish woman characterized as female homosexual in the pro-marital discourse of the period. The following discussion elucidates the changing relationship of the female teacher to the institution of heterosexuality in postwar Ontario, Canada to more fully understand how local perceptions of female teacher gender and sexuality affected teacher-work.[2]

In this chapter I first describe the cultural ethos of the Federation of Women Teachers' Associations of Ontario (FWTAO), with its primary commitment to the never-married teacher. I then trace the declining status of the single female teacher in the post-war period. Second, I show how the female teacher was expected to be heterosexually well-adjusted. The importance placed on heterosexual adjustment, by educational administrators, was intricately tied to the worry about female homosexuality, masculine identified and independent women. I show how the married woman teacher attained the professional stature originally had by the single female teacher.

The FWTAO and the Married Woman Teacher

In the early twentieth century the FWTAO celebrated the image of the single woman teacher as professional par excellence. Her claim to celibacy was indicative of her over-riding commitment to education. As social historian Martha Vicinus wrote of Britain, there was to be seen an "empowering ... [element to] freely chosen chastity, demonstrating how women embraced their unmarried state as a special advantage and virtue. Intense homoerotic friendships replaced the marital union for many career women and those bonds gave them emotionally rich lives while validating self-control and spirituality as sources of personal strength."[3] The single female teacher was most likely to be employed in Ontario's schools until the marriage bans began to lose their force in the mid-twentieth century. The image of the spinster was also celebrated in the United States. She was thought to be a "high-minded, upstanding pillar of the community who selflessly devoted"[4] her life to the school. Fiona (ACPID 69), a retired teacher, interviewed for this study, said that in the post-war period: "I married my job, I mean, I think if I had been married I could not have done this, it would have been impossible. But I think I married my job." As with sexual and marital sanctions applied to a woman religious, female teachers were expected, in many Ontario school districts – particularly city school districts – to remain unmarried. Whether or not all teachers acceded to that pressure is another matter. There were, also, regional differences with respect the extent to which the marriage bar was enforced.

The capacity to renounce sexual passion became a virtue to many working women and this renunciation was evident in dress codes. As historian Martha Vicinus observes of the British context, in the late nineteenth century and through to the early twentieth century "strong bodily control, invariably expressed as heterosexual purity, was an especially important part of community life"[5] for independent working women. Recalling her normal school training, Fiona (ACPID 069) said that the candidates "had to be prim and proper. We had to . . . be dressed just appropriately, almost . . . nun-like . . . we had to be very well dressed and covered up." Mya (ACPID 092) also agreed that "women were expected to . . . dress neatly . . . to be clean of person . . . sound in all moral and physical ways and [to wear] skirt[s] and blouses, dresses, stockings, proper shoes . . . [and skirt length was] definitely below the knee, probably mid calf. You didn't wear anything shorter than that at that time and nobody thought anything of it." In her discussion of British boarding schools, Vicinus also notes that "Headmistresses had a distinct notion of proper behavior and little compunction about invading a teacher's classroom or private life."[6]

The Ontario educational community embraced a professional enculturation model dependent on strict discipline and moral regulation in the early twentieth century. Outlandish taboos were placed on out-of-school activities. Mya confirmed this focus on regulation by explaining that it was taboo to be seen "carousing, going to a dance and dancing too close to your partner . . . [and] you were not seen at unseemly places like the local tavern" by the community in which you lived." At this time, women teachers were also dismissed for boarding in socially "inappropriate" houses, for moving between boarding houses, and for being "out late . . . smoking, or drinking or whatever. Your life wasn't your own. So, if they could find anything you shouldn't be doing, it was no good" (Holly ACPID 017). Holly also spoke about a teacher who was living in a "boarding place [that] wasn't suitable, so she rented an abandoned farmhouse, and lived there. And the board said she couldn't live there without a chaperone, because she had a boyfriend. So she had to hire a young girl who wasn't going to school to be her chaperone."

The married female teacher, by contrast, was thought to be an occupational transient, under-qualified, uninterested in professional development, and torn between divided loyalties to her family and the school. She could not be looked upon as having a true professional calling because she was already committed to a husband or fiancé. Members of the FWTAO believed that married women teachers hampered professional growth in the early to mid-twentieth century. Federation leaders introduced resolutions at their annual meetings designed to restrict married woman teacher access to the schools of Ontario.[7]

United States and British schools were already dropping marriage bans by the 1930s, but the Ontario women teachers' federation remained insistent upon the bans. For example, teacher historian Elizabeth Graham contends that the "Federation urged boards to give preference to the unmarried woman except in cases where the married woman teacher [was] the sole support of the family and that only during wartime, and periods of teacher shortage, did they relent upon their opposition to her marital stature."[8] This was also the case in Manitoba. Married teachers in this province "had public opinion more on her side . . . [but] ironically the [Manitoba] organization of Women Teachers did not see the issue [of the marriage bans] as a priority."[9] Apolonja Maria Kojder also observed that the Saskatoon Women Teachers' Association supported the marriage bans until the teacher-shortage forced them to let go of their preference for the single female teacher.

As the 1950s wore on it became increasingly evident to the FWTAO executive that married women were already, despite their pleas, employed throughout the province in substantial numbers. Ontario rural schools were dominated by married women. In one rural district it was reported that 72% of the teachers were married.[10] As Heather (ACPID 044) reflected upon her teaching career, she said when "I moved out of the city in the early '50s, and came up here [to a northern Ontario community] . . . there were more married women in the profession [than in the city schools] . . . And these married women were leftovers from the war, where married women were called upon to come into the classroom and take over due to the shortage of men." The Canadian census also confirms that in "1931 only 3 per cent of all women teachers were married . . . By 1951, 28 per cent of women . . . .in teaching were married."[11] This was the most significant demographic shift pertaining to the Canadian teaching population in the twentieth century.

The Fall of the Vestal Virgin

FWTAO leaders did not believe that married women were true professionals but the teacher-shortage caused by the baby boomers (now entering into Ontario schools) led them to admit married women to membership, if only reluctantly. Those leaders were also influenced by the provincial Department of Education representatives at their annual meetings who urged them to involve married women in their organization. For example, Ontario Chief Inspector V. K. Greer attended the 1943 annual meeting of the Federation and stated, on behalf of the Department of Education, that "due to the aid of married teachers and teachers from other provinces, Ontario was not suffering from [teacher] shortage to any great extent."[12]

The Canadian federal government insisted that the contributions of married women in the profession should be recognized and that they should not encounter obstacles to tenure. For example, in 1954 the Women's Bureau of the Federal Department of Labour was established to facilitate a "greater understanding of the contribution of women in the labour force"[13] and they decided that married women in the occupational realm were to be a special focus of study. In Circular 174, the Ontario Minister of Education requested that women continue on with their teaching appointments after marriage and this request was subsequently printed in the School-master, the ministry's official organ. The Working Party on the Supply of Women Teachers reported in 1950 that "despite bold efforts to estimate requirements for four years ahead and to provide additional training places,"[14] the supply of women teachers was still insufficient.[14]

Influenced by the pressure to better understand the married woman teacher phenomenon, the FWTAO conducted a large-scale survey of the general policies and working conditions of married women teachers in Ontario public schools in 1955. That survey revealed that Ontario school boards tended not to adopt discriminatory hiring practices and were eager to appoint married women to meet the escalating need for teachers. This finding was substantiated by the interview data. For example, Holly (ACPID 017) recalled that she got married shortly after her first teaching appointment and was not forced to leave the profession: "The secretary of the board came almost on bended knee, would I please come and teach? They couldn't get a teacher." By 1958, the FWTAO found that "52 percent of women teachers [in the province] were single, 41 percent married, [and] 6 percent in religious orders."[15]

Shortly after the study had been completed the women teachers' federation came to accept that married women teachers were an important presence in the profession. In 1952, the Federation Status Committee prepared an influential report with a significant section devoted to the married women teacher. The report read as follows: "The committee observed that married women were greatly needed and had a valuable contribution to make, that the attitude of some teachers, trustees and inspectors was somewhat upsetting; and that married status has nothing to do with professionalism. It was advised that this group make recommendations about the importance of procuring home help when necessary and that married status is not an excuse for evading responsibility nor for neglecting professional reading."[16] In the same year, the FWTAO educational finance committee presented a report to the Annual Meeting delegates which stated that there "should be no discrimination against married women teachers in regard to salary or terms of employment," married women should be engaged on the same basis as single teachers. However, if a Board has a policy in effect at the time the teachers are employed or when they marry, the teachers are necessarily aware of it and therefore accept it. If a change in policy is desired, the salary committee should approach the Board."[17]

The reversal in the position taken on the married woman teacher question was first evident in the late 1940s. For instance, in 1949 the Federation, along with the Ontario Public School Men Teacher's Federations (OPSMTF), published an article entitled "When a Teacher Weds: Are Marriage and Teaching Incompatible?" in the *Educational Courier,* a joint publication of the two associations. The essay, by acclaimed United States author Lucille Ellison, began with the personal statement that she "wished marriage to play the same part in my life that it does in the life of a man, and before marriage to be prepared for a possible incompetency on the part of my husband, as well as for widowhood."[18] Arguing that married women teachers are more normal and emotionally well adjusted sexually than their single counterparts, Ellison condemned the once sanctified ideal of the vestal virgin. Historian, Alison Oram, also notes that in Britain single female teachers were increasingly seen as abnormal and their childless state unnatural in this period. "Spinster teachers' lack of participation in motherhood was not only inauspicious for the future of the state and of the [White] race but, if they didn't watch out, it could also be psychologically harmful to themselves."[19]

In the United States, spinster teachers were sometimes recognized as "mannish lesbians"[20] and this recognition began to permeate the Canadian public imaginary as the mid-twentieth century grew near. Vicinus points out that "Although the single woman's sexuality 'active, failed, or denied' was most frequently discussed in code, it was always an issue for the opponents of women's single-sex communities and institutions"[21] in the early twentieth-century British context. Sexologist Richard von Krafft-Ebing was responsible for equating lesbianism with feminist initiatives in the workplace and his work in the budding field of sexology was influential in post-war North America. Single sex societies like female teachers' associations were looked upon with new wonderment and suspicion. Concern about the all-female composition of the Ontario elementary school women teachers' federation was expressed as a need to promote "wholesome" living, a code word for normative female heterosexual adjustment.

Postwar Fear of the Female Homosexual and the "Mannish" Woman

The post-war Zeitgeist embraced the ideal of heterosexual marriage, traditional gender roles relegating women to monogamous familial units where their identities were shaped by motherhood, marriage and household domesticity. Females were to find happiness in companionate marriage and their sexuality was to blossom within the confines of the matrimonial bed. Educational advancement for women was looked upon with suspicion and romantic female friendships forged over the war years were now thought to be abnormal.

In this period all working woman were, in different ways, shunned but in education the long-term single female teacher was regarded with contempt because she seemed to defy conventional gender roles. Despite their preference for married women, Federation leaders attempted to defend the long-term single working teacher by insisting that she needed her income and that elementary school teaching was an extension of the traditional female role, involving motherly love and otherwise feminine tasks. If life-long, single, female teachers committed to the profession did not come across as feminine, motherly and altruistic they were vulnerable to accusations that they were, somehow, abnormal or un-natural. "The professional woman was an imprecise entity, a paradox, a blur."[22] Carolyn Strange wrote, in her study of the single female worker in the early twentieth century, that "Both the New Woman and the working girl conjured up fears of sexual disorder."[23]

Higher education for women was associated with an unattractive, spinster-like persona and teachers were cautioned against attaining advanced degrees. For example, Heather (ACPID 044) was surprised by her male principal's attempt to dissuade her from taking university courses because he felt that "the men won't be able to keep up" and that this would thwart her attempt to find a husband. When questioned about the impact of her principal's comments, Heather revealed that she did take him somewhat seriously because at that time a "single woman was a nobody." Speaking of the 1950s in particular, she recalled with disdain a single woman teacher who "had no intention of marrying, but she was very clever, and was very stupid at the same time. She was [one of] the first woman teachers in Ontario to get her PhD in education, but she couldn't carry on a conversation with anybody. People avoided her. She's just not approachable."

Mental hygienists believed that when single women make healthy adjustments to the unmarried state they can avoid emotional sensitivity and "oldmaidish compensatory behavior."[24] As argued by psychoanalyst Karl Abraham, celibate women "deprived of normal genital gratification tend to surliness as a rule. A constant tension of the line of the nostril together with a slight lifting of the upper lip seem to me significant facial characteristics of such people."[25] Of course, the only legitimate expression of female sexuality was in the "normative" heterosexual and monogamous marital unit, and so the single female was often thought to have been denied sexual gratification. She was, therefore, vulnerable to unflattering images of the maladjusted spinster.

The importance placed on heterosexual availability was evident in Ontario normal schools. For example, Heather was impressed by a music teacher at Normal who "talked about how we should dress, we should wear high heels, and of course there was no such thing as slacks in those days, and makeup, and she talked about nail polish. She said it should be very light or clear, but if you're going to wear the bright red, make sure it's neat, and not have it all chipped and so on. And then she went into lipstick, and she said girls looked better with lipstick on, and they should wear some. And so, if you had a problem about clothes or anything like that, you felt you could go to her, and talk to her." The need to make Normal hospitable to the marriage-minded teacher candidate is also evident in the *Journal of Education*. That journal argued that "Girls take less readily to segregation during training or do not submit to the circumstances which compel the single, more mobile, teacher to take up work in an area remote from home and highly expensive in necessary travel and services."[26] Wilma (ACPID 010) also recalled the emphasis on marital availability when she sought guidance about her practicum placement at an Ontario normal school. Her instructor did not coach her on the finer points of pedagogical methods, but on her need to apply make-up. The instructor asked: "You ever thought of wearing lipstick and a little bit of rouge? That was her comment to me. I'm thinking, No! I'm not here for you to tell me I should be wearing make-up."

Heterosexual marriageability was now seen to be integral to teacher training. Master teachers of education sought to cultivate a new, more attractive heterosexual image. The most outlandish example of the new focus on marriage was given by Martha (ACPID 002) who recalled a psychology master at Normal who "used to fuss with the girls over their diamonds. Lots of the girls got diamonds while they were there … [The psychology instructor] had a little place on the blackboard. He gave the girls that got diamonds stars … So I can remember … [the female candidates] going in there after Christmas, 'Oh! … see my diamond!' … And he'd put on a little star." Although there seems to have been an acceptance of engagement rings at the Ontario normal schools, Martha did remember being "told to take off your ring a few days ahead [of a school interview] if you happened to have one, so your finger didn't show a sign that a ring was missing."

The emphasis on heterosexual marriageability was not unencumbered by contradictions for women. Popular perception suggested that females wanted to marry, that they wished to present themselves as heterosexually desirable and available to the eligible bachelor, but it was also believed that too many women did not offer themselves to their spouse in the marriage bed. For example, Morgan Winters wrote about the problem of unconsummated marriages and suggested that the phenomenon was to be attributed to the many women who are unwilling to have hetero-sex as normal, healthy people.[27] Such women were said to be "spoiled and thwarted children."[28] The assertion that adult women behave like "children" was often conflated with pre-mature sexual development and, sometimes, with female homosexual-ity. Sexologists, in the post-war period, tended to believe that homo-sexuality signaled an arrest in early adolescent development. That association was made explicit in the analysis given by medical doctor, and key player in the Canadian mental hygiene movement, Samuel R. Laycock, who believed that "Many individuals who never develop a wholesome sex life are insecure persons who are immature emotion-ally. Most sex deviations are an immature expression of the sex impulse."[29] Women were sometimes designated "polymorphously per-verse" which meant that their sexual capacities were not confined to adult genital contact in a heterosexual union. Sketching the prototype of the female homosexual, Laycock wrote that "many female homo-sexuals are masculine in their characteristics . . . [and explains that fail-ure] to identify with the womanly qualities of their mother" incites an arrest in "normal" female psycho-sexual development characteristic of the female invert.[30]

Patsie (ACPID 110) said she recalled a debate in the school com-munity about sexual deviance in the 1950s. Frustrated with the discus-sion, this teacher explained that administrators "wanted people who were certified sexual deviants to be given the heave ho by the profes-sion and . . . remember[ed] standing up and saying, asking [sarcastical-ly], where do you get a sexual deviant certificate?" Concern about male homosexuality was also evident in the Ontario Public School Men Teachers' Federation (OPSMTF). The organization received a report from the chairman of the Counselling and Relations Committee out-lining profiles of the sex deviant in the mid-1950s. Throughout the report, the executive of the men teachers' federation learned that a "certain proportion of our male and female population will always be homosexuals."[31] Suggesting that the "problem" was a matter for the church and the state, the report advised the executive to regard the sexual pathology as a "private matter unless it involves force or is an affront to the public."[32]

Mya (ACPID 092) reflected on a lesbian colleague in her teaching days and surmised that you "had to keep. . . [your sexual orientation] hidden up to recent years." This was the case for many homosexual teachers, male and female, who wished to avoid community scandal and professional castigation. Mya confirmed that "if you happened to be homosexual . . . that was not accepted. If it was found out, you were gone or your life was made so miserable that you left because nobody would have the guts to stand up and say, we will not accept this but they made your life so miserable." Another teacher (ACPID 052) recalled a disturbing case of a teacher who had to leave her teaching post "technically" because of a bad accident [and was put on Workman's Compensation by an intolerant administration], but even before the accident occurred the School Board "had been trying to get rid of her. She was very mannish, homosexual and I really think she was probably persuaded to leave."

In some instances female teachers covered for their homosexual colleagues in the hope of preventing dismissal. For example, Jackie (ACPID 004) spoke fondly about a female colleague who was dismissed for homosexuality. The maligned teacher was allegedly engaged in relationships with both men and women, drank excessively, and because of her alcoholism, was often late or absent from work. Jackie offered the following description of the situation: "we all really like her, it was funny, and she was . . . She knew her English, I'm telling you, she was just . . . She . . . I think she had her MA and I don't know whether she maybe even got her PhD, but she was just a character. We used to cover up for her all the time. She'd be drunk and she'd . . . We'd have to . . . We'd call up, and we'd send somebody down to get her to school." Jackie also reported that the teacher was drawn to a senior female student who "did jump shots automatically playing basketball." Georgina (ACPID 005), another teacher employed at the same school, described the same bisexual teacher as "brilliant . . . and [surmised that] maybe [she] had other problems too . . . Back in those days, you know, nobody talked about lesbians and homosexuality."

Given the strong social expectation to partake in courting rituals leading to marriage in the post-war period, those women who were uninvolved in matrimonial pursuits were more likely to be designated abnormal than in earlier decades. Although some women who opted out of heterosexual family units would not be considered lesbian by contemporary standards, all long-term unmarried women teachers were vulnerable to innuendo or accusations of latent homosexuality. Closely knit friendships between women who lived together, platonic or otherwise, were likely to be rendered pathological not because they were visibly homoerotic, but because they represented a rejection of heterosexual familial structures and traditional gender roles. Some single female teachers who may have had homosexual predilections maintained that it was simply more convenient to live alone or to live with another woman given the demands of the teaching profession.

The Rise of the Married Female Teacher: Heterosexuality and Domestic Bliss

By the 1960s the status of the married woman teacher had changed. This was especially apparent in the organizational culture of the FWTAO. For example, Kay Dwyer, a regular writer for the *Educational Courier,* a joint publication of the FWTAO and the OPSMTF, wrote that school boards now understood the married woman teacher with children to be an "integral part of our present day classrooms." She was now believed to be a psychologically well-adjusted mother and housewife with only "wholesome" inclinations. Dwyer then proceeded to write that "Popular ideas are that many teach to escape household drudgery or to supplement a husband's marginal income – or that some are thwarted wives and mothers who feel the classroom will give them a power over destinies which they cannot experience in their own homes."[34] Dwyer argued that "most [married women teachers] come from happy, well-run homes and are teaching to enrich their own lives, the lives of others, and to raise their family's standard of living."[35]

The professionalism of the married teacher was now thought to be driven by a will to self-sacrifice, much like the earlier caricature of the spinster. Prior to 1950, the single female teacher, designated spinster, was thought to be martyr-like and, as argued by Vicinus, she "transformed this passive role into one of active spirituality and passionate social service."[36] This is similar to the newer caricature of the married women teacher in the 1960s. The more recent Federation portrayal depicted the married female teacher also as selfless, altruistic, and philanthropic. This construction was necessary to garner social approval of the married woman teacher and to assure a conservative public that she was not selfish and, thus, unfeminine.

As described by Dwyer, the married woman teaches purely from a "love of children and a desire to help them, force of habit, or that they just couldn't be happy without teaching. Some felt there was a scarcity of teachers and that they should help. Others said they became more interesting people when they could teach and take part in the many extramural activities of the school."[37] Another married woman is said to "help deserving students supplement their meager [financial] resources to get high school and university educations. Another gives a good part of her salary to educate a priest in Japan. Others had relatives who needed financial help, and taught school because they didn't think it fair to burden husbands with the responsibility."[38] The discussion concluded with a call for the long-term, committed and psychologically well-adjusted married teacher as opposed to the, allegedly, socially awkward and reclusive spinster. The loss of the more "mature" married woman from the profession was described in yet another context as "wastage . . . [and] in the United States . . . this phenomenon is described as 'female fallout.'"[39]

The heterosexually well-adjusted woman was no longer to be hidden from school children. This is evident in the growing acceptance not only of married female teachers but of pregnant teachers in the late 1960s and 1970s. Although female teachers continued to be asked to resign upon pregnancy in some school districts, it was less likely that they would loose their jobs because it was less taboo than in earlier decades. Many challenges were being made to school policies requiring that woman resign upon pregnancy, or, the moment in which "pregnancy becomes apparent."[40] As argued in an article on "anti-mother" discrimination: "Whether pregnancy is apparent or not is not the business of busybodies. Neither is pregnancy anything to hide from children. More, the systematic conspiracy of yesterday to hide from children the fact of pregnancy contributed not a little misery to many children as they grew up. It helps children to have a wholesome attitude towards pregnancy if they see that teacher, as well as mother, takes it as a normal thing and carries on with her work."[41] The argument that pregnancy was "normal" and "natural" was interspersed with concern about those women teachers (spinsters) who could "manage the children of other mothers but were not having children of their own. . . . This group of teachers with [presumably sexually based] phobic illnesses encountered difficulty in producing children, largely as a result of . . . [unhealthy] identifications with their mothers."[42]

Many Ontario women teachers in the 1960s refused the image of the spinster teacher because of the strong negative connotations associated with spinster teacher gender identity. As Susanna (ACPID 072) explained, she did not adopt the older teacher persona with the "glasses on your nose and the bun in the back of your head and . . . oxfords." She also said that she had "many spinster aunts who are teachers and I swore I would never teach." Reticent about the image her aunts embodied, Susanna explained that she perceived her aunts to be "bossy and domineering . . . [and that she] didn't want to see . . . [herself] that way." Speaking about British fiction, Vicinus writes that "foolish maiden aunts were confined by comedy with remarkable ease, but in real life they could be frightening portents of a world upside down"[43] and this sketch was also salient in the 1960s Canadian context.

The spinster image once celebrated by early advocates of teacher professionalism was now seen to be unhealthy and associated with latent homosexuality. Female teachers were compelled to renounce the old-maid persona if they wanted to be seen as "normal." Mya (ACPID 092) recalled that her own teachers were unmarried "maiden ladies . . . [but that for her generation] marriage was fine" and so she got married in 1962 and some of her students attended the ceremony. In an article on why women teach, published in the Ontario elementary school teachers' magazine, there is an attempt to differentiate the modern teacher from the spinster who was seen to be a social outcast. The author writes:

> It may seem strange to parents, but teachers are very much like other people. We are just as interested as the general run of mankind in fashions, the weather, the consequences of nuclear fallout, the arts, and the latest scandal . . . and when we go to a party we would like to be treated as people and not as a race apart. We are also just as sensitive as other people about the kind of humor aimed at us. Jokes about

ethnic minorities are now considered in poor taste, but the teacher is still fair game. We smile politely the first hundred times we hear the joke about the three sexes – male, female, and teacher.[44] The separation between the caricature of the teacher and the more normative (marriageable) female was, also, reflected in rental advertisements in city newspapers: the adds asked for a "teacher or lady."[45]

Social historian Bonnie Smith writes that a "modern sensitivity to the possibility of there being a 'third sex'"[46] emerged as women entered into professional cultures. Because gender roles were so rigidly defined, transgressions of defined roles signaled new and distinct gender identities. Of course, the spinster persona pre-dated the mid-twentieth-century public concern about female sexual deviance, but never before had the construction of the spinster been recognized as an embodiment of sexual and gender identity transgression. This made the spinster teacher identity increasingly difficult to inhabit. Women teachers' federations in Canada and Britain refused to speak outwardly in support of the unmarried teacher in the 1960s.[47] One unmarried Canadian teacher wrote a letter of complaint to the FWTAO stating that "a great many [younger teachers] regard older teachers – none too secretly alas! – as old hags or bags or squares."[48]

Historians P.T. Rooke and R.L. Schnell speculated that the attitudes held by the morally indignant married teacher about her single colleague "must have annoyed all those other single women who had pioneered in the work force earlier in the century and proven themselves steady, resourceful, and responsible while opening careers for married women."[49] A similar state of affairs can be seen in reports about the animosity between the single and married women teachers in the work place. Pauline (ACPID 074) explains: "There were a couple of us that were single . . . and we were higher paid because we worked our way up the grid by taking courses and there was always comments made about, well you're single, I mean you can take more courses than we can because you know, we have family responsibilities. And I remember at one point, we said well you chose that. That was your choice and we chose to go this route." Donna, a very successful, unmarried, art teacher relayed that her students "got quite a lot of prizes in art and so . . . we got a prize for the best display . . . and some of those married ladies who'd been teaching for a long time were quite angry. They had got those prizes before." Edwards also identifies animosity between married and single women teachers in her research and suggested that "many of the unmarried staff disliked married women and envied their social and sexual status."[50]

The Heterosexual Idea of Beauty and the Lecherous Male Principal

In the 1960s female teachers were expected to dress in ways that were appealing to heterosexual men. At this time, Cynthia (ACPID 026) recalls "we couldn't wear pants, we could wear a miniskirt but we couldn't wear slacks ... which seems strange, and there was one Superintendent who had the reputation of not liking pantsuits, so the idea was, well make sure that your pantsuit, your tunic top, could pass as a miniskirt, and if so and so arrives, take your pants off." Some women who refused to adopt the heterosexual feminine ideal of beauty were seen to be social outcasts. For example, Heather (ACPID 044) spoke in an unflattering way about a former single teacher: She wore "Very dowdy clothes, like ... if you remember Eaton's catalogues, and women's house dresses, she'd wear one of those. A string around the back. And she was quite wide in the hips, so that didn't do her any good either." Given that this teacher was "quite attractive" her choice of dress was seen as unfortunate.

Women teachers across the province were protesting the no pantsuit policy for both practical and principled reasons having to do with equity. Wendy (ACPID 042) confirmed that they "couldn't wear trousers to school. You could wear a miniskirt and high heels, but you couldn't wear trousers. And I can remember being the ... [first in my school]. I wore a trouser suit to school, and got away with it, then everyone started doing it." Marion (ACPID 089), another teacher in the same community, recalled that "Part of the transition [governing dress] was being able to wear slacks to school and the principal that I was teaching for at the time that transition happened [and the principal] wanted approval of what you were going to wear so you had to bring in and show him what you were wearing ... this is the pantsuit I'm going to wear to school."

Many women interviewed identified sexism to be the problem with school administrative culture. Having had enough of what she referred to as the "chauvinist" environment, Teri (ACPID 070) decided to cross-dress at her principals' meeting: "My first principals' meeting, there's me and the thirty-nine guys, so they all come in their suits, so I thought, I'm going to go in a suit too. So away I go to Toronto and buy this wool suit" which she wore to the shock and bewilderment of the men in attendance. As confirmed by social historian Lillian Faderman, many professional women "felt themselves forced into dress and behavior that was also characterized as 'masculine' . . . [and so they wore] 'man-tailored suits', shirtwaists, stiff collars and four-in-hand ties to work" not always because they preferred to cross-dress, but because they needed to repudiate "feminine furbelows" in order to be taken seriously.[51] Because pant-suits were discouraged it was difficult for female teachers to pursue administrative roles that required a "masculine" presentation of self.

In psychological studies, women who repudiated their femininity were said to be distinguished by the way they "refrain from wearing attractive clothes, dancing, and participation in general in anything in the sphere of the erotic."[52] For psychoanalyst Karen Horney, the frigid woman (read homosexual) often displayed "distinct masculine attitudes and strong feelings of aversion for the feminine role. The secondary sex characteristics . . . voice, hair, bones . . . of some of this group tend toward the masculine, but most of them have an absolutely female habitus."[53] There is an unmistakable parallel here to be drawn between the spinster teacher and the female homosexual. Both were, in various ways, described to be masculine in appearance, to have unusually rigid facial features, disturbing complexions, as well as unfeminine dispositions and habits of mind.

Inappropriate references to female sexual practices were used to dismiss professional accomplishments and to prevent upward career mobility. For example, Paris (ACPID 040), a female administrator reflected upon the frustration she felt when male administrators would "make disparaging remarks [about how she] . . . got . . . [her position] . . . Who did you sleep with and then things now that would never be allowed were allowed at that time and you wouldn't dare say boo. And I know it affected my whole career that I never wanted it to be said that they couldn't fire me because I was the sole support for three children. I was going to be the very best teacher that you could possibly be and so that I would get there by my merit not because someone was sorry for me that I had three children to bring up."

Judith (ACPID 023) was approached by a trustee about her administrative aspirations in the 1960s. She explains: he said "did I want to become a vice-principal, and he'd make sure I got one, and I found out afterwards that he'd had a relationship with a woman teacher, and she'd got a vice-principalship out of it." Daphne (ACPID 014) also knew "of one case . . . where there was an affair between the principal and one of the teachers, and he helped her up the ladder . . . And then she had to move, which was so often the case. If there was any trouble between male and female, or if she got married, then it was the female that moved on and the man who stayed."

Some teachers adopted masculine traits to move up the administrative ladder. As Linda (ACPID 041) revealed: "The only female administrators in the board that I met . . . [in the mid-1960s] were all single women. Never married. Very tight, very proper, very unwomanish . . . you almost had to adopt the male way of operating in the world." The same teacher recalled that female teachers were not heard when they spoke at school meetings because the men were too busy "looking them up and down. So, almost if you were pretty, you'd want to put a bag over your head if you wanted to have credibility." Female teachers pursuing administrative positions were caught in a double-bind; denounced for their masculine presentation of self, or reduced to a sexual object for heterosexual male administrative visual pleasure.

Retired women teachers recalled episodes of sexual harassment from male principals. Because female teachers were sometimes evaluated on their ability to appeal to the aesthetic preferences of male administrators, it was difficult to maintain the right to sexual and gender self-determination. For example, Linda said that she "just went by the furnace room and the vice-principal called me in . . . [and] he made a real, tried to make a real pass with me and um, I refused, you know, I refused totally and oh he was insistent that he would kiss me and all this kind of stuff and I said, no way . . . [and] I got out of there and I [reported the incident to the principal] who . . . always gave me a glowing report, said that under the conditions that they thought they better move me to a junior school." This same teacher also reported that most women who experienced sexual harassment kept the incident to themselves, evaded questions, or re-located to another school to avoid "talk." Linda recalled that in the mid-1960s the male administrators she worked for would "stand at the bottom of the stairs and look up our skirts, because in '65, '66 that's when we all had mini-skirts and we were all young and female." Holly (ACPID 017) spoke of "a good friend, who was teaching in a school over here, a nice looking young girl. She was being harassed by the principal. She rebuffed his advances, and he made it very miserable for her. And she came to me for help. I referred her to Federation. I don't know just what went on, but she was moved to a school just up the road." Reflecting on the period leading up to the 70s, Wendy (ACPID 042) said that "One of the worst problems we had in our schools would be romantic affairs with women teachers and principals, and that is really tough, because again the power . . . and what is a woman to do if the principal is hitting on her. If she denies his affections, he can make her life hell, so that was often . . . an innocent woman would be transferred because a principal had started the affair."

Conclusion

The eradication of the marriage ban in education was not an unmitigated feminist gain for female teachers. Although married women were permitted to work, mother, and wed without fear of dismissal the long-term single female teacher fell from professional grace and became a laughable caricature. The never-married teacher was more likely to be seen as "unwholesome," a social outcast in the post-war period. The marriage bars enabled women to opt out of heterosexual familial structures without fear of persecution; their calling was to education and they were permitted to live independent lives or with women of their choosing. There was also more room to depart from traditional expressions of femininity. In the post-war period the teacher who chose – for whatever reason – to remain unmarried was marked as a social and psychological enigma.

The educational community saw the gender and sexual identity of the lesbian, or, life-long single female teacher, as an anomaly, a peculiarity to be explained in the postwar period. The postwar emphasis on heterosexual marriage, conventional femininity, and motherhood made unmarried women into social outcasts. The bourgeoning knowledge of female homosexuality and female gender inversion, developed by European and North American sexologists and psychologists, were used by many educational "experts" to construct the single female teacher as a pathology. Mental hygienists and advocates of teacher professionalism in Ontario contributed to the denigration of the life-long single female teacher as latent homosexual, as "mannish" woman, as emotionally maladjusted and as social deviant in a period inhospitable to variegated gender and homosexual identifications.

Notes

[1] See: Frieda Forman, Mary O'Brien, Jane Haddad, Dianne Hallman and Philinda Masters, eds., *Feminism and Education: A Canadian Perspective.* (Toronto: Centre for Women's Studies in Education, Ontario Institute for Studies in Education, 1990); Mary Kinnear, "Mostly for the Male Members: Teaching in Winnipeg, 1933-1966," *Historical Studies in Education/Revue d'histoire de l'education 6* (1994), 1-20; Alison Oram, "Embittered, Sexless or Homosexual: Attacks on Spinster Teachers 1918-39," in *Not a Passing Phase: Reclaiming Lesbians in History 1840-1985* ed. Lesbian History Group (London: Women's Press, 1989), 99-118; Alison Oram, "Serving Two Masters? The Introduction of a Marriage Bar in Teaching in the 1920s," in *Not a Passing Phase: Reclaiming Lesbians in History 1840-1985* ed. Lesbian History Group (London: Women's Press, 1989); Cecilia Reynolds and Harry Smaller, "Ontario School Teachers: A Gendered View of the 1930s," *Historical Studies in Education/Revue d'histoire de l'education 6* (1994),151-169; Cecilia Reynolds, "Too Limiting a Liberation: Discourse and Actuality in the Case of Married Women Teachers," *Feminism and Education: A Canadian Perspective* ed. Frieda Forman, Mary O'Brien, Jane Haddad, Dianne Hallman and Philinda Masters (Toronto: Centre for Women's Studies in Education, 1990),145-165; Cecilia Reynolds, "Hegemony and Hierarchy: Becoming a Teacher in Toronto, 1930-1980," *Historical Studies in Education/Revue d'histoire de l'education 2* (1990), 95-118.

[2] Overt discussion about homosexuality and masculine gender identifications had by genetic females is often thought to be inappropriate for life-history interviews, and so the interview data used, for this chapter, come from a small minority of teachers who were willing to talk openly about gender and sexual identity transgressions. This group of women tended to have personal friendships with former colleagues who were lesbian or to have had family members who were homosexual and were, thus, more thoughtful and vocal on the subject. The interview data have been supplemented with archival case studies, professional education and popular magazines articles, teacher federation reports, academic journals and newspaper reports relating to teacher dismissal to ensure that the oral history testimony is compared to other primary source materials.

[3] Martha Vicinus, *Independent Women: Work and Community for Single Women 1850-1920* (Chicago: University of Chicago Press, 1985), 289.

[4]Jackie M. Blount, "Spinters, Bachelors, and Other Gender Transgressors in School Employment, 1850-1990," *Review of Educational Research 70* (2000), 87.

[5]Martha Vicinus, Independent Women, 42.

[6]Ibid., 179.

[7]See: Sandra Gaskell, "The Problems and Professionalism of Women Elementary School Teachers in Ontario, 1944-54" (Ph.D. diss., OISE/University of Toronto, 1989); Doris French, *High Button Bootstraps* (Toronto: FWTAO, 1968); Mary Labatt, *Always a Journey: a History of the Federation of Women Teachers' Associations of Ontario, 1918-1993* (Toronto: FWTAO, 1993); Pat Stanton and Beth Light, *Speak With Their Own Voices: A Documentary History of the Federation of Women Teachers' Associations of Ontario and the Women Elementary Public School Teachers of Ontario* (Toronto: FWTAO, 1987) and FWTAO Archives, Annual Meeting Minutes, 1934-1960.

[8]Elizabeth Graham, "Schoolmarms and Early Teaching in Ontario" in: *Women at Work: Ontario, 1850-1930* (Toronto: Canadian Women's Educational Press, 1974), 196.

[9]Kinnear, "Mostly for the Male Members," 10.

[10]FWTAO Archives, Annual Meeting Minutes, 1954, 10.

[11]Reynolds, "Too Limiting a Liberation: Discourse and Actuality in the Case of Married Women Teachers," *Feminism and Education,* 151.

[12]FWTAO Archives, Annual Meeting Minutes, 1943, 3.

[13]Mair Davies, "Women Under the Microscope," *Food For Thought* 17:6 (August 1957), 384.

[14]*Journal of Education,* 1950, 434.

[15]FWTAO Archives, Annual Meeting Minutes, 1961, 9.

[16]FWTAO Archives, Board of Directors Meeting Minutes, December 1952.

[17]FWTAO Archives, Finance Committee Report, 1952.

[18]Lucille Ellison, "When a Teacher Weds: Are Marriage and Teaching Incompatible?," Kansas Teacher (1937), Reprinted in *The Educational Courier* (June 1949), 13.

[19]Oram, "Embittered, Sexless or Homosexual, 104.

[20]Blount, "Spinters, Bachelors, and Other Gender Transgressors,," 89.

[21]Vicinus, *Independent Women*, 32.

[22]Bonnie Smith, *The Gender of History: Men, Women, and Historical Practice* (Cambridge: Harvard University Press, 2000), 197.

[23]Carolyn Strange, *Toronto's Girl Problem: The Perils and Pleasures of the City, 1880-1930* (Toronto: University of Toronto Press, 1995), 9.

[24]Samuel R. Laycock, *Mental Hygiene in the School* (Toronto: Copp Clark Press, 1960), 81.

[25]Karl Abraham, *Selected Papers of Karl Abraham* (New York: Basic Books Inc, 1927), 391.

[26]*Journal of Education*, 1950, 435.

[27]Morgan Winters "Four Crises in Marriage," *Chatelaine,* March 1951, 54.

[28]Ibid, 54.

[29]Samuel R. Laycock, "How to protect your child from sex deviates," *Chatelaine,* April 1956, 93.

[30]Ibid., 94.

[31]OPSMTF Counselling and Relations Committee Report, 1956, p. 2.

[32]Ibid., 2.

[33]Kay Dwyer, "The Married Woman Career Teacher is Here to Stay," *The Educational Courier 24* (November and December 1963), 14.

[34]Ibid, 14.

[35]Ibid, 14.

[36]Martha Vicinus, *Independent Women*, 5.

[37]Dwyer, "The married woman career teacher" 14.

[38]Ibid., 14 -15.

[39]"We look divine as we advance, have we seen ourselves retreating?," *The Educational Courier, 35,* (1964), 11.

[40]Ibid.

[41]Ibid, 12.

[42]Karem J. Monsour, "School Phobia in Teachers," *American Journal of Orthopsychiatry 31* (1961), 348-349.

[43]Martha Vicinus, *Independent Women,* 32.

[44]"Why Teach?," *The Educational Courier 35* (1965), 15.

[45]"Rooms for Rent," *The Educational Courier, 24* (November-December 1963), 26.

[46]Smith, *The Gender of History,* 185.

[47]Oram, "Serving two masters? 134-148.

[48]Cited in Pat Stanton and Beth Light, *Speak With Their Own Voices: A Documentary History of the Federation of Women Teachers' Associations of Ontario and the Women Elementary Public School Teachers of Ontario* (Toronto: FWTAO, 1987),125.

[49]P.T. Rooke and R.L. Schnell, *No Bleeding Heart: Charlotte Whitton, A Feminist on the Right* (Vancouver: University of British Columbia Press, 1987), 200.

[50]Elizabeth Edwards, *Women in Teacher Training Colleges, 1900-1960: A Culture of Femininity* (New York: Routledge, 2001),129.

[51]Lillian Faderman, *Odd Girls and Twilight Lovers: A History of Lesbian Life in Twentieth-Century America* (New York: Columbia University Press, 1991), 20.

[52]Karen Horney, *Feminine Psychology* (New York: W. W. Norton & Company, 1967), 194.

[53]Ibid.

Section Two
Leadership Beyond the Classroom

7
Assuming Leadership: Women Superintendents in Twentieth Century Ontario

Janice Wallace

Dr. Madeline Hardy, Assistant Superintendent of Special Services and the Director of Education, London Board of Education, 1975-86. Dr. Hardy was the first female director of a large, modern urban board in Canada. *Photo courtesy Madeline Hardy.*

Women have always assumed both formal and informal positions of leadership in Ontario's education system, but as Ontario's school boards amalgamated and became increasingly bureaucratized in the mid-twentieth century, women were largely excluded from administration. Since then, women have struggled to assume positions of formal leadership both individually and collectively. In this chapter, I explore the narratives of four women administrators who became superintendents of education and whose lives demonstrate the complex ways in which they understand and take up the systemic discrimination they face as leaders.

Unlike the bureaucracies of business and government, schooling has occupied an ambivalent position between the public and private domains of social activity in western democracies. Benn[1] contends that, on the one hand, the activities of teaching, particularly in the early grades, have been constructed as an extension of mothering. On the other hand, many aspects of teaching – particularly at the intermediate and senior level – and the organization of schooling are premised on narratives of power and control, which are most often aligned with "the rule of the father."[2] For many decades, Ontario's provision of education took place in small one or two room schoolhouses that dotted a largely rural landscape. During this time, many women were both teacher and school administrator. However, most of these schools served elementary students and, although deeply embedded in the life of the community, teachers were under the direct supervision of male inspectors who ensured that a highly prescriptive course of studies was followed. Therefore, although teachers in these small rural schools – even those who were school administrators – often enjoyed a significant degree of autonomy,[3] they were never far from the gaze of the community and the inspector.

That autonomy was diminished even further as rural boards amalgamated, schools consolidated, educational systems became more bureaucratized and position status became attached to hierarchical positions that reflected gender norms. Feminist historians[4] have drawn attention to the congruence of the increasing bureaucratization of educational organizations and decreasing opportunities for women to achieve high status positions. As educational organizations became increasingly bureaucratized in Ontario, women became increasingly over-represented in those areas of education most closely aligned with the activities of mothering (although pregnancy in the workplace was perceived to be troublesome) and under-represented in formal positions of authority in educational bureaucracies.[5]

Not surprisingly, then, women who took up work in schools that was most often associated with males, such as administration, found themselves troubling the gendered order inside educational organizations. Given their complex position between the public and private spheres of human activity, however, it is not surprising that the four women administrators whose narratives inform this paper found that assuming leadership within the fraternal-patriarchal[6] constraints of their work was a complex process. The words of the women in this study demonstrate not only the ways in which they negotiated their path through personal desires, career goals, and the gendered constraints of educational organizations, but also the ways that they simply got on with the work of creating worthwhile educational opportunities for the children in their schools and school systems despite the complex location that they occupied.

The four women whose experience I explore in this chapter performed gender[7] roles within the social and historical context in which their understanding of the shifting discourses around ideas of "leadership" and "woman" were constituted over time. As Scott[8] argues, "the actions of women (and men) do not spring from who they are, but rather who they are depends on their repeated performance of acts that constitute their identity over time."[9] In other words, gender is a role that is played and, in much the same way that actors interpret and reinterpret roles within the social and historical context in which their role is performed, the role of "woman administrator" is performed within a particular social and historical context and is interpreted through gendered identities formed by "repeated acts within one's surroundings, either in resistance to or in compliance with local expectations."[10] I will argue that the women administrators in this paper played out two gender scripts[11] – dutiful daughters and troubling women – in their coming to an understanding of their role as women administrators, but each interpreted the role in her own way.

Genevieve (ACPID 136) and Paula (ACPID 190) rewrote the script of the "dutiful daughters" of the postwar generation who "stayed close to home, made a contribution of service to the community, and often sacrificed her own wishes to satisfy the needs of the organization."[12] Judith (ACPID 023) and Lauren (ACPID 050) were the "troubling women"[13] for whom second wave feminism raised questions about the scripts available to women in educational organizations. Their re/interpretation of each script was complex and provides insights about how women in senior administrative positions understand themselves as women and as administrators, as well as the intersection between these subjectivities as they played out their roles in educational organizations.

Women Assuming Leadership

While the careers of the women administrators in this chapter are diverse in many respects, the one noteworthy commonality is that they occupy a bureaucratic position that is still unusual in Ontario: administrators of education at the superintendent or senior administrative level of the education hierarchy. They are all white women who became administrators prior to the implementation of formal gender equity policy in the mid-1980s by the Ontario government to encourage greater participation by women in positions of authority.

Because so few women gained access to senior bureaucratic positions, there is little historical literature on the unique challenges that they faced or on the strategies that they employed in dealing with those challenges. An emergent literature in the United States[14] is helpful but the political and social context in which American superintendents do their work is markedly different than the context in Ontario and other provinces in Canada. For example, Blount[15] explores the ways in which the shift in the United States from electing to appointing superintendents in relatively small school districts with local control disadvantaged women. However, legislative control of education in Canada is a provincial responsibility in which local boards appoint the senior administrators of education[16] within the requirements of provincial education legislation. These governance nuances suggest that, while there are many similarities, there may be significant differences between the experience of women superintendents in Canada and the United States. This chapter will attempt to address the particular challenges of senior women administrators in Ontario's education system.

The educational careers of the women administrators whose experience I explore in this chapter span the years 1944 to 1996. All became senior administrators with their boards of education and/or Ontario's Ministry of Education: one by the middle of the 1960s, two in the mid-1970s, and one at the beginning of the 1980s.[17] These time periods are important in relation to second wave feminism in Canada as well as emergent attention to gender equity policy in Ontario. I will return to this discussion later but will first turn my attention to a brief discussion of the roads to administrative work that each participant took in the last half of the twentieth century.

Paula began teaching in northern Ontario in 1944. Her first teaching assignment was in a burgeoning mill town in northern Ontario that attracted many French-speaking families from Quebec. Paula was particularly challenged in teaching reading to her class, which was comprised of all grades and students whose first language was French. Demonstrating the entrepreneurial spirit that was characteristic of her entire career, she sought answers for her dilemma despite – or perhaps because of – her remote location. She recalls,

> I hadn't the slightest idea of how to teach reading, I really didn't. I mean after a year of teachers college I just didn't have that kind of background, and I kept wondering how I could help these children, and I looked at the book and it said that W.S. Gray had written the book and he was at the University of Chicago, and so I thought well I don't know where else I could get any help in reading . . . and I spoke to my inspector . . . So I decided then, that summer, that I would start finding out something about reading, and that's when I went to the University of Chicago . . . They had a special course for teachers of reading, so I took that, and then not very far from that was Evanston where the National College of Education was, and that's where they introduced the whole approach to reading, which was the experience approach . . . at National it was exciting, they had these children who were using their own experiences as the basis for their writing and reading, and so I was just taken with that.

Paula went on to become a highly respected reading specialist and special education consultant before becoming a senior administrator in the Ministry of Education in the mid-1970s. She retired in the mid-1980s.

Genevieve began her teaching career in the early 1950s and immediately pursued undergraduate and graduate studies at a university in southwestern Ontario and Columbia in New York. Like Paula, her primary interests were reading and special education and by the mid-1960s she was reading supervisor for a large urban board of education. She then became a professor and research associate for several years before taking on more administrative responsibilities as assistant superintendent in the mid-1970s and then was appointed director of a large urban board in southwestern Ontario – one of the first females in Ontario to take on this senior administrative position. Genevieve retired in the mid-1980s.

Lauren took up her teaching career in the mid-1950s rather reluctantly since her interests were medicine or politics. However, as she says, "at my stage of living, you really had two choices, nursing or education, and it seemed the route to go initially . . . I also had an urge to get away from home, so I thought it was a good route to go, and a secure route at that stage which was important for a young woman in the 50s." Her choice turned out to be one that she came to enjoy but her restless energy took her on some interesting detours outside provincial educational bureaucracies. For example, two years after beginning her teaching career in northern Ontario, she became a teacher and then administrator of a residential school for Native children. Her interest in First Nations education and building opportunities for Native children caused her to make another move to a vice-principal position in a northern town where Native children were being integrated into the provincial system. By the mid-1960s, she was a school principal and later studied for her supervisory officer's papers. She became an assistant inspector and was very active on the provincial executive of the Federation of Women Teachers' Association of Ontario (FWTAO) before retiring in the early 1990s.

The fourth participant is Judith who began teaching in the late 1950s. She taught for many years but made her goal to become a principal very clear to her board at the end of the 1960s. However, those wishing to become school principals in Ontario were required to complete additional qualification courses but, at that time, participation was not open. Instead, candidates for the program were chosen from those identified by boards of education. This practice was a major problem for women since mostly male principals and board administrators generally chose from among their male peers. Judith's persistence and strategic action through FWTAO eventually wore down resistance to her candidacy. She describes the process this way:

> I realized things had to change, so, because I was then very active in Federation, what I set about doing was changing the structure. My first application to be a vice-principal went in in '67. Well, my interest was expressed in '67. In those days you had to go to a superintendent, an inspector had to agree, and mine refused, refused for three years to submit my application. He said I would not, I did not make a good subordinate. [Laughter]. Those were his very words . . . I put an application in absolutely every year for 13 years.

Finally, in 1980 she became a vice-principal and by 1989 was a superintendent of schools for a large urban board in south-western Ontario. She retired in the mid-1990s.

"Dutiful Daughters": Paula and Genevieve

In many ways, Paula and Genevieve appeared to play the role of dutiful daughter – that is, they complied with the expectations of their families and communities for young women's behavior and career choices, and in their later careers as educational administrators, they generally complied with the expectations of Ontario society for women's behavior in positions of hierarchical power. Like many young women of their generation, both Genevieve and Paula deferred to the wishes of their parents when making their initial decision to become a teacher[18] Genevieve remembers that:

> Dad thought I should go to Normal School, that that would be the best thing for me to do, so he took me to [a local store] and bought me a fur coat and a wool dress and I went to Normal School. I just loved it. And 50-some years later it's all history, but that's the story.

When asked why she became a teacher, Paula also recounts her deferral to her parents:

> Well actually the decision wasn't mine . . . I was quite young and . . . . we were in the war, and my mother and dad thought the best thing for me to do would be not to work in a munitions factory, but to get an education, which I did. So then mother just arranged for me to get on a train at that time . . . She thought the best thing for you to do is to go up to teachers college. So I've never regretted it, but it was

not something that I had set down as a goal . . . Then I came back to [my home town] area and we looked desperately for a place for me to stay, for me to teach, and there were several places, but they were all small places with a teacherage. And my dad had a terrific sense of humor, and he took us to one and he said "I don't know, [Paula]" he said [laughter], "I'm just afraid you'd burn the whole thing down." [laughter]. He didn't have much faith in my responsibility.

Eventually, Paula found a job in northern Ontario and vividly remembers her trip into the community which was located on a railroad line:

> So actually I guess it was September the 1st or something that we got in there, and my trip into the school area was on a hand car. The train didn't stop at [the community] . . . so I went into my first school on a hand car . . . And the funniest part of it was that this was the first daughter, the eldest, going off to her first job, so mother made sure that I had my best clothes on, a hat, and a spirella garment.[19] And so here I was on this hand car and it was hot, it was awfully hot, and in this spirella garment, a new coat, and a new hat, so that was my introduction. . . .

The complexities of gender identity are evident in these stories in which two young women deferred to their parents' wish that they become teachers and enacted that role, with their parents' encouragement, in conformity with the dress codes and demeanor for "proper" young women. Indeed, these dress codes were reinforced in teacher preparation programs well into the 1970s and so it is little wonder that neither gave any thought to resisting these codes despite the discomfort or inappropriateness for climate and duties that they may have imposed.

While conforming as dutiful daughters in dress and demeanor, Paula and Genevieve found that their teaching careers prompted a deep interest in enabling more equitable opportunities for students who were struggling with reading skills or had special learning needs. Both had enjoyed a significant degree of autonomy in small rural schoolhouses in their early careers and had also encountered students with significant learning needs for which they felt ill-prepared by their teacher education programs. As a result, unlike many "dutiful daughters" who fulfilled their teaching and family responsibilities close to home, they both pursued graduate studies in large cities in the United States quite early in their careers in order to gain professional knowledge – but it was knowledge that conformed to traditional care-giving concerns for women: reading and special education.

This juxtaposition between conformity and non-conformity with traditional behavior for women continued throughout their careers. For example, both followed career paths that they each describe as somewhat accidental and, while unusual, remained firmly inside the boundaries of acceptable – even exemplary – professional practice. As a result of their graduate work and their availability for sharing their knowledge in professional settings, both were offered career opportunities as education consultants with boards of education and then moved on to other opportunities – Paula with a publishing company and Genevieve in a faculty of education. It was not until the mid-1970s that both took on administrative roles – Paula as a superintendent of curriculum for the Ministry of Education and Genevieve as a board superintendent.

Neither woman consciously decided not to marry[20] but, because they did not do so, they were free of the constraints that many married women experienced[21] at that time and were able to pursue their teaching interests without having to worry about the traditional responsibilities of married women. In other words, they were able to perform traditional gender roles for single women while accepting non-traditional career opportunities as they became available. That is not to say that they did not feel the effects of gender on their work and careers. When Paula was chosen as superintendent for a Ministry district, for example, she was confident in her abilities, which had been honed well in various consultant's positions and administrative work with the Ministry, and was strongly supported by the respect she had built across communities in the north for her work. She also recognized that an emerging discussion around gender equity in administrative positions opened up the possibility that she would be chosen for a position that had always been held by a man. Despite the icy reception she received at her "welcome" reception, she was confident that she would be able to win over the men whom she would now supervise and that they would not have the political clout to dislodge her from her new position. She says:

> When they went out into the region, my respect was so high I think
> people knew me so well, and they respected the things I stood for,

that [my male colleagues] really couldn't [get rid of me]. And I think most of them finally decided well O.K., I guess she's O.K., you know . . . A couple of the old fogies didn't, but . . . There was another chap who applied for the position, and he was a secondary person, very fine person, but he didn't have a lot of creativity, so when the Ministry decided to select the regional director, I think they selected me . . . because I probably had more to offer. The other thing was they wanted a woman, too. The Ministry felt that they needed more women. The Federation was offering a lot of leadership workshops so I think the reason that my career went as it did, I guess, is because of the people around me. The people who were willing to try.

While Paula benefited from an emergent discourse in the 1960s that questioned why there were so few women in administration, men were still able to act on their organizational privilege with relative impunity. For example, Genevieve had been sexually harassed as a young teacher but had not had organizational support to help her understand what had happened to her or provide ways to deal effectively with her harasser. Instead, she avoided the problem by not taking a position with the board in which he was later employed.

While both women acknowledged that gender played some role in their careers, there was considerable ambivalence about its role in their work as senior administrators. For example, Genevieve recalls:

> I don't think I ever played the female role, you know, and I didn't play the male role either. *I always tried to be a person rather than a man or a woman, and tried to be a professional,* and I don't know, I just didn't seem to have any trouble. I think if you're competent, that's the main thing. If you're competent and people see that you're competent, and you can produce results, you'll get where you want to go, and you're doing it for the right reasons, and I think people somehow thought that I was doing it for the right reasons . . . I wasn't saying I want to do this, but I want this done for these children.

When Paula was asked whether she felt that being a woman was an advantage to her work as an educational administrator, she replied, "Well I never felt that it was a disadvantage. I didn't have to use my womanly wiles, you know. Everybody I worked with was very professional." Yet, when asked to describe her leadership, she answered, "I don't know, I just did what comes naturally I guess. I had to prove myself. I never asked them to do anything that I wouldn't do too. When they had to go out on the road, I went out too. We did workshops together and so on, so that after awhile they came around."

Both women talked about their work in terms of preferred female behavior – caring, focussed on others, child-centred – and in a way that was "proper" or non-sexualized. They remained the "dutiful daughter" within patriarchal organizations and disapproved of the use of female sexuality as a tool for gaining approval or motivating compliance. Instead, they sought to minimize the possibility that others would construct them as possessing sexual power and would not explore this possibility even when it might have seemed an obvious explanation for some of the behaviors they encountered. For example, Paula observed: "When I got the job as regional director, it was the wives of the men that let me know that [me being in that position] wasn't such a great thing." However, she did not attribute their disapproval to the wives' concern about their husbands working with a single woman. Instead, she offered this explanation.

> Well, one of the women said 'you know, men die of heart attacks, that's what's going to happen to women.' And I said well I just can't see myself dying of a heart attack right now. I guess their husbands probably had built up the position as being so stressful, whereas I didn't find it stressful. I found it very exciting.

Paula's immediate movement from a discourse of sexual power to one of professional competence is not surprising given the fear of women's sexuality[22] and emotionality[23] in organizational settings. As many feminist scholars have argued,[24] Western Enlightenment meta-narratives have relegated women to the private sphere of the body, emotions, and non- rationality. Women administrators represent a disruption to the public sphere of organizational activity in which the rational objective work of the mind is privileged. Thus, those dutiful daughters who occupy administrative positions learn to minimize the disruption that they represent in the gender order of organizations in order to get on with the work that they wish to accomplish.

"Troubling Women": Lauren and Judith

Unlike Genevieve and Paula who remained dutiful daughters, Lauren and Judith were often "troubling women" who challenged the gender order in their organizations and resisted the gender roles they were expected to play. Both came to teaching somewhat reluctantly but found that their teacher education program provided a liberation of sorts and careers that were a satisfying challenge. In Lauren's case, although she describes her parents as very supportive, she also saw going away to school as a liberation from the constraints imposed on young women living at home and an opportunity to explore social opportunities. The teacher education program itself, however, was unsatisfying intellectually. She describes some of the limitations of her program of studies:

> There was far more emphasis put on our behavior and our dress than what was put on the actual creative aspects of teaching. You were handed a little gray primer and you were to march through that. Nobody said 'let's take these explorers and make them wonderfully interesting and fascinating to the kids.' It wasn't quite Napoleonic, that you weren't to be on page 12 on September the 2nd, but darn close to it . . . They certainly stressed decorum and all the rest of it, and I mean you wouldn't have dreamt of going and teaching with a pair of pants on. Just simply had to wear the accepted uniform.

Her words signal a restlessness with traditional gender roles that continued in her first teaching job. She was hired by a northern Ontario community to teach in a one room school, and enjoyed a high degree of autonomy but soon found the life of a classroom teacher less than stimulating. She resigned after two years of teaching to explore other options in the post-war economic boom but eventually returned at the request of an inspector who had encouraged her to think about administration. When it became obvious that administrative opportunities were scarce in the mid-1950s for women in the public school system, Lauren took an administrative position as a vice-principal in a residential school for Native children. However, she found that, like the provincial school system, the federal system that provided Native education on reserve and in residential schools was not open to promoting women to principals' positions. She left to take a position in a provincial system where her experience in a residential school made her uniquely qualified for an administrative position in a public school in the early 1960s when provincial schools began integrating Native children into public school classrooms.

Lauren became a principal in the mid-1960s and one of the few women administrators in Ontario at that time who had completed the requirements for superintendent's papers. She was asked to act as an assistant supervisor and travelled throughout the north as a supervisor of teachers. She eventually returned to school administration and became very active on the provincial executive of the FWTAO. Lauren was well aware that she was a rarity and equally aware of her vulnerability in that position:

> When I started there just were not female principals. They came in the '60s when I did, a few of them, but we still were not that many. I mean we went to a principals' convention in the fall in [a city in northern Ontario] and I mean you could count us on one hand . . . You just simply had to be on your toes constantly. You had to be ready with good ideas, you had to be a good listener, and you also had to try and get out for a drink with the boys now and again. That's the reality of it. And with the [name of male administrator who was known for his inappropriate sexual behavior] around, you also had to develop a good right punch [laughter].

Lauren's pragmatic awareness of what it meant to be a woman in an administrative position included an awareness that access to important organizational knowledge took place in the informal interactions among men so she ensured that those networks were open to her as well – but judiciously and with an awareness that she would act rather than be victimized..

For Judith, who completed her teacher education in the United Kingdom, attending university was both a social and intellectual liberation. Judith reports,

> When I went off to the Faculty of Education, it was a combination of getting a picture of a bigger world in terms of interacting with guys (Judith had attended an all-girls' school), not that I hadn't interacted with guys before 'cause I belonged to the Council for Education and World Citizenship which took me to some very interesting places and meeting interesting people, but never in quite that kind of learning environment, and so it was not a growing year in terms of how my career would take off, but it was a growing year in terms of recognizing my own competence for the first time.

Judith's growing sense of competence, which was obvious at the elite all-girls' school that she attended as a scholarship student, was reinforced when she learned that she was seen as a leader by both males and females. That knowledge was important to her in the battles that lay ahead.

After marrying and starting a family, Judith continued her studies after immigrating to Canada and it was then that she became aware of and active in second wave feminism. As already noted, she declared her interest in an administrative position in 1967 but she was not appointed to such a position until 1980 partly because she was perceived as troublesome because of her participation in various feminist causes.

> I think that the most powerful influence was when the Royal Commission Report came out in '68, and I had already started to be asked to be in Federation . . . I think I was doing sort of a not-for-credit sociology course at [a university] for interest, because feminism was really starting to blossom at that time, and when I read the Royal Commission Report, I became quite angry about the fact that it was systemic. I think up until that time I could pretend it was just, well not pretend, but believe, you know, you're a young person and you're putting your husband through school, and you're doing a whole lot of things, you know. But I realized that there were very strong systemic barriers in [my board] to women becoming administrators . . .So I think it was after that Royal Commission Report and then doing graduate work, that I realized things had to change.

Troubling women are seen as troubling in at least two ways: by troubling the accepted order in the organization and also by being seen as trouble to the organization. Lauren and Judith qualified as "trouble" on both counts but their willingness to resist stereotypes and take on unpopular causes eventually won support. For example, while Lauren took the same "genderless" position about her work as Genevieve and Paula, she took advantage of the less traditional possibilities that were available to women in the north and enacted gender in a very different way. In describing her community work, she recalls:

> I don't know that it was different than men. I think you had to take part in the community, and just simply be in there. I was fortunate in that my husband was a [member of a charitable organization] so I had that outlet, but I also was a member of the Business and Professional Women's, and therefore I sat on the Chamber of Commerce as their representative. I was a volunteer member of the, in fact I was on the Board of Directors for, the Red Cross in Ontario, and the volunteer coordinator for Northwestern Ontario during the plane crash and all those wonderful things, fires and so on, and consequently second in command of the Emergency Services. So I did the type of jobs that

men could do and just simply made myself an indispensable part of the community, and by doing that, you tended to be treated as an equal. For a while there was a, you know, "let's wait and see what this gal's gonna do" kind of thing, and then afterwards when you said you were going to do a job and it was done, they were there with you working as a team.

While Lauren troubled the gender norms of community activity, Judith troubled the practices of her school board. She took on a highly controversial cause because of her disdain for the punitive disciplinary measures she encountered in her first Canadian school. To her horror, she discovered that her principal, a retired military man, allotted a certain number of strappings to all of the teachers in his school, including the early primary grades. Not only were the teachers expected to use their quota but the strap was often administered to children while being broadcast over the public address system so that the entire school heard the proceedings. Judith refused to use her quota and eventually took on the issue of corporal punishment in education for her doctoral research and as a political project. She recalls:

> When the Hall Dennis report came out, it had that clause about punishment, and that just resonated with me. So when a trustee, backed by all the Board, [brought forward] a motion to abolish corporal punishment in [name of city], the shit hit the fan in this community. I mean every radio, every letter to the editor, the teachers mobilized within 24 hours, the teachers mobilized to fight it. I saw what was happening and I was just a teacher in a classroom, but I wrote a note to [the trustee] who brought the motion and said, "Look, I'm just a teacher out here, but please hold the course. You are 100% right." And what happened, and this is what brought me into sort of a leadership role in [name of city], 'cause until then *I'd just been in the background, like causing trouble, but in the background.* The Board decided to set up a committee to look at the issue of corporal punishment, so [name of trustee] said "well I'm gonna suggest we have a teacher and I have a name here," and put my name forward. So I became Chair of that committee . . . there were two of us who were against corporal punishment, so we undertook the largest study that was ever done anywhere on corporal punishment, which is still sort of a standard.

Judith's political activism included work with the FWTAO to advocate for more women in administrative positions as well as work with other groups advocating for women's rights and issues such as violence against women.

While Judith and Lauren worked for many of the same educational goals that Genevieve and Paula did, they seemed less concerned with enacting traditional gender roles in doing so. This is somewhat puzzling, given that they were both married and, in Judith's case, had children. While they were expected to assume more traditional gender roles, they never saw their choices as "either/or" and from the beginning of their careers expressed an interest in and did not hesitate to demonstrate leadership in their school systems and communities. Lauren just rolled up her sleeves and made sure that she was involved in community activities where much of the informal decision-making was taking place among men while Judith worked within the formal networks of power, including the FWTAO, to "cause trouble" around issues of women's and children's welfare.

Being a "troubling woman," however, not only required enormous energy but meant that one's enactment of gender was highly visible. Caught between the demands of two "greedy" organizations – school and home – women leaders were expected to perform their role in each domain not only well but in a way that demonstrated that they "deserved" to be a part of a male domain while not "neglecting" their care-giving role at home. Dutiful daughters often managed to be dutiful to their organizations because they did not have the daily demands of husband, home, and children. However, women whose family responsibilities were unmediated by a reworked gender order between the public and private found that they had to perform in each domain as though the other did not exist. Judith wanted to be seen as competent and was quite aware of the ways in which judgements about her leadership could be shaped by masculinist norms and so, like many of the women who became school administrators in the 1960s and 1970s, she attempted to ensure that there was no room for criticism. She recalls:

> What most women do, in my observation, is we go overboard, trying never to compromise, you know, and have anyone say 'oh well, she's slipped off early' or 'she stayed home because the kid was sick' or whatever. And I think I went overboard the other way, you know, when I was pregnant, making sure I worked, every duty I was supposed to work, and so on. But I think the women are vulnerable on

standards in those two areas. One is the sexual innuendo, flirty stuff, and the other is the family responsibilities interfering.

While taking care of children and family was paramount, the problem of women's bodies and any evidence of their sexuality in roles of organizational authority are evident throughout Judith's comments. Like "the dutiful daughters," she was very aware that women's sexual power was dangerous in organizational settings if one wanted one's work to be taken seriously. She did not participate in the "flirty stuff" despite the fact that it might have been powerful in the short term – a route chosen by some of her female colleagues – because it diminished her ability to take on political battles around issues that she cared about and made her more vulnerable to the control of male colleagues. All four women, in fact, recognized that "women who pursued administrative advancement and yet did not manage their femininity usually faced covert as well as overt resistance, sometimes even hostility"[25] from both men and women.

Assuming Leadership Rethought

In this chapter, I have explored how four women who became senior administrators in Ontario's education system made sense of their position of leadership in an era when women administrators were very rare. Both Paula and Genevieve interpreted the "dutiful daughter" script as they enacted gender norms that were common in the 1950s. They continued to enact these scripts in their administrative work in the mid-1970s and were uncomfortable with women whom they perceived to be troublesome. For example, when Paula was asked whether any women educators had difficulties, she replied:

> Well, I had a couple of girls on staff, for example, who were consultants, who, either they were sort of down on men, kind of thing, you know, and they were insulting to them, and they'd say, "well we shouldn't cater to them." Nobody was catering to them. I think you accept a person on a professional level, so I think some of the women who have had difficulty in the directorships are women who, for some reason, feel that they have to flaunt the whole woman bit.

Paula did not name herself as feminist, but she seemed to be drawing on a particular reading of the feminist discourses that informed many of the policies for which FWTAO advocated during the 1970s and

1980s: "liberal feminism with its emphasis on individuals and proce-duralism, and cultural feminism's advocacy of caring and sharing."[26.] Paula saw these women who were "down on men" as unfair because their actions were gender-specific – antithetical to liberal feminist ide-ology – and their actions as uncaring and divisive – antithetical to cul-tural feminism.

For Paula and Genevieve, their careers were perceived to have lit-tle to do with their gender and more to do with their professional knowledge. In many ways, they were right; their professional knowl-edge and experience were substantial and at least equal to and some-times superior to those men with whom they worked and whom they supervised.[27] Yet they still described their positioning as senior admin-istrators as almost accidental – the result of their educational prepara-tion and professional competence and the openness of others to their enthusiasm for child-centred pedagogy – rather than following a career trajectory. In fact, like many women in administration, their careers did not move through the line positions of hierarchical organ-izations. Instead, they became consultants and subject specialists. Working their way into senior levels of administration, however, required not only an organizational awareness of their clearly superi-or professional knowledge but also a political awareness precipitated by the uncomfortable questions raised by second wave feminists about the privileged access to administrative positions that men enjoyed.

Both Paula and Genevieve began teaching during the postwar years when women were being actively encouraged to relinquish the "men's work" they had taken up during the war and to embrace sub-urban life and have babies. Preferred gender roles for their generation did not include jobs outside the home, let alone careers. However, they moved into senior administration just as questions about these gender norms and what they meant to women's careers began to receive some attention in Ontario's Ministry of Education and its boards of educa-tion. By the late 1970s, FWTAO was gathering statistics that clearly showed gender imbalances by hierarchical position but there was sig-nificant resistance[28] to women occupying positions of authority. Genevieve and Paula, however, were not only highly competent – and seen to be so by their communities – but were women who were not going to rock the organizational boat as women but as professionals. While one could argue that they were demonstrating a form of "wimpish femininity,"[29] Blackmore argues that to do so is to ignore "the harsh realities of women's life histories"[30] where women were censured heavily if they did not enact local gender norms. Genevieve and Paula, whether consciously or unconsciously, performed gender in a way that was congruent with their life histories and considered appropriate in their local context and, in doing so, allowed them to get on with work that they cared about passionately.

By the 1960s, when Judith began with and Lauren returned to the public education system in Ontario, the women's movement in Canada was publicly questioning gender norms for women in both the public and private sphere of activity and practices in schools that privileged boys. By the time the Royal Commission on the Status of Women was called by Prime Minister Pearson in 1967 and published its 167 recommendations in 1970, Lauren was a practising administrator in northern Ontario and Judith was still trying to gain admission to the qualifying courses to become a principal, but both were acting strategically in their local settings as well as through provincial women's organizations to open up opportunities for women. As spaces opened to enact gender differently, however, they were required to balance responsibilities at home and school – neither of which had been altered to reflect women's dual roles. Judith struggled with this as she ascended the educational hierarchy but even more with understanding the women who resented women who were attempting to "do it all." She observed:

> Women of that generation felt they had made a choice, and so there was resentment and there was that competitiveness that you, how dare you think you could have it all. And I've had that said to me, you know, and what kind of mother could you be, you know. I used to cart my babies off to Federation meetings in Toronto when I had to go and speak, and I mean that environment it was great, and it was encouraged, because they wanted to get the sense that you can have the whole. But it wasn't amongst the women who had kind of, you know, moved within the system, and that was the competitiveness I think.

Her words speak to the complexity of the discursive location of senior women administrators and the animosity that sometimes emerged between them. Those who were "allowed in" to the top echelons of the men's club of educational administration in the mid-1970s were required to perform a normative gender role even as they stepped into a world that was ruled by male norms, most often as single women. In order to survive, Genevieve and Paula practised what Catherine Marshall[31] calls a "politics of denial" about the gender discrimination they experienced in order to get on with the work at hand and, although they expressed sympathy for those women who were juggling family and work responsibilities, did not actively seek to change organizational practices that would have made this juggling act more humane.

Those women who had been denied access to positions of authority or, like Lauren, had become administrators and discovered how discriminatory practices were in doing their work, and whose consciousness of gender discrimination had been raised by involvement in or exposure to second wave feminism during the 1960s, were often resisted by both men and women as they sought to rework the gendered division of labor at home and work. Judith spoke of the difficulty women had speaking to one another about the challenges they faced as they sought new ways to enact gender in both the public and private sphere. It was particularly difficult – even dangerous – to do so at the senior administrative level.

As a result, all four women spoke about a certain degree of isolation that they experienced in their role as a senior woman administrator. Most spoke of the importance of family and friendships that emerged in their professional interactions. Lauren, for example, commented,

> Most of my close friendships in the profession would have come out of the federations, and I have maintained those friendships. Either that or I would have a situation where I was mentoring younger women who were wanting to get into a principalship . . . in a sense it's lonely at the top.

They also spoke about the joy of having opportunities to travel to other countries to study school systems throughout the world, taking time to research educational issues of interest, and knowing that their work had made a significant difference in the lives of students, families, and professional colleagues. In fact, all four women continued to be involved in projects of interest following their retirement that were motivated by the same interests that had animated their practice as senior administrators.

The historical experience of the four women administrators in this chapter demonstrates that assuming leadership in Ontario's educational system is a complex process of enacting gender within and in resistance to patriarchal social and organizational gender norms. Both "dutiful daughters" and "troublesome women" performed gender in conscious and unconscious ways as they negotiated the daily contradictions and shifting positions of women in senior administration. Their life histories demonstrate the efficacy of knowing women's lives in order to consider strategic action for what lies ahead as women continue to assume leadership in bureaucratic systems that remain resistant to them even as they occupy formal positions of authority.

Notes

[1] Caroline Benn, "Preface," in *Women Teachers: Issues and Experiences,* ed. H. DeLyon & F. Widdowson Migiuolo, xviii-xxvi (Milton Keynes, U.K.: Open University Press, 1989).

[2] Carol Pateman, *The Sexual Contract* (Oxford: Polity Press, 1988); Jill Blackmore, "Educational Leadership: A Feminist Critique and Reconstruction" in *Critical Perspectives on Educational Leadership,* ed. John Smyth, 93-131 (London: Falmer Press, 1989); Jackie M. Blount, *Destined to Rule the Schools: Women and the Superintendency, 1873-1995* (Albany, N.Y.: SUNY Press, 1998).

[3] Blount, *Destined to Rule the Schools*, 156.

[4] For example: Alison Prentice, "The Feminization of Teaching" in *The Neglected Majority: Essays in Canadian Women's History,* eds. Susan Mann Trofimenkoff and Alison Prentice (Toronto: McClelland and Stewart, 1977); Kerreen Reiger. " The Gender Dynamics of Organizations" in *Gender Matters in Educational Administration Policy: A Feminist Introduction,* eds. Jill Blackmore and Jane Kenway (London: Falmer Press, 1993).

[5] I have provided a fuller discussion of these phenomena elsewhere in Janice Wallace, "Conservation, Conciliation, or Conversation: Discovering a Meeting Place for Gendered Values in Educational Organizations," *Journal of Educational Administration and Foundations 13* (1998): 9-29. See also, Janice Wallace, "Learning to Lead: Women School Administrators in Twentieth Century Ontario," *Oral History Forum, 24* (2004): 87-107.

[6] Carole Pateman, *The Sexual Contract.* (Stanford, CA.: Stanford University Press, 1988).

[7] Judith Butler, *Gender Trouble: Feminism and the Subversion of Identity* (New York: Routledge, 1990).

[8]Jennifer Scott, "The Linguistic Production of Genderlessness in the Superintendency" in *Reconsidering Feminist Leadership in Educational Leadership*, ed. Michelle D. Young and Linda Skrla, 81-102 (Albany, N.Y.: SUNY Press, 2003).

[9]Scott, *The Linguistic Production of Genderlessness in the Superintendency,* 85.

[10]Scott, *The Linguistic Production of Genderlessness in the Superintendency,* 85, italics added.

[11]While recognizing that the notion of "roles" is problematic in feminist analysis, it continues to be a useful conceptual tool for thinking about the possibilities for women with which they struggle in shaping their lives and careers. For further discussion, see Pat Armstrong & Hugh Armstrong, *Theorizing Women's Work* (Toronto: Garamond Press, 1990) and Jill Blackmore, "Troubling Women: The Upsides and Downsides of Leadership and the New Managerialism" in *Women and School Leadership: International Perspectives*, ed. Cecilia Reynolds, 49-70 (Albany N.Y.: SUNY Press, 2002).

[12]Cecilia Reynolds, "Changing Gender Scripts and Moral Dilemmas for Women and Men in Education, 1940-1970" in *Women and School Leadership: International Perspectives*, ed. Cecilia Reynolds (Albany N.Y.: SUNY Press, 2002) 32.

[13]Blackmore, "Troubling Women: The Upsides and Downsides of Leadership and the New Managerialism," 49-70.

[14]For example, Jackie Blount, *Destined to Rule the Schools;* C. Cryss Brunner (ed.), *Sacred Dreams: Women and the Superintendency* (Albany, N.Y.: SUNY Press, 1999); Margaret Grogan, "Laying the Groundwork for a Reconception of the Superintendency from Feminist Postmodern Perspectives" in *Reconsidering Feminist Leadership in Educational Leadership*, ed. Michelle D. Young and Linda Skrla, 9-34 (Albany, N.Y.: SUNY Press, 2003); Linda Skrla, "Mourning Silence: Women Superintendents (and a Researcher) Rethink Speaking Up and Speaking Out" in *Reconsidering Feminist Leadership in Educational Leadership*, ed. Michelle D. Young & Linda Skrla, 103-128 (Albany, N.Y.: SUNY Press,2003).

[15]Blount, *Destined to Rule the Schools,* 82-87.

[16]In some Canadian provinces, the most senior administrator for a board of education is called a superintendent (e.g., Alberta). However, in Ontario, that same position is designated as director. Senior administrative positions immediately beneath the director in the hierarchy of Ontario's educational organizations are designated as superintendents.

[17]I am purposely identifying general periods of time rather than specific years in order to preserve the anonymity of the participants. Likewise, I will identify geographic regions quite generally. Because these women's administrative careers were (and still are) unusual, specific year numbers and geographic locations might identify participants.

[18]In Wallace, *Learning to Lead,* 87-107, I discuss the comment I heard repeatedly when interviewing participants for this study – that there were only three acceptable career choices for young women at the time: teacher, nurse, or secretary.

[19]A spirella garment was a type of corset that many young women wore at the time to ensure that their bodies conformed to traditional standards of beauty.

[20]While both Genevieve and Paula suggested that it was never a conscious choice not to marry, as Genevieve put it, "It just never happened." Genevieve was engaged in the early years of her career but that relationship ended. She did eventually marry when she retired.

[21]Until the mid-1970s, many boards imposed a marriage ban that required women to resign from their teaching position once they were married. However, many married women sought employment with boards who interpreted the ban loosely depending on their employment needs or they continued to teach in part-time or substitute teacher positions. In addition, women were expected to resign once their pregnancy became obvious. The implications of these policies for women whose families required their income was often devastating. For further discussion, see Wallace, *Learning to Lead,* 87.

[22]Jeff Hearn & Wendy Parkin, *Sex at Work: The Power and Paradox of Organization Sexuality* (New York: St. Martin's Press, rev. ed.,1995).

[23]Stephen Fineman, "Introduction" in *Emotion in Organizations,* ed. Stephen Fineman, 1-8 (London: Sage, 1993).

[24]Blackmore, *A Feminist Critique and Reconstruction;* Susan Hekman, *Gender and Knowledge: Elements of a Postmodern Feminism.* (Boston: Northeastern University Press, 1990); Cecilia Reynolds, "Feminist frameworks for the study of administration and leadership in educational organizations" in *Women and Educational Leadership in Canadian Education,* eds. Cecilia Reynolds and Beth Young, 3-18. (Calgary, AB: Detselig Enterprises, 1995).

[25]Blount, *Destined to Rule,* 108.

[26]Jill Blackmore, *Troubling Women: Feminism, Leadership, and Educational Change* (Buckingham, U.K.: Open University Press,1999) 196.

[27]Both women had a graduate degree and significant experience as educators and administrators before taking on their senior administrative roles. See Cecilia Reynolds, "Changing Gender Scripts and Moral Dilemmas for Women and Men in Education, 1940-1970" in *Women and School Leadership: International Perspectives,* ed. Cecilia Reynolds, 29-48

[28]Wallace, *Conversation, Conciliation, and Conversation,* 9-29.

[29]Valerie Walkerdine, "Femininity as Performance," *Oxford Review of Education* (1989): 267-279, cited in Blackmore, *Troubling Women*, 195.

[30]Blackmore, *Troubling Women,* 195.

[31]Catherine Marshall, "The Politics of Denial: Gender and Race Issues in Administration," in *The New Politics of Race and Gender,* ed. Catherine Marshall, 168-175. (London: Falmer Press, 1993).

8

Organizing in Contradiction: Women Teachers, Unionization, and the Politics of Feminized Professionalism

Rebecca Priegert Coulter

Teachers protest at Queen's Park. *Photo courtesy of The University of Western Ontario Archives, London Free Press Collection, Dec. 18, 1973.*

Historically, women teachers have inhabited a world where they were both subjugated by and active agents of the state, where they exercised pedagogical authority in the classroom but experienced the controlling surveillance of the partriarchal gaze, where they negotiated identities in the interstices between the discourses of professionalism and domesticity. The contradictions of their ambivalent social locations were further sharpened when they began to work together collectively for their mutual benefit in the late nineteenth and early twentieth centuries. At that time, women teachers began organizing their own professional associations or federations in several Canadian provinces but only the Federation of Women Teachers' Associations of Ontario (FW) enjoyed lasting success.[1] For eighty years it was a powerful voice for the women who taught in public elementary schools around the province. By looking at one of the most remarkable chapters in women's separate organizing not only in Canada but internationally, we can begin to probe the ways the leaders of the FW at the provincial and local levels understood and negotiated their contradictory positioning, how they both used and opposed discourses of professionalism and femininity, and how they produced meaning for and from their own activism.

The Federation of Women Teachers' Associations of Ontario was created in 1918 as a province-wide organization which brought together under one umbrella a number of locally based Women Teachers' Associations (WTAs). According to Bertha Adkins, the first secretary-treasurer, its goals were "to improve the status of women teachers and to secure a spirit of co-operation and mutual helpfulness among its members."[2] For eighty years, until 1998, the FW represented female, public school elementary school teachers, initially through a voluntary membership system and then, with the passage of *The Teaching Profession Act* (TPA) in 1944, through the compulsory membership requirement set out in by-laws made under that act.[3] Throughout its history, a number of efforts were launched, sometimes by the men teachers and occasionally by some women, to amalgamate the FW with the Ontario Public School Teachers' Federation (OPS) which represented male, public school elementary teachers. Finally, after a series of lengthy and costly court battles and a decision by an Ontario Human Rights Commission Board of Inquiry that the by-laws made under the TPA compelling membership on the basis of sex were discriminatory, the FW and the OPS decided, in 1996, to form a new organization, the Elementary Teachers' Federation of Ontario (ETFO).[4] The transition to the new structure was completed in 1998.

During its eighty year history, the FW made important contributions both to the improvement of the material lives of female elementary teachers in Ontario and to the development of the Canadian women's movement. The FW's in-house histories and a small number of scholarly works review these contributions[5] and confirm the successful efforts to improve women teachers' wages, working conditions, pensions and professional status. The FW also supported the women's suffrage movement of the late nineteenth- and early twentieth-centuries as well as the second wave of Canadian feminism in the late 1960s and early 1970s. The FW was instrumental in the birth and continued nurturing of the National Action Committee on the Status of Women, the umbrella organization that was formed by a diversity of feminists following the 1970 release of *The Report of the Royal Commission on the Status of Women.*[6] The FW also assisted with the struggle to include the equality clause in the *Canadian Charter of Rights and Freedoms,* funded anti-violence initiatives in schools and communities, and developed a range of non-sexist curriculum materials for school use.[7]

At the same time, as Sawaya reminds us, women's desire for professional status can reveal "not only fractures within women's fight for equality but also how women's history is imbricated in the dominant ideologies and institutions of . . . capitalism."[8] Why did women teachers, even as they took up equity and social justice agendas, appear to re-inscribe dominant gender norms and trap themselves within constraining boundaries of social conformity? Was it because the heroic narrative of the FW was "built on assumptions of white and Protestant hegemony"[9] and on dominant cultural views of class and femininity? When women's equality rights conflicted with professional aspirations, why did the leadership of the organization often opt for the latter, even in the face of opposition from grassroots members?

To confront these difficult questions about the history of the FW raises ethical and political concerns for me. How can I tell some of their stories without betraying the trust of the women who, during interviews, shared their lives and views with me? They may well be shocked, individually and collectively, to see themselves revealed in ways and circumstances not always flattering. And for a feminist educator to be critical of the FW seems at best disloyal and at worst politically naive in an era when anti-feminists or post-feminists could easily mis-use critical commentary. In this context, I must emphasize that I remain convinced that despite any failings, the FW was an important organization for women teachers and for women more generally. At the same time, I agree with Cynthia Cockburn who argues that, ". . .

elaborations of paradox and confusion are painstaking and often painful. But it is precisely out of the process of bringing such contradictions to consciousness and facing up to illogicality or inconsistency, that a person takes a grip on his or her own fate. Politically, it is of vital importance that we understand how we change."[10]

Almost without exception, women teachers who were active in the FW at the local and provincial levels emphasized their commitment to professionalism and rejected any characterization of the organization as a union. Of course, debates which set up an oppositional dualism between unionism and professionalism are not uncommon in the helping professions and many studies of teaching and nursing are replete with discussions of this dynamic.[11] Nonetheless, there was something astonishing about hearing FW leaders speak vehemently against unions. Only Deborah (ACPID157), an FW leader in the last two decades of the twentieth century and someone who had previous experiences of a union while working at the post office before entering teaching, had no compunction about calling the FW a union.

> I mean I couldn't distinguish for you the difference between a professional organization and a union because it seems to me that if you've got the right to grieve and you've got a, a body that's going to do that grieving for you, that that's a union, not just a professional body. So, no, it didn't vary much. It certainly, FW was involved in all aspects of a woman teacher's career, in society in general, but I certainly thought one of their important roles was advocacy and bargaining.

More common was the view expressed by Mavis (ACPID130) who served on a local WTA executive in the 1950s and 1960s, but taught for many years after that, as well. She stated very forcefully that

> the Federation was not a union. It was a professional federation. You're speaking to a Londoner who was a teacher federation president, and we considered ourselves not a union. We were not the postal workers, we were not the automobile workers, or anything like that. I never heard the word strike when I taught. Never was suggested to me.

When asked to distinguish between a union and a professional association, Mavis responded,

> Well, the professional association to me, like the College of Teachers now, like the standards of the profession, like they kept the standards of certificates up, they published articles that they thought if you

know, this would help you, you'd be respected. The Federation, when it was a professional organization, sort of you felt obliged to dress this way. There was no dress down day. The standards were high. The people that were in the office would always dress beautifully. You'd look up to them. Anytime you had a meeting, that sort of thing, it wasn't well, let's have it at the such-and-such and we'll all have a beer. There was none of that whatsoever. And I think that's the difference. Now it's too much like the postal workers. And, you know, solidarity forever, the union makes us strong. And I'm sorry, I guess I'm not a union person. . . . Now, I said I could strike if somebody, the government or someone was doing something detrimental to the children, and then I'd be the first one out there carrying the sign. But for me, for a little more money, for me for prep time, I thought prep time was what I did before and after school and what I took home at night. And see, I guess I'm too far removed.

Like many teachers, Mavis appeared to draw clear lines between what the Federation did and what unions do and at least part of her reasoning arose from a desire to distance herself from what she saw as working class occupations – postal workers, automobile workers and the like, all notably male jobs in her day. For Mavis, the Federation was about a professionalism that emphasized teacher learning, a commitment to children and certain normalized standards of feminine behavior and bodily presentation. Indeed, Mavis observed "I still can't bring myself to go out in jeans or track pants or something like that, when I go shopping. I don't know, it's just ingrained in me. And so they kept up, the standards were kept up that way."

On the face of it, Mavis is speaking from a position we might call domesticated or feminized professionalism, a professionalism almost guaranteed to promote conformity in gender specific ways. As Lind observed, it is "a very housebroken form of professionalism," the sort of professionalism that "tries to play the other side of unionism"[12] and emphasises duty, responsibility, obligation. Indeed, this approach is very clear in the FW's 1981 booklet of advice for new teachers called "Professionalism: The Heart of the Matter."[13] The very first entry is about appropriate dress for the woman teacher. This is followed by advice on being sensitive and listening to others, having a good attitude and being positive – traditional womanly virtues. The booklet then concludes with a large section on teachers' obligations and responsibilities as they are detailed in the statutes and regulations of the Province of Ontario. Despite the FW's record of social justice work on behalf of women and children, there is no hint here to begin-ning teachers that they might act as transformative intellectuals in their schools or engage in political action on their own behalf or in the wider community.

Ontario teachers rally at Saunders Secondary School. *Photo courtesy of The University of Western Ontario Archives, London Free Press Collection, Nov. 15, 1982.*

Sawaya has argued that the desire for professional status served to contain women's potential to act for radical change[14] and there is cer-tainly evidence to suggest that this was often the case in the FW. At the same time, there is sufficient evidence to demonstrate that many women teachers, especially those in leadership capacities, used the quest for professional status as one strategy to achieve broader equity and social justice goals. In fact, while the theme of professionalism is pervasive in the accounts of all the women leaders interviewed, how they talk about and understand the meaning of "professional" varies. "Professional" became a malleable category, called on in a variety of contexts to smooth over contradictions. It was a term used in differ-ent contexts and at different times for different ends; for example, it was utilized to "soften" what was otherwise tough union or class con-scious talk, but it was also employed to control rank and file militancy, to discipline teachers who strayed too far from acceptable gender norms, to justify certain initiatives seen as masculinist by members. In every case, however, we can see women teachers negotiating understandings of equality and identity and struggling with what it meant to be a woman and a teacher.

Mavis offers a case in-point. Despite her attachment to a feminized professionalism, she was willing to go on strike – to become in her eyes, a despised unionist – to protest against anything that would hurt children. In admitting this, she retains a womanly commitment to nurturing children but combines it with a more explicitly militant edge. In fact, when she was active in her WTA, she fought to improve pensions for the retired women teachers she saw living in poverty, and she argued for maternity leaves even though at the time she herself had no intention of marrying and having children. She also participated in the struggle to achieve opportunities for women to apply for and hold administrative positions, something she was not interested in for herself. When asked if these were not all traditional union issues, Mavis replied in a way that returned her to the anti-union discourse of professionalism.

> They were, they were. But I think that the Federation could have handled those, we always managed to handle them quite professionally without going to a rally and having somebody unionize all the workers there. We didn't need that.

Hannah (ACPID 129), who was both a WTA president and then a provincial president in the 1970s and 1980s, gave fiery speeches about collective bargaining rights and fair treatment for workers in the public sector while in office. In this context, it was surprising to hear her express a strong antipathy towards unions in her discussion about professionalism.

> Well, I think it's a status. You know, you've spent a certain number of years training for a position, and there should be some respect going with that position, and there should be a standing that each person who's in that position should have, and a responsibility of that role that that position places you in. Like the doctors' code of honor, you know, and that's what I think. But I feel as if that's very sadly lacking now. They're treated as a trade union rather than a professional organization, and that's what we used to get away from. It was several times I had trouble, when I was president in Toronto. It was, "Oh yes,

you're from the union," and I said, "Beg your pardon, I'm not from a union, I'm from a federation of teachers." I said we don't just negotiate salaries. We're concerned more, just as much with the standing of teachers and further training of women assistants in the classroom, and assistance with the children, and better ideas for teaching. So I said, that doesn't make us a union, it makes us a federation. A professional organization.

Hannah saw a conflict between union and professional goals and believes the public does, too. In her view, unions were primarily interested in salaries and working conditions and thus were self-interested. She proudly observed, "the year I was president, one of the slogans I brought out was that working conditions for teachers were learning conditions for children. That's one of the slogans I asked to have, we put that on a banner, and that's true." And it is true in important senses, but it is also a linguistic spin that allowed women teachers to camouflage more traditional union demands as demands for improved learning environments for children.

The efforts of women teachers to hang on to what they saw as "proper" and "professional" is reflected even in their descriptions of how they participated in protests and job actions. Hannah, in speaking about the one-day walk-out of teachers that occurred in 1973 to protest the introduction of Bills 274 and 275 in the Ontario legislature,[15] commented that she was "very pleased" with the way teachers protested because "it was always very well controlled. We never got into any fisticuff fights or anything like that. I thought it was done in a very professional way." Cynthia (ACPID026) described her discomfort with strikes and other job actions:

> I always have trouble with this. I can't judge a teacher who does decide to take job action. We only need to look at groups where they don't have some kind of protection, and we see they are taken advantage of, but it is really hard when you are in the public sector serving, whether it's kids in school or people in hospitals or whatever. It's really hard to know the answer to that one. Quite different from depriving a company of their profit.

Cynthia resolved her ambivalence in her own way.

> Now we were on the edge of a, what we thought was going to be job action, and I was, I think, second vice-president, which put me in a very difficult situation, and so I talked it over with the executive, and

I was going to be in charge of babysitting for the teachers, so I did-n't have to be on a picket line (laughter). Now that's kind of a cow-ardly way out, I guess, but I felt comfortable with that.

Cynthia's case is interesting because she recognized the need for a col-lective organization to protect teachers' rights, she respected the deci-sion of other teachers to strike, and she was willing to support teach-ers on strike by providing the necessary service of child care, albeit one closely connected to a traditional female role, for those on the picket line. She resolved her troubled feelings and held on to her fem-ininity by volunteering to look after children, but in doing so she allowed other women to demonstrate a militancy she could not allow herself.

Members of the FW continually struggled over their identities and over choices about what political strategies to use to achieve their goals. This is not surprising since, as women teachers seeking profes-sional status, they occupied contested ground and were situated with-in a network of contradictions. In the first instance, by seeking careers women challenged dominant norms about femininity and domesticity, norms which set women in the home and not the hurly-burly of the paid work force. Yet teachers used arguments that drew on those very norms to justify their work as teachers, emphasizing how the natural-ness of women's nurturing and caring suited them for classroom work, especially with younger children. Furthermore, by choosing education, teachers entered a field that was profoundly implicated in state formation and the maintenance of the existing social order, a social order that was patriarchal and hierarchical. Women thus occu-pied contradictory territory for their role as teachers was to promul-gate the *status quo* but their very presence in large numbers challenged the established gender regime, a key element of that order. Finally, because the professions were constructed as a male sphere, women teachers seeking professional status were both "outsiders" trying to get in, yet became "insiders" willing to participate in the very culture being criticized.[16] These multiple contradictions posed substantial strategic and political challenges that were played out in the local WTAs and in the FW.

While women teachers generally hewed to a line about federations being professional associations rather than unions, even as they worked hard to improve salaries, working conditions and pensions for their members, they were most comfortable seeing their federation as an organization that enhanced professional growth and leadership options for women, made life better for women and children, and contributed to the creation of a more just society. As Alice (ACPID 253), a provincial president in the 1960s said when asked about the most important contribution of the FW, "Professionalism was the biggest part of it – workshops, seminars, support, etc. You don't get that in a union."

London Public School Women Teachers' Guild Dinner. *Photo courtesy of The University of Western Ontario Archives, London Free Press Collection, Oct. 18, 1938.*

That the primary role of the FW was to provide professional development is a position which is accurately reflected in the views of many classroom teachers who often had difficulty distinguishing between school board and federation activities as a result. The work of the federation in blurring employer and employee relations and creating a particular image of the good teacher can be found in Antoinette's (ACPID 234) story. At the age of 19 and in her first or second year of teaching (she was uncertain which), this teacher was voted in as the "leader" for all grade two teachers in her urban board and, on behalf of the FW, she had to organize monthly meetings of that group. After an initial response which found her "so distressed," "sick to my stomach," and "upset and nervous," Antoinette described her efforts at programming for grade two teachers thus:

> you would try to get a topic that if there was something new intro-
> duced into the curriculum, if there was, or you might talk about
> bright ideas of interesting the children in their reading, their reading
> books or anything new that had come out because it was, things were
> evolving quickly from old-fashioned types of pictures to modern,
> more modern, pictures in a book. Anything new you would try to find
> out, and get a superintendent from the main office to let you know if
> anything came that could be introduced to teachers.

When asked if teachers were supportive of one another at the meet-ings, Antoinette replied, "Oh, yes. They might say, 'I've got a bright idea I would like to demonstrate or show.' Yes, it was nice." Here, again, the federation played a contradictory role. To promote "profes-sionalism" the FW, without any cost to the school board, was estab-lishing routines that expected teachers, in their own time, to voluntar-ily provide professional development; that is, the notion of women's service was emphasized. At the same time, we can also see these meet-ings as self-help support groups, allowing opportunities for women to discuss common concerns and, in contemporary parlance, build a net-work. The experience was "nice." However, the essentially conserva-tive nature of PD activities which emphasized a technical-rational approach to implementing curriculum policies set elsewhere, must ultimately be seen as detrimental to the development of work auton-omy and as constraining to women teachers. It continued to re-inscribe the ideology of the woman teacher as self-sacrificing and obe-dient, as taking the decisions of the male hierarchy in education and making them work.

Of course, the call to "professionalism" was, and often still is, a political strategy used by teachers to promote their employment inter-ests. But the use of this strategy is not unproblematic. For one thing, professionalism implies normalization and Cavanagh's research is crit-ical of the role played by the FW in policing teacher behaviors and assisting the state in defining, maintaining and regulating acceptable conduct for female teachers.[17] Professionalization also remains, at heart, a strategy of exclusion and boundary maintenance[18] which throws up a set of contradictory relations. For example, in the name of professionalism, the leadership of the FW supported enhanced credentials for the elementary teaching force. Whereas at one time young women could prepare for elementary teaching by entering one or two year programs at teachers' colleges immediately after leaving high school, by the 1960s the FW was calling for all elementary teachers to hold an undergraduate degree. Indeed, Dorothy Martin, the executive secretary of the FW from 1961-1973, is reported to have said that her most important contribution occurred when she was able to "overcome tremendous opposition" and present a recommendation to the Minister's Committee on the Training of Elementary School Teachers that all elementary teachers hold a baccalaureate,[19] a recommendation that was accepted as part of the Committee's final report (the MacLeod Report) in 1966 and ultimately implemented by the government in 1973.[20]

At the theoretical and political level, the decision to support degree-holding must be seen as a move to enhance the status of women teachers and strengthen their hand at the bargaining table by moving them more fully into the masculine realm of "reason" and "knowledge" and away from the feminine world of "emotion" and "caring."[21] And, of course, it is foolish to suggest that more education for teachers is a bad thing. But in the practical and concrete reality of the women teachers' world, this new, and retroactive, demand was neither uncomplicated nor accepted with total equanimity. Many teachers were resentful because they felt that their years of service were now being discounted and their competence questioned. They could not see how a university degree was going to make them better teachers, especially when many felt university courses contributed little to classroom teaching.[22] The need to attend night classes and summer school or take a leave of absence from teaching to complete a university degree also often placed financial hardships and new time demands on women, most of whom nonetheless began the long process of acquiring a degree. In the meantime, teachers who already held a degree often felt ostracized by those who did not and this two-tiering of the teaching force brought new tensions in relations among women teachers. Reva (ACPID248), for example, recounts situations where she felt some older teachers were "jealous" or "made fun" of her because she held a degree and they did not.

Divisions in the elementary teaching force can only have been further exacerbated when the official joint publication of the FW and the OPS, *The Educational Courier,* observed that, in tackling teacher education, the MacLeod Report got "to the roots of the crisis in Ontario's under-achieving school system." The Courier went on to assign credit for the changes to the federations, noting,

> It is primarily the work of Federation that saved the day for the schools in the face of hordes of teachers with Grade 13 or less and a year of teachers' college, certified by the Department and hired by the Boards because they were cheap.[23]

This is a rather astonishing condemnation by the leaders of their own members, most of whom were women. That the FW would go along with this only serves to emphasise the way in which the discourse of professionalism could work to create divisions among women teachers and between male and female teachers. Indeed, it is part and parcel of the same discourse which allowed men to criticize women teachers for their lack of professional commitment and construct males as the only true professionals.

Take, for example, the debate which ensued at the April, 1957 Provincial Assembly of the OPS after the executives of the FW and OPS had developed a one-salary policy for all elementary teachers in the public school system. One male teacher, J.B. Beckett, suggested to delegates that

> we should make up our minds whether or not we are professional men teachers. School boards are forcing us to discuss salaries in conjunction with women. This should not be so. We should be acting independently.[24]

In other words, to be a professional really meant to be a man. Delegate W. J. Redford revealed another, rather more self-interested dimension to this anti-woman sentiment. Voicing opposition to a one-salary policy, Redford observed, "When the teacher supply levels off, school boards will be willing to pay men more than women, and this proposal would prevent such an advantage from being accepted."[25] He went on to claim that women sabotage men's efforts at salary improvement, a position expressed by other male teachers who saw women as being too easily content with whatever salary they were paid and as willing to let the men fight all the battles. Because teachers tied improved salaries to professional status as part of their bargaining strategy, these claims about women further reinforced men's views of themselves as the real professionals with a lifelong commitment to school teaching.

However, the men's claim about the ease with which women accepted low salaries is belied by the long history of efforts by FW to achieve equal pay for equal work and by several outbreaks of women's militancy. In 1973, for example, when the government-commissioned Reville Report on Teacher Negotiations was released, Loren Lind, a reporter for the *Globe and Mail,* commented that the document had an "anti-teacher bias" but because the federations had already bought into a soft brand of professionalism and had opposed the right to strike, they could not and did not mount an effective response. The women teachers, he said, were the exception and were "the most caustic. They were able to call it plainly 'an anti-employee document' inspired by an attitude showing 'a kind of contempt for the rights of public employees'"[26] This outspoken, union-identified refusal of the Reville Report raises questions about why, and in what circumstances, female teachers throw off the constraints of conformity.

The disruption of the discourse of professionalism among women teachers occurred on other occasions, as well, when they made common cause with other workers, especially women workers. In 1982, when the provincial government introduced wage controls through Bill 179, *The Inflation Restraint Act*, the leadership of the FW was furious. The provincial president, Doris Harrison, a primary school teacher from London, speaking to a teachers' rally insisted,

> Any Bill that singles out one segment of the population and deprives them of the right to full and free collective bargaining is highly discriminatory and strikes against the fundamental human rights of that segment. It not only poses a threat to all society – but is particularly damaging to the lower and middle income bracket – many of whom are WOMEN [her emphasis]. Women teachers are ANGRY [her emphasis]. Wage controls without price controls are highly discriminatory, for the price controls are in effect flexible guidelines that do nothing to help pay the mortgage or heat the home.[27]

She concluded by promising that the 30 000 women teachers of Ontario "cannot and will not stand quietly by and witness the destruction of the democratic right to full and free collective bargaining."[28]

A month later, the FW made a presentation to the Justice Committee of the Ontario Legislature about Bill 179. Harrison introduced the teachers' brief by talking about the feelings of her membership and, in so doing, revealed what moved the women teachers to anger, an emotion that is, of course, seen as most unwomanly, and, indeed, unprofessional. Harrison began by acknowledging that her membership was "socially conservative," that it tended "to be trusting of governments," that it believed "that governments would act in the best interests of the people." But then she went on to warn that "governments forget at their peril that when people like us are betrayed, our anger is slow and deep and long-lasting." She went on to say,

> . . . I have been around this province for the last month, talking to teachers, and everywhere I have found the same thing. When they first heard about Bill 179, they thought it didn't sound really fair, but something has to be done about the economy, and maybe this is the price they should be willing to pay. But when they look at the Bill in detail, and when they find out who is covered by it and who is not covered by it – and when we talk about the real problems in the economy and the fact that this Bill is not going to solve them, then teachers begin to feel betrayed. And slowly their anger is growing. . . . When governments act cynically to play one group of workers off against another, to let private sector workers believe that public sector workers are fat cats, to try to palm off a piece of legislation that will hurt but will not help, then out there, out in the province where trust and sacrifice will be called for, there will be only cynicism and a sense of betrayal.[29]

What this example illustrates is the ability of the FW to shift from a professional to a unionist discourse, depending on the circumstances, and to name teachers as workers sharing a cause with other workers. Thus, at one and the same time there could be a denial of a union orientation but a claiming of union principles and practices, particularly when a stance of professionalism would militate against taking direct action on issues impinging on women teachers' rights, salaries and working conditions. This shift was, in all likelihood, encouraged by the fact that teachers won the right to collective bargaining and seized the right to strike in the mid-1970s. Activism around negotiations with school boards undoubtedly had something to do with changing a political consciousness about unionization. However, these shifts did not eliminate the commitment to and belief in professionalism, however fluidly understood. Think, for example, of Hannah's (ACPID 129) claims, cited earlier, about the one-day protest (in reality a wild cat strike) against Bills 274 and 275 in 1973 being "done in a very professional way."

If access to collective bargaining began to re-make attitudes towards unions, the women's movement and feminist activism also began to re-shape the politics of professionalism within the FW. The history of the marriage bar and subsequent events illustrate how women teachers changed their views about women and work and the nature of professionalism. When D.J. Baum delivered the final decision of the Ontario Human Rights Commission Board of Inquiry on the membership by-laws made under the TPA, he observed that historically the FW had been less an organization of women teachers and more one of single women teachers. After reviewing the archival documents for the period up to 1953, Baum concluded that "married women teachers were discriminated against *both by their employers and FWTAO*. The discrimination was pervasive. This was a form of job protection for the single woman teacher."[30] He was able to point to specific actions the FW had taken against married women in the 1930s and 1940s and this evidence weighed heavily against the FW's claim that it was a women's equality seeking organization and hence a "special program" protected under the Human Rights Code. Baum's position is, in fact, supported by Doris French who wrote the first history of the FW. As she said, "the FWTAO has not always been above reproach. It is not to their credit that they accepted married women reluctantly. . . ."[31] She also reports that in a 1961 survey about maternity leave, comments made by members of FW revealed the depth of the schism between single and married women teachers. "Why does the Federation encourage the married women with children to work? It's outrageous. No one can do two jobs well," one woman said. Another, revealing attitudes held over from the 1930s, observed, "No married women – except in exceptional cases – should be teaching now that there are single girls out of a position."[32] These comments were made in the same year the FW conducted a survey of rural women teachers and discovered that 71.3% were married and another 6.8% were widowed or divorced.[33]

Even when the FW had left behind any support for the marriage bar, its history as a single women teachers' organization lingered and was reflected in other ways. Certainly, as late as 1980 an FW pamphlet advising teachers how to get a job told married women with children they should include in their applications an explanation about how they intended to manage child care arrangements. Sample entries to guide teachers provided rather extensive detail:

> Married, one child 4 years of age – registered full time in Sunshine Nursery School; part-time housekeeper is in my home from 11:00 a.m. to 5:00 p.m. every week day.
>
> or
>
> Married – one child 2 years of age. My mother resides in our home and cares for the child.[34]

Teachers were further warned that they should "make it plain that you do expect to become a 'career', 'professional' teacher . . . your job commitment comes first, and personal commitments are kept outside of working hours." [emphasis in original][35] The message to women, especially those with children, is unmistakable. Professionalism requires putting the job first. Do not let the profession down by allowing the messiness of a personal life to intervene in the career setting. Here, again, a masculinist construction of professionalism emerges.

Yet, at the same time, the FW was supporting the women's movement and was active in equity campaigns, suggesting again that its history is alive with contradictions and complexities.

The London WTA, in its 1982 brief on Bill 179, made common cause with other women.

> Our concern extends beyond women in the teaching profession. Women comprise one-half of the labor force yet on average earn less than sixty percent of men's wages. According to the Equal Pay Coalition, wage controls will lock two million women into an unfair wage system. Some progress has been made to advance the concept of equal pay for work of equal value for men and women. This proposed legislation with its implied discrimination is indeed a regressive step.[36]

Judith (ACPID 023) explained how the FWTAO supported the women's movement.

> You see, I had become in, I think, '73, the Regional Convenor for the Status of Women Committee provincially, so my area was southwestern Ontario, and I met with colleagues in Toronto – there were five

of us. So we did a lot of things. We worked with, with Rosie Abella reforming the family property law, and we were lucky, we were the only women's group that had money, so all the things that happened, all, the formation of PFLAG [Parents and Families of Lesbians and Gays] and all that was the result of work I could do because of the money, see I could do all the mailings, I could, so in a way the Federation of Teachers played an absolutely pervasive influence around the province with any women's groups that were going, because the others didn't have money. Whether it was setting up a women's shelter or whatever, we were always called in because we could get, you know, yes, we can get money for mailings, yes, we can get, yes, we'll bring in a speaker, and I brought in all kinds of speakers, like Flora MacDonald and Judy LaMarsh and Laura Sabia.

Hannah (ACPID 129) also commented on the ways in which the FWTAO funded shelters for battered women and how women teachers always contributed money and goods to local shelters. She saw protecting mothers as a way of also protecting children but returned to the rhetoric of feminized professionalism by commenting, "I think that was one of the great things of Women's Federation. We were far more interested in the care of the children than we were in the care for teachers in lots of ways. But I don't think the public saw it that way, which was a shame. . . ."

Just as so many Federation activists struggled to avoid the unionist label so, too, did feminism present challenges to the ways in which women teachers saw themselves. Where Judith was committed to the women's movement and identified herself as a feminist working to eliminate structural inequities, Hannah quickly re-defined similar activities as "caring for children." Lee (ACPID 132), who accepted some of the feminist analysis of women's experience, claimed, however, that

> there were still some times when we'd go down to Toronto, come back and say, "No, no. Some of these issues are too strong for us." We can't, you can internalize them, but a lot of times you couldn't act upon it in the north in the small communities because you, it doesn't fit with that lifestyle.

Recognizing the realities of women teachers' lives, Lee also noted that many women could not get involved in the FW because "they were held back by their husbands" who opposed participation in "this women's militant group." Speaking of the 1970s and 1980s, Lee concluded,

> So that's the mentality that overflowed, not just sort of in the public generally but also into the school system and anything FW. If the male was (sigh) a male chauvinist in the family, then, then that woman suffered. Not physical abuse but this would be more emotional, I think.

As Lee suggests, teachers, like other women workers, had to negotiate the difficult terrain of gendered social relations in the workplace and in domestic arrangements but her refusal to acknowledge physical abuse by a husband as a possibility in teachers' lives is telling. The ascendancy of a discourse of professionalism that initially saw a rupture between marriage and work and later in the twentieth century urged a separation between the concerns of work and home, militated against a recognition that the personal was also political in teachers' lives. Teachers helped other women who needed to escape to shelters, but as white, middle-class professionals earning independent incomes, they did not collectively tend to acknowledge domestic violence as a factor in their own private lives.

The introduction by the provincial FW of affirmative action policies as a strategy to get more women teachers into administration presents another example of ambivalence about feminism. Gina (ACPID195) was clear that she "wanted to know that if I got a position, I got it because I earned it." Beth (ACPID 227) remembered the challenges which confronted her.

> I became president of Women Teachers' Federation at a time when affirmative action came into being. And I hardly knew anything about affirmative action and here I was president of a, of an association, a large association of women and how to introduce the concept to them which was very challenging because most women, most women teachers were very against affirmative action. They had the American model which was bra burners and hate men. And they really had difficulty with it and they were very challenging sometimes in comments and behaviors and, and so on.

Deborah (ACPID157) also commented on the challenges she received from women teachers who argued that all the FW did was talk about women's issues when there was far more to teaching than that. Deborah observed, however, that many women teachers would say, "'I'm not a feminist. I'm for equal opportunity' or 'I'm a humanist' or

'I'm no women's libber but . . . " and then they would go on to explain their feminist philosophy even though they didn't know they had one."

Like all organizations, the FW had its internal struggles about the role it should play and what its goals and objectives should be. Women from different political backgrounds and regions of the province, working in different social circumstances across a variety of decades, debated the meaning of professionalism and supported or eschewed unionism and feminism. Large numbers of women teachers saw the wisdom and utility of a women's federation, while many others did not. However, the Federation of Women Teachers' Associations of Ontario is often named as a strong example of the benefits of women's separate organizing where separate organizing is viewed as "the strategic reflection of gender significance and specificity."[37] Linda Briskin, Canada's leading scholar on the question of women's organizing, speaks positively about the success of the FW as "a strong feminist voice both for women teachers and in the women's move-ment" and suggests that the FW has effectively balanced autonomy with integration into the wider world of teacher unions.[38] As Briskin sees it,

> The structural location of the FWTAO is key to its strength. It is both autonomous from other teachers' unions – a fully separate union – and integrated as an equal member into the larger umbrella structures such as OTF [Ontario Teachers' Federation]. It has equal status at the bargaining table with the OPSTF; that is, they bargain together, but as two separate autonomous units. This degree of autonomy produces not only a degree of legitimacy– FWTAO is seen as a force with which to contend – but also a strong voice to repre-sent the specific concerns of women teachers in the primary sector [i.e., elementary schools].[39]

These observations are not, however, quite as straightforward nor as unproblematic as they seem at first blush. How did the FW con-struct and interpret the "specific concerns of women teachers"? The FW's earlier stance on married women teachers, especially those with children, resulted in differential treatment and, I think, we can argue that the FW's emphasis on careerism and professionalism, and the ten-dency to what was often a fairly blunt or crude liberal feminist analy-sis at best, also throw up questions about the nature of the FW's sep-arate organizing in practice. For example, as Hoover's research points out, some collective agreements negotiated by mixed sex unions contained better provisions for maternity and family leaves than those negotiated for Ontario public elementary teachers.[40] This forces us to consider a negotiating paradox for in some cases, a traditional, conservative, or even a so-called "family values" stance at the bargaining table will result in better actual conditions with respect to maternity and family leaves for women. The grounding assumptions about women's roles are reactionary and intended to reinforce the "naturalness" of mothering, but the lived result is better for women teachers with children in the short term.

Separate organizing also raises the problem of over-identification as women. Historically, the FW saw its members as gendered but gave little regard to ethnicity, race, class or sexuality; that is, the tendency was to see women teachers as an homogenous group and to focus on an essential woman in opposition to the "other," namely man. This is not surprising for a federation of women teachers who felt frequently, and correctly, that male teachers were seeking amalgamation in order to access the larger resources of the women's federation and control the women teachers. Furthermore, in elementary teaching, women experienced the sexual division of labor on a daily basis and lived with the fact that women taught and men managed. But the over-identification of women teachers as women also led to a neglect or forgetfulness about women's other identities and to an image of the FW as a white, middle-class organization.

One story highlights the kind of very troubling questions that must be put to the work of the FW. In the mid-1990s the Federation passed an affirmative action policy with respect to their own governance, specifying the number of seats to be held by visible minority women (one out of six for each region of the province), thereby finally recognizing the need to take account of differences. Commenting on this action, Vanessa (ACPID 249), who had served as a president of the FW in the early 1970s, said, there are "not enough of the Anglo-Saxon and European left anymore." She then added, "I suppose I dislike policies at any level which show 'favoritism.' People should 'rise' because of their ability and skills." Ironically, this is exactly what was said by those who opposed the affirmative action policies of the FW and the Ministry of Education designed to increase the numbers of women in educational administration. To what extent can we say that for the FW, women could be female but could not lay claim to other identities?

The over-identification as women, and the focus on separateness, can also be seen as contributing to a deficit model of organizing founded on the belief that being more like men would produce equality. Many of the FW's programs for women were in keeping with a liberal feminist approach and hinged on efforts to improve self-esteem, develop women's assertiveness, and enhance individual skills in areas such as parliamentary procedure. Teachers who can recall Federation offerings beyond professional development activities do remember workshops "teaching me to be aggressive" or those on leadership. This is probably because what was often most visible were actions linked to efforts to increase the number of women in administration. Regular classroom teachers seemed remarkably unaware of the work of their own federation with respect to matters such as pensions and maternity benefits and even when experiencing employment difficulties do not always appear to have called on the Federation for help. Even someone like Brianna (ACPID 245), who was a strong supporter of and actively involved in the FW at the local level, did not ask for help when she found she was being under-paid as a result of a mix-up with her qualifications. There is a suggestion here that the FW narrowed its vision to the "separate" and, as is all too often the case with unions, neglected the "organizing" in its own constituency. This might help explain why, when the end came for FW, there was remarkably little outcry from the rank and file. By positioning the women against the men and emphasising this dynamic, the FW had ignored both internal differences and the coherent analysis and educational work necessary to assist women teachers in developing a deeper understanding of the strengths of separate, autonomous structures and a consciousness of themselves as gendered subjects.

Furthermore, there appears to be a long history of accepting the inevitability of the eventual demise of the FW. French recounts a partial history of the debates about amalgamation and demonstrates that as early as the 1930s even some FW leaders felt uncertain about the need for a separate organization. She quotes Etta Lane, the FW president from 1933-35, who felt that, "So many problems would be handled more efficiently by the united efforts of all."[41] In contrast, Florence Irvine, the president from 1958-59, "accused the FWTAO of a 'disgusting ambivalence' on the question [of amalgamation], warning that such a move would 'undermine the original and tenaciously held objectives . . . to further the welfare and interests of women teachers'."[42] French, herself, believed, "It is almost bound to happen, at some future Annual Meeting, that well-intentioned women teachers, to prove that they are neither old maids nor feminists, will vote to amalgamate with their male colleagues."[43] One FW activist, who later became a provincial president, predicted the demise of the FW in the early 1960s and reported that the senior leadership agreed with her but explained to her that the FW strategy was to delay the inevitable.

Many women leaders in the FW, however, resisted amalgamation and saw benefits for women in having their own organization. For Beth (ACPID 227) the local WTA offered new challenges when she reached a level in the school system where there was no more potential for personal growth and promotion. Caroline (ACPID 125) observed that in her day, the WTA "was the only place where women could really exercise their brain power, and not be, not worry about being quoted" or put down because they were smart. Genevieve (ACPID136), who became a very senior administrator in a school system, acknowledged that the Federation offered women experiences they would not otherwise have had. She noted that being on a WTA executive helped "to give them [women] exposure and to give them opportunities to meet people in the system, and to help them to develop leadership skills and to make them more confident." Gail (ACPID 133) became an acting vice-principal twice but got no training, which was not a problem she said, "because I had my leadership through the Federation." Noting that she had once been a "mild, meek person," Gail now boasted that she had changed and was prepared to speak up for herself. She and Beth both felt that young women teachers abandoned the FW because they did not understand that the rights they took for granted – maternity leaves, advancement opportunities, a well-funded retirement – were the result of decades of struggle by the women's federation. Of course, this begs the question: Why did young women not understand the benefits of belonging to the FW?

When the FW disappeared in 1998 and the women and men elementary teachers established a new union, the Elementary Teachers' Federation of Ontario, many of the female teachers who had been activists and leaders in the women's federation in the last three decades of the twentieth-century mourned the loss of their organization. Caroline (ACPID 125) described her feelings in this way: "I was devastated. I was so sad. I cried. I must say I was angry. I'll admit I cried for half a day." She regretted the loss of the FW because "for the group of women in my cohort, that was our only opportunity to learn leadership skills externally, and to work in the big picture, as opposed to being a leader in the home. That was our only opportunity to start that, working for the federation."

When Hannah (ACPID 129) heard that the FW would no longer be a separate organization for women, she

> felt dreadful, felt very hurt and upset, and I felt frustrated because I felt they just don't know what they're letting themselves in for. You know, I felt they'd suffer in the end and I feel in some ways they have. I've had more than one teacher complain to me and say, "Gee, you know, things are not the way they used to be."

Although it has now been several years since the FW ceased operations, Deborah (ACPID 157) claims "my heart still aches that it's not there today." This is a sentiment that was echoed over and over again. Even many of the women who had come to believe that some form of amalgamation was inevitable were troubled and upset at the loss of a strong, separate women's organization.

Throughout its eighty year history, the FW had provided a structure that allowed women teachers to exercise some control over their working lives. It provided an independent voice for women teachers and an opportunity for them to negotiate on their own behalf and work in concert with and for other women. However, within their organization, women struggled with one another over the role of their Federation and their contradictory identities as women, as teachers, and as women teachers. They sought to make meaning within and against the dominant discourses of professionalism and gender. Ultimately, the FW provided a setting for many women teachers to define and re-define their subjectivities and engage with the political and social questions which inevitably shaped the lives of all classroom teachers.

Notes

[1]See, for example, Alison Prentice, "Themes in the Early History of the Women Teachers' Association of Toronto," in *Women's Paid and Unpaid Work: Historical and Contemporary Perspectives,* ed. Paula Bourne, 97-121 (Toronto: New Hogtown Press, 1985); Harry Smaller, "'A Room of One's Own': The Early Years of the Toronto Women Teachers' Association," in *Gender and Education in Ontario,* eds. Ruby Heap and Alison Prentice, 105-126 (Toronto: Canadian Scholars' Press, 1991); Wendy E. Bryans, "'Virtuous Women at Half the Price': The Feminization of the Teaching Force and Early Women Teachers' Organizations in Ontario" (MA thesis, University of Toronto, 1974); Apolonja M. Kojder, "The Saskatoon Women Teachers' Association" (MEd thesis, University of Saskatchewan, 1976); Apolonja M. Kojder, "The Saskatoon Women Teachers' Association: A Demand for Recognition," *Saskatchewan History 30* (1977): 63-74; Apolonja M. Kojder, "In Union There is Strength: The Saskatoon Women Teachers' Association," *Canadian Woman Studies/Les cahiers de la femme 7* (1986): 82-84; Mary Kinnear, "'Mostly for the male members': Teaching in Winnipeg, 1933-1966," *Historical Studies in Education 6* (1994): 1-20. See, for England, Sarah King, "Feminists in Teaching: The National Union of Women Teachers, 1920-1945," in *Women Who Taught: Perspectives on the History of Women and Teaching,* eds. Alison Prentice and Marjorie R. Theobald, 182-201 (Toronto: University of Toronto Press, 1991). For an example from Australia, see Kay Whitehead, "'Many Industrial Troubles Are Due to the Presence of Female Labour': The Women Teachers Guild in South Australia, 1937-42," *Historical Studies in Education 8* (1996): 25-41.

[2]Bertha Adkins, "Federation of Women Teachers' Associations of Ontario" *The School* VII (April 1919): 535.

[3]Following the formation of the FW in 1918, public secondary school teachers founded the Ontario Secondary School Teachers' Federation (OSSTF) in 1919 and male public elementary school teachers set up the Ontario Public School Men Teachers' Federation (OPSMTF) in 1920. The OPSMTF later dropped the "men" from its name to become the OPSTF. These three federations, along with the Ontario English Catholic Teachers' Association (OECTA) which represented anglophone elementary and secondary teachers in the publicly funded Roman Catholic schools and the Association des enseignantes et des enseignants franco-ontariens which represented teachers in the francophone schools, were the five affiliates that combined under the umbrella of the Ontario Teachers' Federation as set out in *The Teaching Profession Act, 1944.*

[4]The membership case alleging discrimination on the basis of sex was initiated by a woman named Margaret Couture, later Tomen, with the support of the OPS. For this reason it is often called the Tomen case. For background see, Mary Eberts, Florence Henderson, Kathleen Lahey, Catherine MacKinnon, Sheila McIntyre and Elizabeth Shilton, *The Case for Women's Equality: The Federation of*

Women Teachers' Associations of Ontario and the Canadian Charter of Rights and Freedoms (Toronto: FWTAO, 1991). See, also, D. J. Baum, *Final Decision, Board of Inquiry in the Matter of a Complaint Made by Margaret Tomen and Linda Logan-Smith* (Toronto: Ontario Human Rights Commission, 1994).

[5]The three in-house histories are Doris French, *High Button Bootstraps: Federation of Women Teachers' Associations of Ontario, 1918-1968* (Toronto: Ryerson Press, 1968); Pat Staton and Beth Light, *Speak With Their Own Voices* (Toronto: FWTAO, 1987); Mary Labatt, *Always a Journey: A History of the Federation of Women Teachers' Associations of Ontario, 1918-1993* (Toronto: FWTAO, 1993). See, also, Rebecca Coulter, "Gender Equity and Schooling: Linking Research and Policy," *Canadian Journal of Education 21* (1996): 433-452; Hanne Mawhinney, "Institutionalizing Women's Voices, Not Their Echoes, Through Feminist Policy Analysis of Difference," in *Feminist Critical Policy Analysis: A Perspective from Primary and Secondary Schooling,* ed. Catherine Marshall, 216-238 (London: Falmer Press, 1997).

[6]Royal Commission on the Status of Women in Canada, *Report of the Royal Commission on the Status of Women in Canada* (Ottawa: Information Canada, 1970).

[7]See, French, *High Button Bootstraps;* Staton and Light, *Speak With Their Own Voices;* Labatt, *Always a Journey;* Coulter, "Gender Equity"; Nancy Adamson, Linda Briskin and Margaret McPhail, *Feminist Organizing for Change: The Contemporary Women's Movement in Canada* (Toronto: Oxford University Press, 1988); Jill Vickers, Pauline Rankin and Christine Appelle, *Politics As If Women Mattered: A Political Analysis of the National Action Committee on the Status of Women* (Toronto: University of Toronto Press, 1993); Judy Rebick, *Ten Thousand Roses: The Making of a Feminist Revolution* (Toronto: Penguin Canada, 2005).

[8]Frances Sawaya, *Modern Women, Modern Work: Domesticity, Professionalism, and American Writing, 1890-1950* (Philadelphia: University of Pennsylvania Press, 2004), 10.

[9]Kathleen Weiler, "Reflections on Writing a History of Women Teachers," in *Telling Women's Lives: Narrative Inquiries in the History of Women's Education,* eds. Kathleen Weiler and Sue Middleton (Buckingham and Philadelphia: Open University Press, 1999), 43.

[10]Cynthia Cockburn quoted in Pamela Sugiman, *Labour's Dilemma: The Gender Politics of Auto Workers in Canada, 1937-1979* (Toronto: University of Toronto Press, 1994), 3. Ehical and political dilemmas similar to the ones I raise are discussed in Michelle Fine, Lois Weis, Susan Weseen and Loonmun Wong, "For Whom? Qualitative Research, Representations, and Social Responsibilities," in *The Handbook of Qualitative Research,* eds. Norman K. Denzin and Yvonne S. Lincoln, 107-131 (Thousand Oaks: Sage, 2000).

[11]See, for example, Pat Armstrong, "Professions, Unions, Or What? Learning From Nurses," in *Women Challenging Unions: Feminism, Democracy and*

Militancy, eds. Linda Briskin and Patricia McDermott, 304-321 (Toronto: University of Toronto Press, 1993); Kathryn McPherson, *Bedside Matters: The Transformation of Canadian Nursing, 1900-1990* (Toronto: University of Toronto Press, 2003).

[12]Loren Lind, "Judge Reville and Ontario Teachers," *This Magazine is About Schools 6* (Winter 1972-73): 23-24.

[13]Federation of Women Teachers' Associations of Ontario, *Professionalism: The Heart of the Matter* (Toronto: FWTAO, 1981).

[14]Sawaya, *Modern Women, Modern Work.*

[15]Bills 274 and 275 were introduced in 1973 by the Progressive Conservative government under Premier Bill Davis and were designed to restrict the use of mass resignations as a bargaining strategy, deny access to collective bargaining and introduce compulsory arbitration. As a result of the teachers' protest rally, the largest to that date ever held in Ontario, the bills were withdrawn, and in 1975, the government introduced *The School Boards and Teachers Collective Negotiations Act* which gave teachers full collective bargaining rights. See Stephen B. Lawton, George Bedard, Duncan MacLellan and Xiaobin Li, *Teachers' Unions in Canada* (Calgary: Detselig, 1999), 31-32.

[16]For a fuller discussion of these issues see, for example, R.D. Gidney and W.P.J. Millar, *Professional Gentlemen: The Professions in Nineteenth-Century Ontario* (Toronto: University of Toronto Press, 1994); Anne Witz, *Professions and Patriarchy* (London and New York: Routledge, 1992); Sawaya, *Modern Women, Modern Work;* Sandra Acker, *Gendered Education: Sociological Reflections on Women, Teaching and Feminism* (Toronto: OISE Press, 1994), especially part 2; Elizabeth Smyth, Sandra Acker, Paula Bourne and Alison Prentice, eds., *Challenging Professions: Historical and Contemporary Perspectives on Women's Professional Work* (Toronto: University of Toronto Press, 1999).

[17]Sheila Cavanagh, "The Heterosexualization of the Ontario Woman Teacher in the Postwar Period," *Canadian Woman Studies 18* (Spring 1998), 65-69; Sheila L. Cavanagh, "The Gender of Professionalism and Occupational Closure: The Management of Tenure-related Disputes by the Federation of Women Teachers' Associations of Ontario, 1918-1949," *Gender and Education 15* (2003), 39-57. See, also, her chapters in this book.

[18]Witz, *Professions and Patriarchy.*

[19]Edward Lynas, "L. Dorothy Martin," *The Educational Courier 44* (October, 1973), 16- 17.

[20]R.D. Gidney, *From Hope to Harris: The Reshaping of Ontario's Schools* (Toronto: University of Toronto Press, 1999).

[21]For a fuller discussion of feminist theory in this regard see, Jo-Anne Dillabough, "Gender Politics and Conceptions of the Modern Teacher: Women,

Identity and Professionalism," *British Journal of Sociology of Education* 20 (1999): 373-394.

[22]This is a recurring theme in the oral interviews. See, also, *Educational Studies Committee, A Survey of the Problems of Female Rural Elementary School Teachers in Ontario, 1960-61* (Toronto: FWTAO, 1961), 108. A similar observation is made for Britain in Philip Gardner, "Reconstructing the Classroom Teacher, 1903-1945," in *Silences and Images: The Social History of the Classroom,* eds. Ian Grosvenor, Martin Lawn and Kate Rousmaniere, 123-144 (New York: Peter Lang, 1999).

[23]Quoted in French, *High Button Bootstraps*, 154.

[24]Quoted in R.A. Hopkins, *The Long March: History of the Ontario Public Men Teachers' Federation* (Toronto: Baxter Publishing, 1969), 209.

[25]Ibid.

[26]Lind, "Judge Reville and Ontario Teachers," 23.

[27]Doris Harrison, "Address to the Teachers' Rally Opposing Wage Controls, 21 September 1982," in personal collection of Doris Harrison; copy of the original held by author.

[28]Ibid.

[29]Doris Harrison, "President Accuses Government of Creating Social Unrest," *FWTAO Bulletin, 4* (1982-83), 1. Reprinted by the Ontario Secondary School Teachers' Federation as Doris Harrison, "A Lesson for the Legislature: 'Teachers Are Slowly Becoming Angry'," Federation Update 10, no. 5 (25 October 1982), 1.

[30]Baum, *Final Decision,* 189-90.

[31]French, *High Button Bootstraps,* 133.

[32]French, *High Button Bootstraps,* 133-34.

[33]Educational Studies Committee, *A Survey,* 31.

[34]Federation of Women Teachers' Associations of Ontario, *Getting a Teaching Position* (Toronto, FWTAO, 1980), 10.

[35]FWTAO, *Getting a Teaching Position,* 18.

[36]"WTAs Stand Firm," *FWTAO Bulletin 4* (1982-83), 4.

[37]Linda Briskin and Patricia McDermott, "The Feminist Challenge to the Unions," in *Women Challenging Unions, eds. Briskin and McDermott,* 13.

[38]Linda Briskin, "Union Women and Separate Organizing," in *Women Challenging Unions,* eds. Briskin and McDermott, 104.

[39]Ibid.

[40]Barbara Hoover, "Reflections of Women Teachers' Careers in Their Collective Agreements" (M.Ed Directed Research Project, University of Western Ontario, 1994).

[41] Quoted in French, *High Button Bootstraps,*129.

[42] Quoted in French, *High Button Bootstraps,* 130.

[43] French, *High Button Bootstraps,* 205

Section Three
Perils and Pleasures

Department of Education, Ontario

JUNE, 1919

SECOND CLASS PROFESSIONAL EXAMINATION

NORMAL SCHOOLS

HISTORY

1. (*a*) Give a series of topics on pioneer life, suitable for a Form II class.

(*b*) Write the matter of one of these topics as you wonld give it to a class.

2. (*a*) Describe your method of conducting a review lesson in Form III on *either* "The Discovery of America" *or* "The Capture of Quebec, 1759."

(*b*) Make the blackboard summary which should appear at the end of the lesson.

3. Explain fully and definitely your method of using the authorized text book on English History in Form IV.

4. Outline your plan of a lesson with a Form IV class on *one* of the followiug :—

(*a*) The work of Jacques Cartier.

(*b*) The Fathers of Confederation.

(*c*) The Norman Conquest.

(*d*) The Reform Bill of 1832.

5. (*a*) Give reasons why civics should be emphasized in our schools.

(*b*) How would you conduct a lesson on the Municipal elections?

(*c*) When would you teach such a lesson?

9

Nervous Narratives: Female Teacher Maladies in the Twentieth Century

Sheila L. Cavanagh

I had been around the bend three times, and quite literally, very crazy and in the psychiatric ward and taking heavy duty drugs and shock treatment, the whole bit. So with this in my history, I knew I was approaching the edge, so I quit [teaching]. A very sad ending to a career that was never marked by remarkable success actually. At my best, I was competent and there were little pockets here and there of something better than that, you know (ACPID 066).

Overcrowding in London's Elementary Schools. *Photo courtesy of The University of Western Ontario Archives, London Free Press Collection,Sept. 7, 1945.*

Feminist historiography has yet to focus upon the female teacher who was less than the sanctified professional ideal of quiet competency, cognitive rationality, and social diplomacy. Questions are rarely asked by feminist historians about female teacher nervous breakdowns, and their associated maladies. The idea that female teachers could have been anything but virtuous and emotionally sound is counter-intuitive to those who put the teacher upon a pedestal. Feminist historians who wish to depict the female teacher as professional par excellence (and endeavor to protect her from negative press) choose not to write about her rendezvous with madness. Although female teachers suffering from nervous strain, anxiety and a host of other psychological ailments were most certainly a minority, important questions must be asked about their presumed gender comportment, their relation to prescribed moral codes governing socially acceptable feminine conduct, and their relationship to the institutions of heterosexuality and motherhood in the post-war period.

School administrators including principals and trustees, inspectors, superintendents of education, federation representatives, parents and other concerned parties in the Ontario educational context used psychology and mental hygiene literature to make sense of individual teacher maladies but little is known about the gendered designation of madness in Ontario education. Despite the fact that mid-twentieth century popular culture was replete with images of the female teacher as nervous Nelly, as thwarted spinster, as tyrannical disciplinarian, as socially awkward, and vulnerable to melancholic reclusiveness, little has been done to interpret these images in the Canadian educational context.

It is evident that psychological studies and educational reports tend to construct teacher personality maladjustment and nervous tension as a predominantly female disorder. This is, in part, because the vast majority of teachers at this historical juncture were women. It is also because there was a strong cultural association between women and madness in North American culture[1] in the nineteenth and twentieth-century. A good example of the gendered character of madness in European culture can be found in the genesis of the word hysteria. Hysteria (most often associated with early twentieth century nervous conditions in North America) was derived from the ancient Greek word for uterus[2] investing it with a feminine connotation. Although hysteria came to be a more generic term in the modern period – no longer tied exclusively to the female reproductive organ – women continued to be the most frequent "clients for private and public psychiatric hospitals, outpatient mental health services, and psychotherapy"[3] throughout the twentieth century.

This chapter reveals what I am calling the "nervous narratives" of women teachers. I consider what official and testimonial accounts of madness tell us about how female teacher social subjectivity was understood in the mid-twentieth century, an historical period that began to relax its moral prohibitions on teacher marriage and motherhood. I am not concerned with what these narratives reveal about the psychology of individual teachers, but with the social and historical construction of female madness in the mid-twentieth century educational context.[4] As cultural historian Peter Logan writes in his discussion of nervous narratives in social criticism, there is a "linkage between nervous bodies and social conditions . . . [which like] a canary in a mine shaft . . . [sing a] warning song."[5] In other words, nervous bodies and their associated narratives "expose unresolvable conflicts within the existing social order"[6] and say much about the social conditions that produce the emotional trauma the nervous body acts out. Maladies have been associated with female voicelessness and lack of power in dominant societal institutions. For example, feminist scholar Shoshana Felman argues that hysteria is a manifestation of the "impasse confronting those whom cultural conditioning has deprived of the very means of protest or self-affirmation" and so I suggest that the various teacher maladies illustrated in this chapter be read as a culturally and historically specific response to life and work as teacher.[7]

Rendezvous With Madness: A Case Study

Emma Swanson (a pseudonym) was a single, middle-aged, female teacher who graduated from a provincial normal school in 1935 with an interim second class certificate. According to the Department of Education reports, she had a highly varied and mobile career leading her to serve in at least six different schools in Roman Catholic Separate school systems. One inspector commented on her various housing arrangements in one, particular, school district:

During 1947-48 she has boarded in three different homes and boarded herself from Nov. 1-17th in a cottage. [She] left her first boarding house . . . because she "Can't stand that woman [with whom she lived because] she gossips" . . . [The teacher said] she can live cheaper in a cottage. She found the cottage too lonesome and begged [another woman of the community] to board her . . . [She then] quarreled very bitterly with [her new house-mate] over some remark made at the supper table relative to nuns or convents. [Shortly thereafter she moved out and into another living situation with a third woman who] speaks of her as a fine girl and is willing to board her in September.[8]

There is no evidence to suggest that this teacher sought to attain a permanent second class certificate although she did have notable expertise in physical training and agriculture. Her inspector reports were far from stellar but she was getting by until February 14, 1948. On this day, she received a sarcastic valentine from one of her pupils which was (according to the inspector report to the Department of Education) meant to embarrass and mock Swanson. The valentine read as follows: "With your voice and my Celery, we can't be beet"[9] (salary and beat were spelled as if they were vegetables). The teacher, clearly agitated and disturbed by the valentine, wrote an angry (and paranoid) letter to the child in response:

Send this valentine to Father . . [the district priest]. It will make him happy. The pupils in Protestant schools are not allowed to insult the teacher. They know better. The Catholics are too ignorant. Do not spend your weekends in impurity. I know who you people are – nothing but dirt and the essence of it. With the Principal, Staff, and Inspector running on me and picking at me, the pupils are following their example.[10]

The troubled teacher wrote a second letter to an area ratepayer accusing him of conspiring to dismiss her after she had received the valentine:

You were paid well to get me to leave the school, so you can go now and get your money. You can sport some money from the Catholic Church. It will suit you fine because you are so mean and low-lived . . . [Referring to a student who was suspended Emma Swanson wrote] you wanted him to run on me and torment me . . . Then you put that mean sneak of a daughter of yours up to come and tell all the other children to go into the basement and smoke me out. The teacher later accused her principal of sending the boy [who was suspended] to her room to torment me.[11]

She later insisted in another letter to the Department of Education that her "services as teacher were perfectly satisfactory until the valentine came, and that is why they [the School Board] threw me out, and it was not I who sent it."[12] Swanson later admitted that she had reacted badly to the boy's message in the pseudo love-letter (referring to her angry and paranoid response in the above quoted letters) but explained that the "sarcastic valentine vexed me so badly, that I scarcely knew what I was saying or writing."[13]

After being contacted by the secretary-treasurer of the school board that employed Swanson, the Ontario Teachers' Federations (OTF) asked the teacher to resign. The OTF Relations Committee also requested that she submit a psychiatric report. Inspector reports attesting to the teacher's erratic work habits and un-agreeable manner were reviewed by the Department of Education. One inspector commented in detail on her manner of dress and on the awkward interpersonal relations Swanson had with pupils, teachers, parents and her principal. Focusing on her dress, the inspector wrote: she "dressed in a manner that was very noticeable. To be quite frank she looked like a scarecrow. The pupils called her an old witch, and openly ridiculed her throughout the section. I never heard these remarks myself as the children didn't say such things during my presence."[14] The Inspector also wrote that Swanson was neurotic and suffering from what he thought to be a "persecution complex." He felt it was appropriate to comment on her personal appearance, her manner of dress and personal hygiene. The Inspector wrote that she was "very untidy . . . Her landlady told me that during the year she hadn't used as much as one pail of water for washing. That isn't very much water for a ten month period. It is quite possible her landlady was correct for . . . [she] carried with her an offensive odour."[15] To complete the portrait, another inspector described the troubled teacher as neurotic, erratic, visibly noticeable with respect to her manner of dress, witchlike and not unlike the popular caricature of the scarecrow.

In this nervous narrative there was an association between female teacher gender identity, beauty and madness. That a life-long single female teacher could be so vexed by what many in the period would regard an innocent schoolboy prank must be understood in relation to mid-twentieth-century ideas about the sexually thwarted and maladjusted gender identity of the spinster. The marriage bans, which were enforced in many Ontario rural districts right through the 1950s, coupled with the not so subtle (and unflattering) caricature of the maiden lady teacher, produced the conditions in which it was possible to over-react to an otherwise benign valentine. The single career teacher lived with the societal construction of the melancholic, slightly laughable and pathetic spinster-like image that permeated educational culture and some were deeply troubled by it.

The single female teacher could have escaped public speculation about her gender and sexual identity development were it not for the writings of Sigmund Freud suggesting that even the unmarried – supposedly celibate – woman was a sexual being. Prior to the international circulation of Freudian psychoanalytic writing about female sexuality, it was customary to regard the spinster as asexual: as a "prim model of sobriety and diligence."[16] Freudian ideas about female psycho-sexual development challenged public perception of spinsters by investing everyday mundane activities with sexual significance. Everyone (including children) were sexual beings in the psychoanalytic schemata and even a seemingly benign gesture – including a choice of career as teacher – suggested repressed sexual wishes, displaced or sublimated desire. The choice of becoming a teacher was, therefore, sexually significant. As a result, innuendo and speculation abounded about the nature of female teacher sexuality and its accompanying maladjustments in academe, professional circles, and at the level of community folklore.

Speaking about the psychological community, Mini Carson confirms that "popular sociology and culture in the war years and afterward [reflect] ... the fear that women's wartime independence and responsibilities might release a dangerous female sexuality that would corrupt American family life."[17] The concern about undomesticated female sexuality, also, led to a concern about the accomplishment of femininity, a marker of normal psychosexual development, and a curiosity about the gender of the female who deviated from traditionally defined feminine social scripts. This concern was especially evident in an Ontario article published in a teachers' professional magazine in 1939. The author worried about the educational system being increasingly dominated by "man-hating" and "overly-aggressive women" and feared that such teachers would educate a generation of "sissy men."[18]

A journalist with *Macleans,* a popular Canadian magazine, spoke candidly about what he referred to as the "Ichabod Crane concept of the schoolmarm." He repeated the legend which had by then reached mythical proportions in educational folklore about the "little boy ... who, when asked to name the sexes, said: male, female and school-teacher."[19] A similar fable was repeatedly told about the young boy who said: "that lady looks kind of queer, mamma; is she a school-teacher? No, Jimmy, she's just seasick!"[20] These colloquial tales are based on ambivalence about the societal restrictions placed on the lives and activities of female teachers but, more importantly, they signal to a belief about the single female teacher and her gender augmentation.

The failure to marry was sometimes understood to be a grave social misfortune predisposing women to neurasthenia, hysterical outbursts and untold emotional turmoil. For example, a Canadian professor at Mount Allison University stated that there are two general kinds of teacher: "teachers and time-servers (those who are using teaching as a means of getting to some other profession, and those waiting to get married.) You rarely hear of anyone in the latter class having a nervous breakdown, but among the former it is common enough to be alarming."[21] In an often quoted study of 700 maladjusted school teachers in the US, the principal investigator concluded that "although the state of being unmarried is not a cause of the psychosis [studied], it is a potent factor in that it leads to a realization that one is in some respect inadequate to meet the social situation."[22]

Cautions about female teacher undesirability to heterosexual men given by John Sullivan, professor of educational psychology at Wayne University, suggested a correlation between teacher physical appearance and mental health. He urged women in the profession to be concerned with comprtment and appearance.

> Clothes that are drab and colourless, hair poorly or uninterestingly done, body odour or offensive breath, do not serve to attract children to us. Our tone of voice or the way in which we speak may have considerable bearing upon teacher-pupil relationships. A loud, rasping

voice not only tires the listener, but serves to drive him away from us.[23]

Other articles printed in *The Educational Courier* on teacher beauty suggested that a solid mental outlook is established by the purchase of "smart clothes and [the use of] a good beauty parlor."[24] Too often the teacher's "frock was dark and shapeless; her collar tight and high; her shoes broad and unimaginative. Her nose was long and pinched at the end; her eyes small and deep-set; her lips narrow and severe."[25] This caricature of the dowdy and unattractive spinster was central to the narrative construction of the, allegedly, maladjusted spinster who was emotionally shaken by the aforementioned sarcastic valentine.

Teacher accommodation was identified by mental hygienists, in the early and mid-twentieth century, to be relevant to mental health. For example, Doctor James Rogers, Chief of the Division of Physical Education and School Hygiene for Washington, wrote that "good houses can not always be rented, and in 'boarding around' the single teacher does not in many communities find conditions such as to keep her physically or mentally trim for her best work, and she is likely to 'move on' as soon as she can do so."[26] Ontario female teachers reported a connection between living accommodations and nervous tension. For example, one female teacher wrote to the Department of Education that she was "not hard to please but liked a quiet place and would rather not board where there are children of school age ... a comfortable boarding house is half the battle in teaching school."[27] In this instance, the teacher could not locate a place to board without school-age children and, as a result, resigned saying that she was a "bundle of nerves." In her letter of resignation addressed to the secretary-treasurer of the school board she wrote: "my nerves could not stand it [the boarding house]. I am not a very healthy person and inclined to be nervous."[28]

Professional Responses to Complaints about Female Teacher Mental Health

It is difficult to ascertain the number of teachers suffering from nervous anxiety, psychological turmoil, and other ailments associated with madness and so it is difficult to know how common mental breakdowns – like the one had by Emma Swanson – are in Ontario's educational history. Statistics on teacher mental health were not assembled by teachers' organizations in the mid-twentieth century and individual cases tended to be surrounded by a cloak of silence at the professional level. Teacher organizations like the Federation of Women Teachers' Associations of Ontario (FWTAO) dealt with cases related to mental health by encouraging the teacher to resign or to apply for early retirement; by assisting the school board in launching procedures necessary for dismissal; and by encouraging sick-leave. As a matter of course, the FWTAO would recommend suspension of the teacher's license until the disenfranchised member could produce a report from a psychiatrist giving her a clean bill of mental health. In some instances, the FWTAO executive advised individual teachers to be examined by medical doctors and psychiatrists. In a few cases the Federation urged teachers to commit themselves to mental institutions.

The FWTAO did not keep extensive records relating to individual cases of dismissal and the only evidence of "mental health" cases in the OTF archive relate to policies and studies conducted on what psychiatrists, in the mid-twentieth century, referred to as mental illness. For example, in the 1940s the OTF recommended suspension for teachers suffering from nervous anxiety and mental illness. Eileen Gladman, chair of the OTF Relations and Discipline committee, spoke about "personality problems, such as the emotionally disturbed, the alcoholic and the deviant"[29] in the profession, and questioned the committee about the role of the OTF in facilitating access to medical services for troubled teachers. The OTF circulated a memorandum stating that it was "getting more cases of teachers who should not be teaching because of inefficiency or because of personality defects and it is felt that it would assist the O.T.F. Relations Committee . . . if policy and procedures in the matter were considered."[30] The following year the OTF sent a letter to the Department of Education recommending that a "panel of psychiatrists be set up when considering the returning of a certificate to a teacher whose mental health was in question."[31] There is no evidence of which I am aware to suggest that such a panel of psychiatrists was appointed but the request indicates that the issue of teacher mental health was a concern of the professional education community. The OTF archive also contains a letter written by a secretary-treasurer, of a northern Ontario school board, request-

ing that the Department of Education look "after physical examinations of students entering normal school [and that] boards of exam-
iners in the various normal schools . . . be used as boards so that mentally unwell teachers may be referred . . . More applicants were being
excluded now because of mental instability than had been possible in
previous years."[32]

Medical experts in Canada and the United States made female
teachers the subject of numerous psychological and psychiatric journal articles in the first half of the twentieth century.[33] The research
questions reflected an overarching concern about female psychological constitution and its susceptibility to psychoneurosis and neurasthenia (psychiatric designations). A report published in the *Journal of
Educational Psychology* claimed that of 100 women who taught, a third
were emotionally unbalanced and many others needed psychiatric
guidance.[34] It was also established in a second study that of 51 female
teachers "35.2% were emotionally maladjusted to a serious degree;
28.8% were socially maladjusted and 49% were unhappy in their home
life."[35] The National Education Association suggested that as many as
37.5% of teachers interviewed had "persistent worries which inter-
fered with their sleep, with their efficiency in teaching and with their
health."[36] After reviewing these troubling reports, Leo Alilunas
warned that North American "education has not in reality become
cognizant of the significance of teacher mental hygiene."[37]

The focus on female psychological development was also evident
in governmental publications in the Canadian context. In one extensive handbook on teacher health published by the Ontario
Department of Education and the Department of Health in 1938 it
was written that the number of women teachers who were "incapaci-
tated as a result of the so-called 'nervous breakdown' indicates the
extent to which poor health prevails"[38] among them. Canadian doctor,
Ira Wile, also confirmed that "problems of the personality adjustment
[among women teachers is] . . . . increasing in significance in this age
of heightened neuroses and mental disorders."[39] Christine Smith of
the Canadian Mental Health Association stated emphatically:

> breakdowns among teachers due to physical or emotional disorders
> are not rare. Now and then a teacher suffers from recognizable emo-
> tional or nervous disability requiring a period of rest and possibly

treatment; and in some cases a complete change of employment and environment is recommended.[40]

In *Mental Hygiene: A Manual for Teachers* co-authored by Associate Medical Director of the National Committee for Mental Hygiene, J.D. M. Griffin; Professor of Education Psychology at the University of Saskatchewan, S.R. Laycock; and Associate Professor of Psychology at the University of Toronto, W. Line, the claim was made that "teacher's mental health is very definitely of interest in regard to its influence on the children; for our classrooms are extremely socialized, and the children are numbered among the teacher's intimate associates."[41]

In 1931, psychiatric consultant to the American National Committee for Mental Hygiene, Clara Bassett, wrote that the "teacher's personality make-up has a great effect upon the reactions of children under her care [and this] cannot be denied."[42] Doctor Frances Mason also queried: "What is the effect upon young children of being with teachers warped or distorted ideas toward life?"[43] Frank Loweth wrote that a "teacher teaches by what she is more than by what she says."[44] Referring to detailed and careful study, the Joint Committee on the Teaching of Health insisted, in 1938, that the "health of the class as a whole improves or deteriorates according to the health of the teacher."[45] There can, in their view, be no mistaking the impact a teacher has on the health of pupils. It was also cautioned in *The Educational Courier* that the teacher's "own inhibitions, frustrations, mental and emotional blind spots, will profoundly affect every child with whom she comes into contact, and may in some cases do much damage, damage which cannot be easily seen, checked or measured in its incipient states."[46]

Societal fears about working women, changing social structures associated with modernity, and the collapse of the nuclear family all exasperated the overarching concern with female teacher mental health. Educational authorities and advocates of teacher professionalism challenged both the idea that female teachers were predisposed to nervous illness and that they were familial outcasts. For example, Dr. C.C. Goldring, Director of Education in Toronto, insisted that "teachers come from solid, substantial, respectable, well-integrated families and by the very nature of their work they get satisfaction by giving a great deal of themselves." He also reported that the "mental health of school teachers is very, very good – better than that of people in many other fields."[47]

Despite the earlier anxieties expressed about working women, there did seem to be a general consensus that teachers were not especially prone to neurosis. This was confirmed in an influential study of New York city teachers conducted by Doctor E. Altman. Altman established that "the proportion of psychotic persons in teaching is no higher than for the general population."[48] In 1936, Harry Rivlin added credibility to the position by stating that "teachers are not especially subject to psychosis."[49] By 1940, a significant number of North American psychologists and mental health practitioners insisted that there was no "evidence to show that the teaching profession is more likely to cause mental strain than any other profession, or that teachers need psychotherapy any more than do other citizens." Speaking for the OTF executive members, the secretary-treasurer of the organization said that

> we do not feel that mental ill-health is any more prevalent among teachers than among any other profession, in fact statistics would indicate the contrary, but we do believe that mental ill-health in the teacher is apt to affect the students and so it is perhaps more serious than in the case of many other workers; and for that reason we are extremely anxious to find some means of handling this problem in a way that will be to the greatest help to our members and to the students in the schools.[51]

At the ninetieth annual convention of the Ontario Educational Association, in 1950, Dr. Griffin insisted that "teachers are like most of the rest of us and are subject to the same stresses and strains."[52] Noting also that teachers are composed of a good cross-section of our Canadian citizenry, he explained that we can "expect the same incidence of emotional illness as in other groups."[53] Even more reassuring was the sentiment expressed by Dr. C.C. Goldring, Director of Education in Toronto, that "teachers come from solid, substantial, respectable, well-integrated families and by the very nature of their work they get satisfaction by giving a great deal of themselves."[54] He also reported that the "mental health of school teachers is very, very good – better than that of people in many other fields."[55]

Experts insisted that mental breakdowns were reducible to the question of personality adjustment. The problem lay with the psychological adjustment of individual teachers and not with teacher work. For example, representatives of the Department of Education and the Department of Health for the province of Ontario asserted that

> the important factors in preserving mental health are largely under one's own control. Teachers often try to excuse their nervousness and poor emotional control by laying blame upon the difficulties under which they teach, and the special strain which teaching is supposed to involve. Others prefer to blame their grandparents and complain or boast that they have inherited an exceptionally sensitive and nervous disposition. These excuses should be recognized for what they are – simply evasions.[56]

Doctor Frances Mason studied seven hundred maladjusted teachers and concluded that the "school can hardly be held accountable to any appreciable extent for the mental breakdown of the teacher . . . [but of the cases that due pertain to work related stresses] failure of promotion after having studied and worked hard for it seemed to be the outstanding cause."[57] Observing the significant role administrators play in shaping the working conditions of teachers, Doctor Rogers pointed to a "direct relation existing between the type of principal and the state of health had by teachers."[58] He also contended that over the course of a typical day the teacher is exposed to "general nervous wear and tear [along with] those mental insults to the nervous machinery which have as real an effect as if they were mechanical blows or doses of bacteria or other poison."[59]

Although occasional references are made to the arduous nature of teacher work, it is the teacher who was thought to be responsible for harnessing interpersonal resources to cope with job-related stress. Assistant Professor of Education at the College of the City of New York, Harry Rivlin, wrote in 1936

> that like all other men and women, the teacher has her personal problems. She may solve them wisely or not at all, but in either case, her method of solution affects her personality and is reflected in class. The teacher's mental health is thus influenced by her own development as an individual, as well as by her success in overcoming the special menaces to emotional stability inherent in the nature and organization of school work.[60]

Marion Welham, columnist for *The Educational Courier,* advised teachers on how to relax and keep free of emotional tenseness resulting from teacher work.[61] Considering the stresses associated with job and economic insecurity in the modern world, Canadian professor Charles Krug advised teachers to follow the basic rules of mental hygiene and to regard the possibility of dismissal without undue worry, nervousness or emotional strain.[62]

Dorothy Rogers also emphasized the importance of teacher attitude toward mental hygiene and the persistent problem of selecting teachers who are prone to nervousness.

> It is well known that many teachers have found their way into a profession for which they are not physically fitted and that the knowledge of hygiene possessed by many of them is low and their indifference to health is correspondingly great . . [for every] one teacher who has . . . a slight immunity to tuberculosis. . . there are ten who possess a nervous mechanism or a mental background which is highly susceptible to nervous exhaustion.[63]

If teachers have a tendency toward "queerness" (meaning odd as opposed to homosexual in this historical juncture), it is because they are "often recruited from those individuals who are shy, reclusive, and studious, but not equipped with the emotional sturdiness necessary to withstand the strain and tension of teaching."[64] In selecting teacher candidates, the Ontario Educational Association acknowledged difficulty identifying persons with personality deficits. "Certain obvious misfits such as stammerers are easy to assess; but it is difficult to measure that elusive quality often referred to as personality."[65] In a study of maladjusted teachers committed to mental hospitals it was found that troubling personality traits such as "neuroticism, anxiety, irritability, selfishness, and eccentricity . . . [were] possessed in childhood and continued throughout life."[66] They were not a product of teaching itself. Professor Charles A. Krug contended that it was a great tragedy that the "people whom we call born teachers – people for whom the profession is a life work – [have] dispositions [that are] are warped and twisted most."[67]

Conclusion

I conclude that the nervous narratives about female teachers articulated by psychological, psychiatric, medical, and educational "experts" point to a concern about single female teacher gender and sexual identity. Of course, the worry about mental health was significant in and of itself, but the extent to which the concern was mediated by ideas about gender and sexuality suggests that there was a parallel concern about the life-long, single female teacher and her personality development. The narcissistic, anti-social, or emotionally turbulent teacher upsets the ideal of female teacher motherly love, moral virtue marked by self-sacrifice, genteel respectability, and feminine sociability. The nervous teacher was, consequently, subject to school-based controversy and was, in some instances, dismissed or forced to resign. She could not adjust herself to the school situation and this was believed to indicate a troubled social, emotional and sexual life. The concern about female teacher personality, madness, and emotional distress spills over onto a more deep-seated concern about female teacher gender identity transgression and homosexuality, in the first half of the twentieth century.

Notes

[1] See Shoshana Felman, "Women and Madness: The Critical Phallacy," *Diacritics, 5* (1975); Sander L. Gilman, *Seeing the Insane: A Cultural History of Psychiatric Illustration* (New York: Brunner-Mazel, 1982); Genevieve Lloyde, The Man of Reason: "Male" and "Female" in *Western Philosophy* (Minneapolis: University of Minnesota Press, 1984); and Elaine Showalter, *The Female Malady: Women, Madness, and English Culture* (New York: Penguin Books, 1985).

[2] Peter Melville Logan, *Nerves and Narratives: A Cultural History of Hysteria in 19th-Century British Prose* (Berkeley: University of California Press, 1997).

[3] Showalter, *The Female Malady,* 3.

[4] Although this study focuses on the discursive construction of female teacher maladies in the educational and psychological literature, one can not help but imagine the case studies reviewed to be, in some sense, an expose of the troubling emotional adjustments of women working in the profession of education under emotionally traumatic and strenuous conditions. Knowing that women teachers lacked power in the educational hierarchy; that they were subject to what we would recognize today to be excessive occupational hazards and job-related stresses; that they were predominantly answerable to men acting as

principals and inspectors, underscoring sexist and patriarchal social relations; that they often lacked control over conditions of boarding, social relationships of every kind; and, finally, that they were subject to disproportionately stringent moral codes, it is tempting to view the psychological profiles presented in the literature as indicative of untold emotional turmoil garnered in the public sphere of professional work. As Frances Donovan suggested in her sociological study of women teachers, the "profession of teaching ... furnishes a fertile field for mental conflict." See Frances Donvan, *The Schoolma'am: Women in America From Colonial Times to the 20th Century* (New York: Arno Press, 1938, 108).

[5]Logan, *Nerves and Narratives,* 2.

[6]Ibid., 4.

[7]See Felman, "Women and Madness."

[8]Provincial Archives of Ontario, RG2, P3, Superintendent of Elementary Education – Complaints, 295/10, 4-815, 1948.

[9]Ibid.

[10]Ibid.

[11]Ibid.

[12]Ibid.

[13]Ibid.

[14]Ibid.

[15]Ibid.

[16]Bonnie Smith, *The Gender of History: Men, Women, and Historical Practice* (Cambridge: Harvard University Press, 1998), 195.

[17]Mina Carson, "Domestic Discontents: Feminist Reevaluations of Psychiarty, Women, and the Family," *Canadian Review of American Studies* (1992): 176.

[18]"Too Much 'Sissy Government,' *The Educational Courier 9* (1939): 39-40.

[19]Max Braithwaite, "Why Teachers Quit," *Macleans,* 1947, 9 and 43-46.

[20]G.E. Valentine, "Escaped – One School Teacher," *Educational Courier 9* (1939): 19 and 22.

[21]Charles A. Krug, "Mental Hygiene for Teachers," *The Educational Courier 6* (1936): 4-10.

[22]Frances V. Mason, "A Study of Seven Hundred Maladjusted School Teachers," *Mental Hygiene, 15* (1931): 584.

[23]John Sullivan, "Teacher Pressure and Child Growth," *The Educational Courier 15,* (1945): 35.

[24]"How is Your Beauty?" *Educational Courier, 16* (1945): 237.

[25]Donovan, *The Schoolma'am,*.13.

[26]Dorothy Rogers, *Mental Hygiene in Elementary Education* (Boston: The Riverside Press, 1957), 19.

[27]Provincial Archives of Ontario, RG2, P3, Superintendent of Elementary Education – Complaints, 295/13, 1948.

[28]Ibid.

[29]Ontario Teachers' Federation Archive, Discipline and Relations Committee Records, 1944 to 1964.

[30]Ibid.

[31]Ibid.

[32]Ibid.

[33]See Leo J. Alilunas, "Needed Research in Teacher Mental Hygiene," *Journal of Educational Research 38* (1944): 653-665; John A. Broxston, "Problem Teachers," *Educational Administration and Supervision 29* (1943): 177-182; Leigh Peck, "A Study of the Adjustment Difficulties of a Group of Women Teachers," *Journal of Educational Psychology 27* (1936): 401-416; and James H. Wall, "Psychiatric Disorders in 50 School Teachers," *American Journal of Physchiatry* XCVI (1939):137-145.

[34]Peck, "A Study of the Adjustment Difficulties," 401-416.

[35]Alilunas, "Needed Research in Teacher Mental Hygiene," 655.

[36]Ibid.

[37]Ibid.

[38]John T. Phair et al. *Health: A Handbook of Suggestions for Teachers in Elementary Schools* (Toronto: The Ryerson Press, 1938), 23.

[39]Ira S. Wile, "The Bases of Personality Adjustment," *School and Society 34* (1931): 586.

[40]Christine Smith, "Mental Health Clinics Serve a Vital Need," *The Educational Courier 21* (1950): 42.

[41]J.D.M. Griffin, S.R. Laycock and W. Line, *Mental Hygiene: A Manual for Teachers,* (New York: American Book Company, 1940), 236.

[42]Clara Basset, *The School and Mental Health,* (New York: The Commonwealth Fund, 1931), 45.

[43]Mason, "A Study of Seven Hundred Maladjusted School Teachers," 585.

[44]Frank J. Lowth, *Everyday Problems of the Country Teacher* (The Macmillan Company, New York, 1936), 50.

[45]Power and Roberts, *Health: A Handbook of Suggestions for Teachers in Elementary Schools,* 23.

[46]"How is Your Mental Health?" *Educational Courier, 16* (1945): 6.

[47]C. C. Goldring, "The Mental Health of Teachers," *1950 Year Book and Proceedings, Nineteenth Annual Convention*, Ontario Educational Association, 25.

[48]E. Altman, "How is Your Mental Health?" *Educational Courier 16* (1945): 6.

[49]Harry N. Rivlin, *Educating for Adjustment: The Classroom Applications of Mental Hygiene* (New York: D. Appleton-Century Company, 1936), 396.

[50]Griffin et al., *Mental Hygiene,* 242.

[51]Ontario Teachers' Federation Archives, official letter of correspondence.

[52]Griffin et al., *Mental Hygiene,* 242.

[53]Goldring, *Year Book and Proceedings*, 25.

[54]Ibid.

[55]Ibid.

[56]Phair, Health: *A Handbook of Suggestions for Teachers in Elementary Schools*, 25.

[57]Mason, "A Study of Seven Hundred Maladjusted School Teachers," 592.

[58]Rogers, *Mental Hygiene in Elementary Education,* 3.

[59]Ibid.

[60]Rivlin, Educating for Adjustment: *The Classroom Applications of Mental Hygiene,* 395.

[61]Marion Welham, "Muscular Relaxation for Teachers," *The Educational Courier 7* (1936): 34-35.

[62]Krug, "Mental Hygiene for Teachers," 4-10.

[63]Rogers, *Mental Hygiene in Elementary Education,* 19.

[64]Donovan, *The Schoolma'am*, 107.

[65]A.C. Lewis, "Selection and Training of Teachers," Annual Report and Proceedings of the Eighty-Sixth Annual Convention of the Ontario Educational Association, (April 1946): 131.

[66]Mason, "A Study of Seven Hundred Maladjusted School Teachers," 595-596.

[67]Krug, *Mental Hygiene for Teachers,* 7.

10

"Girls just want to have fun": Women Teachers and the Pleasures of the Profession

Rebecca Priegert Coulter

The London Women Teachers' Association fashion show, Ivanhoe Hotel. *Photo courtesy of The University of Western Ontario Archives, London Free Press Collection, Oct. 8, 1969.*

211

This is a tale of remembrance, a reclamation of the pleasures teaching provided for women who toiled in the classrooms of this nation across the twentieth-century. It is offered as a move towards understanding women teachers in all their complexities and contradictions, to seeing the fullness of their lives. In arguing for attention to "fun," freedom, and the satisfaction of desire in teachers' lives, I am most definitely not suggesting we ignore the very real challenges that women teachers encountered, and still confront in their work. However, teachers must be seen as agential, creating their own lives not just as teachers but as women, women who could, and did, choose to engage in activities and diversions that brought personal satisfaction and joy. Any history of women teachers is incomplete if it considers only the troubles and not the pleasures a life in teaching could bring.

Much of the historical literature on teaching in Canada reflects the narrative of the brave but long-suffering female teacher good-heartedly managing the one-roomed rural school under less than ideal conditions. On the one hand, it is a sentimental story filled with nostalgia for days gone by and appearing in reminiscences collected by retired teachers or other local historians. It is a tale of mice in the piano, snakes in the teacher's desk, hot lunches cooked on pot-bellied stoves, inspectors' visits, winter blizzards, Christmas concerts – a mythic tale of a loving teacher bringing learning to the young – or as my colleague, Helen Harper, puts it, the story of Lady Bountiful shedding reason and light upon the land.[1] On the other hand, it is also a story, usually told for worthy political purposes by teacher federations, of the trials and tribulations of the woman teacher, isolated in rural communities without the necessary teaching resources, toiling for low or no pay, lacking job security and pension, easily exploited by and subject to the whims of demanding trustees.[2]

It is this latter trope which most often gets picked up by educational historians who, influenced by the pessimism of post-modernism, or, perhaps, the cynicism of the post-modern condition, focus on teachers poorly educated and even more poorly paid, working in abysmal conditions but nonetheless acting as controlling agents of the state, filling in innumerable forms, living in isolation and in fear of inspection, and in some cases, committing suicide.[3] One is left to wonder why anyone would ever enter teaching. Nonetheless, it was this historical tradition which informed my understanding of the past as I began the research on the history of women teachers in twentieth-century Ontario. I was determined to avoid the trap of sentimentality and get to the "real story" of teachers' lives, a story I understood to be one of oppression and gender discrimination. The nearly 200 retired teachers interviewed, however, presented a challenge to any gloomy interpretation of their lives for they almost unanimously insisted that they were happy as teachers and satisfied with what they had accomplished. There were a few regrets but for the most part, they said, they would do it all over again. Even those who recounted professional difficulties, problems, indignities, or out and out abuse, persisted in their positive reading of their careers over-all. How then, short of resorting to claims about false consciousness or the label "cultural dopes," do we make sense of the teachers' refusal to name their experiences "exploitation" even when evidence from their own testimonies and from more generalized empirical data on matters such as wage discrimination and promotional disadvantage suggest this is precisely what it was?

Part of the explanation must rest with the fact that as teachers reflected back on their careers as a whole, they felt proud of what they had accomplished, even in the most difficult of circumstances. Vivien (ACPID 116), who taught in North York from 1949-1959, could not "imagine if I had been a secretary or a nurse. I'm sure I would have done alright and so on, but teaching was very affirming to me. I think it was one of the most affirming times of my life, where I realized that I had a happy life." Caroline (ACPID 125), who began teaching in Toronto in the late 1950s, reiterated,

> I loved teaching. I absolutely loved being with children and teaching and planning the lessons, and seeing how it would develop and all the little quirks that would happen, and seeing in the long term where my students have gone. That, I think, was an absolute joy. . . . To have been part of being able to be a part of a child's life in some way, shape or form. It's been a lot of fun.

Genevieve (ACPID 136), whose career began in a country school outside London in 1950, commented, "I didn't find teaching hard at all. I loved every day that I ever went to work, I just loved it." This is a very consistent pattern. Teachers received a great deal of satisfaction from their work, both in the moment of doing it and in seeing what became of their pupils. Teaching was for them "affirming," "an absolute joy," "a lot of fun" and something they "loved." Even those who might have liked other careers if they had been open to women, spoke glowingly of the pleasures of the teaching profession, of helping young people, especially those with learning difficulties.

These were also women who had grown up in other times and places, whose experiences of life in the first half of the twentieth-century – the world wars, the economic hardships, deaths of family members and friends, back-breaking farm labor – taught a certain stoicism. They learned to count their blessings and survive and, in this context, and compared to what might have become of them, saw teaching as a worthy occupation that brought self-satisfaction and even happiness. Helen Richards Campbell exemplifies this attitude. She faced the difficulties of teaching in a rural school from 1913-1919 fortified by her mother's words which reminded her that "we must light our own lamps, grow and grind our own grain, open our own oysters." She responded to the maternal observation that if you stumble over rocks in your path, think of them as "testing stones. You can get over, around, or through them, or you can trip over them, fall flat on your face and stay there with the rest of the worms." Campbell concluded, "the pupils and I faced apparently impossible problems, but we worked them out."[4] It is this kind of "can-do" attitude, this determination to succeed and make the best of things, that many young teachers brought with them to the workplace. But that is not the whole picture and in this chapter I want to argue that teachers loved their work, not only for itself, but because it held out possibilities for other pleasures as well.

While trying to understand the teachers' positive, and largely uncritical, interpretations of their own careers given in oral testimony, I turned to teachers' diaries, autobiographies, unpublished personal memoirs, letters written to friends and family from school postings around the province, and fictionalized accounts of teaching careers. Reading these I was struck immediately by how much the lives of beginning teachers in the past seemed to reflect concerns and enthusiasms similar to those of young women today. But, of course! For the better part of the twentieth-century, most teachers were, in fact, teenagers; they were really girls just out of the school room themselves. .

When Helen Richards Campbell began teaching in 1913, she was only 15 years old, although she claimed to be 18 when applying to the Ontario Department of Education for a permit because she had been told that no school board would hire a girl in her mid-teens. On her first day of teaching, she remembered, "I was proud. I was humble. I was undeniably scared. And I was close to tears."[5] Helene Brown Weaver emphasized her youth when she recalled the first visit of the inspector to her classroom in the 1940s. He popped in on the 17 year-old beginning teacher with exactly six weeks of teacher preparation on the second day of class to see how she was doing. "He greeted me by name. I was still unaccustomed to being called 'Miss Brown.' It took a while for me to realize that I was a teacher when only three months prior I was playing x's and o's on the back of a Latin text or having chalk fights when the teacher was out of the room."[6] Mildred Young Hubbert made a similar observation in recalling her first year of teaching, 1943-44. "I don't think I did the children a lot of good, but I hope neither did I do them any harm. I was actually just as immature as they were."[7]

The picture of the youthful teacher enjoying play with her pupils much as an older sibling would is prevalent. For example, one teacher recalled,

> when I began teaching in my first rural school I was very young, full of pep, full of fun, anxious that school would be a happy place. I was also very thoughtless! Our September noon hour activity was the building of a raft and riding it on a nearby pond. It was great fun until moms found out. They told me in no uncertain terms what they thought of such a dangerous activity.[8]

Not only was the teacher engaging with her students like a big sister, but the mothers of those children appear to have dressed down the teacher as though she were an older daughter who had been negligent in her baby sitting duties.

This recognition that most beginning female teachers at the elementary level were just out of the school room themselves brings into focus the element of age in understanding teachers' lives and identities. For many young women, "going teaching" offered an opportunity to slip the ties of family oversight and supervision and become independent wage-earners. As Marjorie Madill observed about her decision to teach in the 1920s, "like many another teenager, I was very anxious to get away and begin a life of my very own."[9] Other young women saw teaching as an escape from the drudgery of farm chores and housework. It was common for young farm girls to clean house for their families and for neighbors, cook for farm workers, nurse invalids, scrub laundry, garden in the hot sun, milk cows, feed the pigs, collect eggs, care for chickens, clean and preserve fish, pick and can food, and babysit younger siblings. Ina Lewis noted,

> we girls, we always helped with the milking, and helped with the chickens, and we'd load the grain, and we could mow the sheaves, and when the hay was being unloaded we could drive the team on the fork to pull the hay up. Yes, we – I often think about it – we, for kids, really worked hard. [10]

Lauretta Mills also had experienced the hard and relentless work of farming by the time she entered Stratford Normal School in 1935 and commented about farm life, "Work was plentiful but pay was scarce."[11] Like many other young women graduating from the normal schools in the 1930s, however, she was unable to find work in teaching and migrated to Toronto to seek employment. In the big city, she, and other unemployed teachers, such as Greta Black Tribble, found domestic work as nannies and maids.[12] The long hours and low wages associated with domestic service, coupled with the constant surveillance by employers, made teaching an attractive alternative and when school jobs came open, women took them. Teachers were recognized in their communities, even while sharing the privations of their fellow citizens, and teaching was respectable work, accepted by parents and neighbors alike.[13] It also was an important avenue to the independence that comes with earning money of your own. Teachers were not paid well, but they were paid more than most working women. And even when young teachers sent money home to support a family economy, this, in and of itself, further established them as independent women with disposable income.

Sarah Margaret Peden was forthright about the importance of having her own money and the role that played in her choice of a teaching career in the 1920s. She was not alone in her reasoning.

> Why did I decide to become a teacher? I wasn't prompted by the fact that I had the desire to impart knowledge or to have the satisfaction of educating the ignorant, or contributing to the good of humanity.

True, I found children interesting, and teaching did appeal to me in a degree but none of those things were uppermost in my mind.

My three older sisters were teachers, and when they arrived home on holidays I came to the conclusion that teaching was the profession for me – a long vacation which gave time for travel – enough money for that and also beautiful clothes such as they wore – seal and sable coats, satin and velvet dresses.

As soon as their trunks arrived, I couldn't wait to get to the bottom of them. I tried on all the dresses and jewellery – pirouetted in front of the mirror to the amusement of the family who always passed sarcastic remarks. Wouldn't it be wonderful to be a teacher, and earning enough money to have clothes like this for my own?[14]

Across most of the twentieth-century, the ability to buy new clothing for themselves is a recurring theme in the accounts of women teachers. Ina Lewis said, "it was nice to be earning your own money and buying and getting out to town and picking out a dress or something you liked."[15] Accounts kept by Helena Wallace while she was teaching at Fairbairn in 1903 reveal her expenditures on clothing. In the first seven months of the year, she purchased a coat, two hats, gloves, a dress, and a collar, buckle and ribbon for a total expenditure of $25.95, or nearly 38% of her $69 income. In the same period, she spent $22 on room and board. By midsummer, her budget was anaemic and it was only rescued and propped up through a gift of $10, possibly from her family for a birthday.[16] Helene Brown Weaver's mother taught in the period following World War I. She "was a natty dresser. . . . when she went to a new school she got a whole new wardrobe in the latest style: shoes, suits, hats and gloves which were coordinated. She ordered the finery from the Eaton's catalogue."[17] When Dorothy Morgan got her first pay cheque in 1921, she

went on a shopping spree. First came a gift for each member of the family. I had never been able to give presents before. Then came clothes for myself. I remember particularly a pair of gleaming patent leather pumps and a copenhagen blue taffeta blouse with silk stockings to match – the tops were cotton for the silk came to just below the knee, but no nice girl showed her knees in those days.[18]

Teachers' tales are consistently full of talk about the suits or dresses that they wore on memorable occasions, about the outfits they purchased when visiting Toronto. Even negotiating teams in the 1950s and 1960s would go out together and purchase new hats to mark the opening of discussions with local boards. In London, and probably elsewhere, the Women Teachers' Association sponsored an annual fashion show and even into the 1970s and 1980s, female teachers who called themselves feminists would model clothing for the busy professional woman.[19]

Now, undoubtedly, dressing well, which later became "dressing professionally," was part of the complex pattern of feminine conformity and consumerism, but there is also no denying the part it played in enhancing women's pleasure. The precision with which women remember their clothing only emphasizes this point. Decades after going to normal school in 1934, Greta Black Tribble was still able to recall the wardrobe she had taken:

> . . .a black and white hounds tooth skirt with a 3/4 length coat, a white blouse with lots of tucks and a black blazer to wear with it. Another outfit was a white flannel pleated skirt with a royal blue blazer and knee length socks to match. I loved that outfit and wore it for years. I also had a red dress that Mom had bought me and Dad gave me money to buy a winter coat. I bought a dark green tweed in Eaton's Annex for $12.00. It was tailored with a black belt.[20]

More than fifty years later, Penny Petrone remembers buying her first fur coat, a black raccoon one, that "looked great" and recalls "a chocolate brown silk dress with gold piping around the dropped waist and Peter Pan collar" that she wore to play at a recital.[21]

Just as women teachers took pleasure in personal adornment, they also valued the opportunity to travel that teaching accorded them. In the earliest part of the twentieth-century, young women would travel west to Alberta and Saskatchewan to teach, often over the summer months to earn extra money to support further education.[22] By the 1920s teachers were travelling more often simply for a holiday because they had both some disposable income and vacations. In that period a trip to the Rocky Mountains to go mountain climbing, followed by an excursion to the coast and a tour of Vancouver became popular. Teacher travel persisted as a real pleasure as young women in pairs or larger groups set out together for fun and adventure.[23] In the late 1950s, Celine (ACPID 135) and a girlfriend, another teacher, "gadded off here and there, and we took a train trip across Canada."

Advertisements for travel began to target teachers specifically, offering up inducements to visit other provinces and countries. Taking summer courses in England and on the continent became an increasingly attractive option in the post-war period.

Young teachers also sought the adventure that teaching in different countries offered. In 1921 Eva Pugh Outram of Peterborough arranged with her school board to take a leave of absence so she could change places with a teacher in England who wanted to visit Canada.[25] At the age of 20, in 1944, Mildred Young Hubbert went to the Yukon to teach. Her mother insisted on going with her, Hubbert's salary was only to be $40 a month plus room and board, and an Aboriginal boy was paid more to tend the furnaces than she earned to teach, but as she said,

> None of this mattered. I was setting off on a great adventure to see things few people before me had seen and, with the optimism of youth, was confident all would be well. I would as readily have gone to outer space to teach Martians if the opportunity had presented itself.[26]

Many a young teacher went north as a "great adventure." Jean Cluff Aubry tells of receiving a job offer in 1934 from a place called Nakina. Job offers were few and far between in the 1930s and Nakina was offering "the unheard of salary of $900 a year!" Aubry, impressed with such a "phenomenal salary," and having heard "the old idea that girls going north had such an exciting time (north being around Parry Sound or Manitoulin Island)," accepted the offer immediately. Three days later she finally discovered where Nakina was (a community situated in the Canadian Shield, two hundred miles north of Thunder Bay and accessible only by train) but she went anyway. Despite admonishments from her mother to stick it out to Christmas and then come home, Aubry remained in the north for 28 years, participating fully in the social life of the community.[27] Mary Pat Hay went north to Biscotasing in 1941 despite concerns expressed by her father. With the support of her mother who said, "Go. It will be the greatest experience of your life,"[28] Hay embarked on a voyage north to the little town most famous for having been the home of Archie Delaney, also known as Grey Owl. Her mother was right, said Hay. Bisco' was "the best experience of my life."[29]

Following World War II, teachers went off to ply their trade in Department of National Defence schools on Canadian military bases in Europe. Through an international development program run by the Canadian Teachers' Federation called Project Overseas, teachers went to the Caribbean, Africa and Asia. There was much joy in recounting the excitement of seeing places hitherto experienced only vicariously through geography textbooks. Penny Petrone acknowledges,

> When the Port Arthur Public School Board agreed to give me a two-year secondment to teach in Germany, I was ecstatic. I was asserting my own identity. I was escaping the family despite my mother's admonition that the beaten path is the safe path.[30]

Petrone ended up teaching for three years in Germany and France in the mid-1950s and used the opportunity to expand her horizons.

> I travelled extensively in Western Europe with my teaching colleagues and our male friends in the Services. We were all young and carefree Canadians seeking and finding adventure and romance, new friends and experiences.[31]

Whether in Europe or in Canada, young teachers led the hectic social lives we associate with contemporary adolescence. Their diaries, autobiographies, memoirs and letters recount a mad and merry circle of crokinole, euchre, skating parties, dances, sailing and canoeing, cottage life, visits hither and yon for dinner or tea, trips to town, snowshoeing, hiking. In most cases, teachers were very popular and much in demand as company in their local communities. They became "somebodies" in their own right. As Marjorie Holley Ludgate expressed it, "It's something to be the big frog even though this is a very small puddle."[32] Grace Hastings found her place in 1931, her first year of teaching in a village school.

> Deep down I was lonesome. I was boarding in a home with no running water and therefore an outhouse away out in the back shed seemed not much of a step forward in my budding life, or so I thought. Gradually, however, when I became more aware that the village had many young people my age, I began to pick up an entirely new life. They were a lively bunch, indulging in many activities like tennis, soccer, dancing and partying and outdoor skating on the mill pond. . . . Suddenly I realized that I belonged! I made lifelong friends and got to know and enjoy my life as a resident of the community and church.[33]

Hastings ended up staying in the village for seven years and when she submitted her resignation, "everyone knew that a certain young man and we [sic] were entering into the joys of matrimony come August of that summer."[34]

Greta Black Tribble, who began teaching in 1936 just north of Orangeville, reveals much about the social life of young women teachers.

> I knew quite a lot of people in Orangeville, both girls and boys. I met a boy who worked at Toronto Dominion bank – Merrill Walters from Brockville. We started going out with other couples – Merrill didn't have a car so usually it was with a bunch from the bank. On Saturday nights during the winter we often went to Toronto to see a hockey game or we'd all go to the "show" and meet at a restaurant later, usually one on Broadway called "The Greeks." Lots of kids would be there that I knew and we'd sit around and listen to the juke box.[35]

This is one way young women teachers escaped the surveillance of their communities. Another example can be found in the escapades of Elizabeth Penson and a teacher friend named Lilian. On 14 July 1914 the two of them canoed across a lake to an island, taking a lunch, a supper and, good teachers that they were, exam papers to mark. Penson reveals another purpose of the trip.

> I had got George [her brother] to send me a box of cigarettes – not that I am really fond of them but because Lilian was dying to "try one" and we hardly dared buy them in town. Teachers must be so careful! We smoked them all and Lilian was duly thrilled. No doubt the good people were shocked enough to see us going hatless and in picnic attire on such a godless excursion instead of traipsing meekly to the church. Enjoyed the day immensely but got horribly burned.[36]

Female friendships, such as this one between Elizabeth Penson and her friend Lilian, were important contributors to the pleasures women teachers experienced. Women provided support and camaraderie to one another in schools, and together they socialized, took courses, shared living arrangements and travelled. Mary Pat Hay notes the kindness of her principal and friend, Lilka, and details how, through Lilka, she had many exciting adventures such as travelling a trapline and experiencing a European sauna for the first time, complete with a roll in the snow "in 30 below zero weather." Hay also remembered that

> Lilka arranged many Saturday afternoon surprises – canoeing and motor boat trips up the lake, even an aeroplane ride to a mine thirty miles into the bush, aboard a Lands and Forest's plane. That trip was memorable. The bi-plane shook in every quarter, but the view was magnificent. Unfortunately I was "air sick."[37]

Alice (ACPID 253) acknowledges she could not have become provincial president of the Federation of Women Teachers' Associations of Ontario in the 1960s without the support of her female room-mate who did all the cooking and housework.

Vivien (ACPID 116), who taught in a larger urban school with many colleagues in the 1950s, observed,

> when I was teaching, most of us were young and single, and so we weren't rushing home to look after children and get meals, so we coached, like I coached a hockey team, I mean if you can imagine . . . .ice hockey . . . volleyball, choirs, Christmas concerts, basketball, lots of opportunities to really enjoy the school as a whole rather than just your class. And none of us felt put upon.

Noting that little was required of her with respect to paperwork, Vivien also commented on the professional freedom she felt she had in comparison to teachers today. For her, the school offered social relationships within the context of the workplace and provided an environment, "a great atmosphere," that encouraged a positive morale among teachers. Teachers were friends with one another, partied together and Vivien even dated some of the male teachers.

For many young women teachers relationships with the opposite sex provided considerable fun and even the pleasures which come from the exercise of sexual power. Eva McNab explained that "when you first went to a rural school the young fellows always wanted to be the first to take the teacher out. The first serious one I had was in the second year I taught school. Well, I kinda had been going out with two at the same time."[38] Madge Dickson, on the other hand, got annoyed with all the male attention. Noting that young women moved to the towns and cities for work, leaving young men behind in the country to do the farm work, Dickson commented, "so the teacher got too much attention. I refused dates except on Friday night – but sometimes had to be nearly rude to avoid other nights in the week when I was tired."[39]

Jean Aubry took a different view. Invited to a dance the second night she was in Nakina by members of the school board and their wives, she "eagerly accepted" because she loved to dance. Of the experience she observed:

> Never having been to a dance where one danced with total strangers, I was at first a little hesitant when one man after another stepped up to ask me to dance. However, to make sure I got off on the right foot in a strange place, I accepted all requests and found myself having the time of my life. To have five dances reserved ahead was enough to lift the morale of any young girl.[40]

In 1958 Joan Hall and her friend Louisa travelled out of Toronto to Hillsburgh, a small town where they were to complete their practicum, chosen because Louisa had a crush on a young man who lived there. Hall remembers, "We were carefree and giddy. Here we were, two city girls taking a bus into the sticks with a snowstorm on the way. I felt as if I were going to the country for a holiday. We chatted and giggled all the way."[41] After several adventures, Joan and Louisa arrived at the house where they would be boarding. And as Hall says, fate arrived.

> Later that day we finally met the eldest son. And now, this was surely fate. It was March 11th, my 19th birthday and here I was meeting the man of my dreams. He wasn't tall but he was dark and handsome and 21 years old. It was love at first sight! I was living in a novel and it was going to end "happily ever after."[42]

For Joan Hall it was happily ever after but Elizabeth Penson had a different experience. On March 23rd, 1912 she told her diary the following story:

> I met a boy this winter – so overflowing with the spirit of youth – that I took a fancy to him. He did such rash, unconventional things, was so frank and generous, and yet under all so unexpectedly kind and thoughtful. I thought here there must surely be room for reason and justice. Well, he thought me quiet, so tried to get me out of myself and have a little flirtation. I rather surprised him by rising to the occasion. Finally one evening . . . the conversation turned to the suffragette question in England and from that to women's rights and finally marriage. Then I saw that this man was like all the rest. He granted women a soul – but he must own it![43]

She longed for marriage with the right man, but not at any cost. To

this young man, she expressed her views on women's rights forcefully.

> I said that women should be able to see to their own rights – that it
> wasn't wise to trust the well being of half the nation to the care of
> the other half, without power of appeal. It was like slave owning. A
> good master didn't justify slavery. Mr. Stonehouse was quite shocked
> at this view and I haven't seen him since.[44]

Penson concluded this entry by musing, "How I would love to
meet a man who sees a woman as an individual – a soul, a possible
companion – not a possible purchase!"[45]

Penson's critical perspective was not, however, shared by most of
the young women teachers with little more than fun on their minds.
For example, in what can only be a roman à clef, Elaine Purdie provides an account of a young teacher and her friend Joan who found a
way to get to hockey games. After all "there were two new hockey
players we had our eyes on and we liked to be front and centre in case
they might notice us."[46] The two teachers fooled the community and
engaged in a little temporary petty larceny to achieve their goal.

> Teachers were paid once a month and it was hard to stretch the
> money from payday to payday. We used a code over the phone when
> we wanted to go to a hockey game in Pembroke. (Everyone listened
> in on conversations in the country where several families were on one
> party line and all were nosy about what the teacher was up to). "I'm
> having a Red Cross meeting Tuesday," Joan would say. "I'm having
> one, too," I'd reply. In code this meant that the hockey game was
> Tuesday and the collection taken up at the meeting that day would be
> enough to get us into the game. We only had to do this close to the
> end of the month.[47]

Needless to say, as soon as the pay cheque came in, restitution was
made to the Red Cross jar.

The title of this chapter is taken from a song made popular by
Cyndi Lauper. In her public persona as a rock star, Lauper was the
anti-thesis of the professional teacher in dress and comportment.
Nonetheless, the lyrics of "Girls Just Want To Have Fun," are relevant
to the lives of women teachers. The words express

- an experience of gender discrimination shared with other
  women: "Oh mother dear we're not the fortunate ones";

- a recognition of the power of patriarchy in education: "Oh daddy dear you know you're still number one, But girls they want to have fun";

- a shared lot with other workers: "When the working day is done, girls – they want to have fun," and, most importantly,

- the desire to be loved, recognized and rewarded: "I want to be the one to walk in the sun."[48]

In our time, this song spoke to female adolescents like my daughter and her friends, now in their 20s. Had they been born a few decades earlier, they would have been the young teachers who did their jobs as best they could, but when the day was done, wanted to have fun. It is not that teachers did not recognize problems and issues in the workplace. Of course they did, for how else could we explain the rise of teacher federations or the struggle for pay equity, maternity leaves, job security, and pensions. Women teachers noticed gender discrimination and sexual harassment even when they did not have the language to name it. They saw the nature of their work shifting, and noted their professional autonomy wax and wane. But they were more than martyrs or saints and resist characterization as either. There was a fullness to their lives as teachers that is not captured in sentimental tales, nor in gloomy histories. Young women did not live to teach; they taught to live. And like all young women, they deserved to walk in the sun.

Notes

[1]See, for example, Myrtle Fair, I *Remember the One-Room School* (Cheltenham,ON: Boston Mills Press, 1979); Russell Morton, *Cairnbrogie School: Tales of a Northern Township* (Richmond Hill, ON: Northpine Publishing, 1999); Hazel Andrews, Virginia Drayson, Hazel Farr, Janina Juric and Madaline Wilson, eds., *Telling Tales Out of School* (n.p.: Norfolk Women Teachers' Association, n.d.); Hazel Andrews, Barbara Crabb, Virginia Drayson, Ruth Anne Earls, Janina Juric, Sharon Larabie, Mary Lou Norman, and Madaline Wilson, eds., *More Telling Tales Out of School* (n.p.: Norfolk Women Teachers' Association, 1998). On Lady Bountiful, see Helen Harper, "White Women Teaching in the North: Problematic Identity on the Shores of Hudson Bay," in *Dismantling White Privilege: Pedagogy, Politics, and Whiteness*, ed. Nelson M. Rodriguez and Leila E. Villaverde, 127-141 (New York: Peter Lang, 2000).

[2]See, for example, Doris French, *High Button Bootstraps: Federation of Women Teachers' Associations of Ontario, 1918-1968* (Toronto: Ryerson Press, 1968); Pat

Staton and Beth Light, *Speak With Their Own Voices: A Documentary History of the Federation of Women Teachers' Associations of Ontario and the Women Elementary Public School Teachers of Ontario* (Toronto: FWTAO, 1987); Mary Labatt, *Always a Journey: A History of the Federation of Women Teachers' Associations of Ontario, 1918-1993* (Toronto: FWTAO, 1993).

[3]See, Alison Prentice and Marjorie R. Theobald, "The Historiography of Women Teachers: A Retrospect," in *Women Who Taught: Perspectives on the History of Women and Teaching,* ed. Alison Prentice and Marjorie R. Theobald, 3-33 (Toronto: University of Toronto Press,1991) for a useful, though now dated, review and Susan Gelman, "Select Bibliography" in the same book, 285-301. See, also, Alison Prentice, "Workers, Professionals, Pilgrims; Tracing Canadian Women Teachers' Histories," in *Telling Women's Lives: Narrative Inquiries in the History of Women's Education,* ed. Kathleen Weiler and Sue Middleton, 25-42 (Buckingham and Philadelphia" Open University Press, 1999). Some key studies on the history of women teachers in Canada include Marta Danylewycz and Alison Prentice, "Teachers' Work: Changing Patterns and Perceptions in the Emerging School Systems of Nineteenth- and Early Twentieth-Century Central Canada," *Labour/Le travail 17* (1986): 59-80; J. Donald Wilson, "'I am ready to be of assistance when I can': Lottie Bowron and Rural Women Teachers in British Columbia," in *Children, Teachers and Schools in the History of British Columbia,* ed. Jean Barman, Neil Sutherland and J. Donald Wilson, 285-306 (Calgary: Detselig, 1995); Alison Prentice, "From Household to School House: The Emergence of the Teacher as Servant of the State," in *Gender and Education in Ontario,* ed. Ruby Heap and Alison Prentice, 25-48 (Toronto: Canadian Scholars' Press, 1991); Cecilia Reynolds, "In the Right Place at the Right Time: Rules of Control and Woman's Place in Ontario Schools, 1940-1980," *Canadian Journal of Education 20* (1995): 129-145; Kari Dehli, "They Rule By Sympathy: The Feminization of Pedagogy," *Canadian Journal of Sociology 19* (1994): 195-216. For its recognition of the historical role teachers played in nation-building and the normalization of a Canadian way of life, an important recent text is Jean Barman, *Sojourning Sisters: The Lives and Letters of Jessie and Annie McQueen* (Toronto: University of Toronto Press, 2003).

[4]Helen Richards Campbell, *Four Goblets of Wine* (Kingston: H.R.C. Simcoe Holdings, 1980), 67.

[5]Ibid.

[6]Helene Brown Weaver, *Memories of the Thirties and Forties* (Owen Sound, ON: Elmhedge Press, 1997), 118.

[7]Mildred Young Hubbert, *Since the Day I Was Born* (Thornbury, ON: Conestoga Press, 1991), 236.

[8]Excerpt from anonymous teacher's oral history in Fair, *I Remember,* 113.

[9] Marjorie Madill, "At School in the Nineteen Twenties," in *The Haliburton Era,* vol.1, typescript of women teachers' stories collected for the diamond jubilee of the Federation of Women Teachers' Associations of Ontario, 1917 [sic]-1978. Copy held by author. I am grateful to Ruth Stutt for sending me this material.

[10] Ina Lewis is quoted in Alan A. Brookes and Catharine A. Wilson, "'Working Away' from the Farm: The Young Women of North Huron, 1910-1930," *Ontario History* LXXVII (1985), 286.

[11] Lauretta Mills, hand-written memoir, 52, copy held by author. I am grateful to Lauretta Mills and her son, Dennis Mills, for sharing this memoir with me.

[12] Mills, memoir; Greta Black Tribble, My Life and Times: A Tapestry of Memories, unpublished memoir, copy held by author. I thank Bonnie Herron, Greta Tribble's daughter, for sending me her mother's memoir.

[13] For a good discussion of women teachers in the 1930s see Judith Arbus, "Grateful To Be Working: Women Teachers During the Great Depression," in *Feminism and Education: A Canadian Perspective*, ed. Frieda Forman, Mary O'Brien, Jane Haddad, Dianne Hallman and Philinda Masters, 169-190 (Toronto: Centre for Women's Studies in Education, OISE, 1990). See, also, Cecilia Reynolds and Harry Smaller, "Ontario School Teachers: A Gendered View of the 1930s," *Historical Studies in Education 6/History of Education Review 23* (special joint issue 1994): 151-169.

[14] Sarah Margaret Peden, *A Teacher's Trials and Triumphs* (n.p.: Mission Press, 1967), 1. I thank Edward Goertzen for sending me a copy of this book.

[15] Ina Lewis, quoted in Brookes and Wilson, "'Working Away'," 295.

[16] W. W. Judd, Diaries of Helena Judd at Shortsville, New York, 1866, 1868 and of Helena Wallace at Fairbairn, Ontario, 1903 (London, ON: Phelps Publishing Co., 1995), 55-57.

[17] Weaver, *Memories,* 167.

[18] Dorothy Morgan, *Chalkdust in My Blood* (Cornwall, ON: Vesta Publications, 1975), 25.

[19] The University of Western Ontario Archives and Regional Collection, London Women Teachers' Association fonds, B869, Boxes 1A and 1B, Minute Books; assorted, as yet unaccessioned, binders of annual reports and miscellaneous materials. This collection was donated to the UWO ARC as a direct result of the work of The Woman Teacher in Twentieth Century Ontario research project.

[20] Tribble, *My Life and Times,* section VI, 1.

[21] Penny Petrone, *Breaking the Mould* (Toronto: Guernica, 2001), 159.

[22]Rosalind Rowan, "The Eastern Student as the Western Teacher," *The School* 5 (1916): 97-101; Rebecca Priegert Coulter, "Getting Things Done: Donalda Dickie and Leadership Through Practice," in *Historical Perspectives on Women, Teaching, and Learning,* ed. Elizabeth Smyth and Paula Bourne (Vancouver: UBC Press, forthcoming 2005); unpublished diary of Elizabeth Penson, 12 January 1908-15 July 1912, contains descriptions of her teaching in Saskatchewan in 1909. A collection of Elizabeth Penson's diaries is held by Joan McHugh who generously shared this material with me.

[23]The Penson diaries contain a vivid account of a visit to the west; Penny Petrone, *Embracing Serafina* (Toronto: Guernica, 2000) describes a teacher's travels to Europe with three girlfriends in 1952.

[24]See, for example, a 1928 summer tour of Europe with Miss Gertrude Dixon and Miss Mina C. Nicol advertised in *The Bulletin of the Federation of Women Teachers' Associations of Ontario* 5 (1927): 28; for a later period see specific advertisements urging teachers to "book now, pay later" in, for example, *The Educational Courier* XXXVI (March-April 1966): 76 or attend international summer schools, *The Educational Courier* XXXVI (May-June 1966): 84.

[25]Letter to author from Don Outram, 5 December 2002.

[26]Mildred Young Hubbert, *Because It Was There* (Owen Sound, ON: Stan Brown Printers, 1993), 1.

[27]Jean Aubry, "Memories of a Young School Teacher," copy of a column published in Independence, n.d. sent to author by Mrs. Colin Keen.

[28]Mary Pat Hay, "Remembering," unpublished memoir, 29. Copy of memoir held by author who thanks Mary Pat Hay for sharing this material.

[29]Ibid., 34.

[30]Petrone, *Embracing Serafina*, 9-10.

[31]Ibid., 10.

[32]Marjorie Holley Ludgate, *Walk Up the Creek* (Ste.-Anne-de-Bellevue, PQ: Shoreline, 2001), 14.

[33]Grace Hastings, *My Journey to the Millennium* (Port Perry, ON: Observer Publishing, n.d.), 64.

[34]Ibid.

[35]Tribble, *My Life and Times,* section VIII, 4.

[36]Penson diaries, 14 July 1914 [mis-dated 14 June].

[37]Hay, *Remembering*, 33.

[38]Eva McNab quoted in Brookes and Wilson, 'Working Away,' 294.

[39]Madge Dickson, hand-written memoir, "Teaching in the 1930's," generously shared with the author and in her possession.

[40]Aubry, "Memories of a Young School Teacher."

[41]Joan Hall, hand-written memoir, "A Fateful Day," generously shared with the author and in her possession.

[42]Ibid.

[43]Penson diaries, 23 March 1912.

[44]Ibid.

[45]Ibid.

[46]Elaine Purdie, unpublished short story based on her experience as a teacher. I thank her for sharing this lively story with me.

[47]Ibid.

[48]"Girls Just Want To Have Fun," lyrics by Robert Hazard, copyright Heroic Music (ASCAP), 1979.